Ethical Conflicts in Buddhist Societies

Ethical Conflicts in Buddhist Societies

P Pathak

MD Publications Pvt Ltd
New Delhi
www.mdppl.com

Published by :

MD Publications Pvt Ltd
"MD House", 11, Darya Ganj,
New Delhi - 110 002
Phone : +91-11-45355555
E-mail : contact@mdppl.com
Website: www.mdppl.com

ISBN : 978-81-7533-316-1

Published and Printed by Mr. Pranav Gupta on behalf of **MD Publications Pvt Ltd** at Repro India Limited.

Preface

Buddhism is a pragmatic teaching which starts from certain fundamental propositions about how we experience the world and how we act in it. It teaches that it is possible to transcend this sorrow-laden world of our experience and is concerned first and last with ways of achieving that transcendence. What finally leads to such transcendence is what we call Wisdom. The enormous literature of Buddhism is not a literature of revelation and authority. Instead, it uses ethics and meditation, philosophy and science, art and poetry to point a Way to this Wisdom. Similarly, Buddhist writing on social action, unlike secular writings, makes finite proposals which must ultimately refer to this Wisdom, but which also are arguable in terms of our common experience.

The uniqueness of Buddhist ethics lies in its many outstanding qualities. It is all-embracing and comprehensive without being impractical or impossible to follow. It is free from taboos relating to diet, dress, behaviour etc. which very often pass as ethical principles. It serves the needs of the worldling as well as those of the recluse. It is useful to the rich and to the poor; to the powerful as well as to the powerless. To conform to Buddhist ethics one need not have to be a "buddhist"; and it serves as a norm to measure the ethical standard of other teachings. But Buddhist ethics is only the threshold for those who wish to pursue the Buddha's path to Enlightenment and the end of all ill.

In modern Western society, humanistic social action, in its bewildering variety of forms, is seen both as the characteristic way of relieving suffering and enhancing human well-being and, at the same time, as a noble ideal of service, of self-sacrifice, by humanists of all faiths. Buddhism, however, is humanism in that it rejoices in the possibility of a true freedom as something inherent in human nature. For Buddhism, the ultimate freedom is to achieve full release from the root causes of all suffering: greed, hatred and delusion, which clearly are also the root causes of all social evils. Their grossest forms are those which are harmful to others. To weaken, and finally eliminate them in oneself, and, as far as possible, in society, is the basis of Buddhist ethics. And here Buddhist social action has its place.

I am very grateful to Mr. Pranav Gupta, Director of MD Publications Pvt Ltd, New Delhi, for his kind cooperation and support for this book.

P Pathak

Contents

1

Buddhist Ethics

Life is dear to all. Comparing others with oneself, one should neither kill nor cause to kill. Whoever, seeking his own happiness, harms ... beings, he gets no happiness hereafter. Fundamental features of Buddhism's world-view relevant to ethics are the framework of karma and rebirth, accepted by all schools of Buddhism, with varying degrees of emphasis, and the Four Noble Truths, the highest teachings of early Buddhism and of the Theravada school. In the Mahayana tradition, an increasing emphasis on compassion modified the earlier shared perspective in certain ways.

In ethics as in other matters, Buddhists have three key sources of inspiration and guidance: the 'three treasures' or 'three refuges': the Buddha, Dhamma and Sangha. The Buddha is revered as 1. The 'rediscoverer' and teacher of liberating truths and 2. the embodiment of liberating qualities to be developed by others. In addition, in the Mahayana, heavenly Buddhas are looked to as contemporary sources of teaching and help. The Dhamma is the teachings of the Buddhas, the path to the Buddhist goal, and the various levels of realizations of this goal. The Sangha is the 'Community' of Noble Ones: advanced practitioners who have experienced something of this goal, being symbolized, on a more day-to-day level, by the Buddhist monastic Sangha.

The Dhamma, in the sense of teachings attributed to the Buddha(s), is contained in voluminous texts preserved and studied by the monastic Sangha. The advice and guidance that monks and nuns offer to the laity are based on these texts, on their own experience of practising the Buddhist path, and on the oral and written tradition from earlier generations of monastics and, sometimes, lay practitioners. Lay people are under no strict obligation to do what monks or nuns advise, but rather respect for their qualities and way of life is the factor that will influence them, depending on the degree of the lay person's own devotion to the Buddhist way.

A common source of material for popular sermons is the Jataka collection, containing stories which purport to be of the previous lives of Gotama when he was a Bodhisattva. They occur in the canonical collections of all the early schools, became popular subjects for Buddhist art by the third century BCE, and were also taken up in the Mahayana. The stories often function as morality tales, being full of heroes, heroines and villains. The form of a Jataka is a prologue purporting to be about events in the Buddha's day, the story itself, about a past time, and then a brief epilogue which identifies the Buddha with the hero of the story, and certain disciples or relatives with others in it.

In the stories of the past, Gotama is mostly human, but sometimes a god and sometimes a (talking) animal. In the case of the Theravadin Jataka collection of 547 stories, the form in which we now have them consists of some verses, seen as canonical, set in a lengthy prose frame, which was compiled by a later commentator, probably in Sri Lanka. Many stories are also found in the commentary on the Dhammapada, dating from fifth-century CE Sri Lanka, which gives around fifty Jatakas, plus other stories set at the time of the Buddha.As regards the order of priority among sources relevant to resolving points of monastic discipline - and by extension, one could say matters relevant to lay ethical discipline - the fifth-century Theravadin commentator Buddhaghosa gives:

1. Scripture in the form of Vinaya, but it could be seen more widely for non-monastic matters;
2. That which is 'in conformity with scripture';
3. The commentarial tradition (acariyavada);
4. Personal opinion (attanomati), based on logic, intuition and inference independent of 1–3, but whose conclusions should be checked against them.

Here Damien Keown comments that conscience is not irrelevant, but scripture is 'a check that one's own moral conscience is calibrated correctly', and that 'it is not the text itself that is important, but the fact that it is "in conformity with the nature of things"'. Nevertheless, less scholastic monks than Buddhaghosa might put more emphasis on the living oral tradition and meditation-based insights. Mahayanists would also take 'scripture' to include Mahayana texts not acceptable as authoritative to Buddhaghosa.

The teachings attributed to the Buddha(s) are seen as an authoritative guide to the nature of reality and the best way to live, based on the vast, meditation-based knowledge of such spiritually 'awakened' beings. Such teachings are not to be simply accepted, though, but used, investigated and, as far as is possible for a particular individual, confirmed in experience. This emphasis on testing out the teachings is seen in the wellknown Kalama Sutta. Here, the Buddha advises the Kalama people not to accept teachings simply through tradition, speculative reasoning, personal preferences, what one thinks should be true, or respect for a particular teacher. Rather:

> When you, O Kalamas, know for yourselves: 'these states are unwholesome and blameworthy, they are condemned by the wise; these states, when accomplished and undertaken, conduce to harm and suffering', then indeed you should reject them.

Accordingly, the Buddha then gets them to agree that greed, hatred and delusion (lobha, dosa, moha) are each states which are harmful to a person when they arise. Being overcome by any of them, he or she kills, steals, commits adultery, lies, and leads others to do likewise, so that he or she suffers for a long time (on account of the karmic results of his or her actions, in this life or beyond). The Kalamas are then led to agree that the arising of non-greed, non-hatred and non-delusion is beneficial, without such bad consequent actions and results. Accordingly, these states can be seen to be wholesome, unblameworthy, praised by the wise and conducive to happiness, so that the Kalamas should 'undertake and abide in them'.

Here, personal experience, checked out by reference to the guidance of wise people, is taken as the crucial test of what mental states, and consequent behaviour, to avoid or indulge in. Using this criterion is seen to put a high value on states of mind which are the opposite of greed, hatred and deluded unclarity or misorientation, for they can be seen to conduce to happiness rather than suffering. Moreover, it is suggested that people are trustworthy guides to the extent that they are free of greed etc., as seen in a passage on how there can be a reliable 'awakening to truth'.

A lay person first assesses a monk for the presence of states of greed, hatred or delusion, which might lead to lying or bad spiritual advice. If he sees that the monk's mind is purified of these, he reposes trustful confidence (saddha) in him. A series of activities then follows, each being 'of service' to the next: 'approaching', 'drawing close', 'lending ear', 'hearing Dhamma', 'remembering Dhamma', 'testing the meaning', 'reflection on and approval of Dhamma', 'desire-to-do', 'making an effort', 'weighing up', 'striving'; and finally, 'he realizes, with his person, the highest truth itself; and penetrating it by wisdom, he sees'. Thus there is a progression from trust in one who has overcome greed, hatred and delusion to the development of insight which itself destroys these in the practitioner.

Ethical behaviour is seen as greatly aided by formally undertaking to follow specific ethical precepts, done by reciting or chanting them, whether by oneself or after a monk, who is then seen as 'administering' these precepts to one. Such acts are seen to set up beneficial tendencies in the mind, and to support the sense of letting oneself and others down if one then breaks a precept one has undertaken to follow. Accordingly, the great Mahayana writer Asaṅga said that the essence of ethics is 'To correctly receive it from someone, to have a quite purified intention, to make correction after failure, and to avoid failure by generating respect and remaining mindful after that'.

The role of 'conscience', in Buddhism, is performed by a small group of qualities, starting with hiri (Pali - or hiri, which is also the Skt form) and ottappa, seen as the immediate cause of virtue and as two 'bright states which guard the world'. Hiri is 'self-respect', which causes one to seek to avoid any action which one feels is not worthy of oneself and lowers one's moral integrity. Ottappa is 'regard for consequences', being stimulated by concern over reproach and blame for an action (whether from oneself or others), and embarrassment before others (especially those one respects), legal punishment or the karmic results of an action.

Heedfulness, a combination of energy and mindfulness, is also said to be the basis of all virtues. Mindfulness is alert presence of mind, cultivated strongly in meditation practice, which enables one to be more aware of one's mental states, including intentions and motives. It is complemented by 'clear comprehension' (Pali sampajanna; Skt sampajanya), which acts to guide one's actual behaviour to be in harmony with one's ideals and goals.

REBIRTH AND KARMA

In Buddhism, 'right view' (Pali samma-ditthi; Skt samyak-drsti) is seen as the foundation of moral and spiritual development. While this begins in the form of correct belief, it can go on to become direct personal knowledge. As outlined at M. III.72, preliminary 'right view' is the belief that:

1. 'There is gift, there is offering, there is (self-) sacrifice': these are worthwhile;
2. 'There is fruit and ripening of deeds well done or ill done': what one does matters and has an effect on one's future;
3. 'There is this world, there is a world beyond': this world is not unreal, and one goes on to another world after death;
4. 'There is mother and father': it is good to respect parents, who establish one in this world;
5. 'There are spontaneously arising beings': some of the worlds one can be reborn in (for example some heavens) are populated by beings that come into existence without parents;
6. 'There are in this world renunciants and brahmins who are faring rightly, practising rightly, and who proclaim this world and the world beyond having realized them by their own super-knowledge': spiritual development is a real possibility, actualized by some people, and it can lead, in the profound calm of deep meditation, to memory of past rebirths in a variety of worlds, and awareness of how others are reborn in such worlds.

THE REALMS OF REBIRTH

In Buddhism, one's present life is seen as one of a countless number of lives stretching back into the past, with no discernible beginning to the series. Such lives take various forms. They may be relatively pleasant, as in the case of rebirth as a human or in one of the many heaven worlds. They may be unpleasant, though, as in the case of rebirth as some kind of animal, as a 'departed one' in the form of a frustrated ghostly being, or in one of a number of hells, where life is like an extended nightmare of intense suffering with feelings that are 'exclusively painful, sharp, severe'. The Mahayana poet Santideva, for example, cites the Saddharma-smrtyupasthana Sûtra as describing murderers being eaten alive by birds in hell, 'But each time he is devoured, so each time he is reborn more sensitive than before'.

None of these realms lasts for ever, though, for all end in death and then (for the unenlightened), another rebirth. Thus even life in the hells, though long lasting, is not eternal. This means that there is hope even for Adolf Hitler: at some time in the far far distant future, he might even become enlightened! – if he were to strive to develop moral and spiritual perfection. At the other end of the scale, the life-span in the many heaven worlds varies from 9 million human years (but only 500 'divine years'!) up to 84,000 aeons, an aeon being a huge time-span. And yet even the gods die, to be reborn and die again.

The Buddhist perspective on the cycle of rebirths is that it is not a pleasant affair, but that all unenlightened people are reborn whether they like it or not, and whether they believe in rebirth or not. The process of life and rebirth is not seen to have any inherent purpose; for it was not designed and created by any being. Thus it is known as samsara, or 'wandering on' from life to life. Thus the only sensible aim, for one who understands samsara to some extent, is to strive, firstly, to avoid its more unpleasant realms, and ultimately to transcend it altogether, by attaining Nirvana (Skt; Pali Nibbana), and to help others to do so. Most Buddhists therefore aim to attain a heavenly or a human rebirth, with Nirvana as the long-term goal. Buddhist heavens, then, are this side of salvation; for Nirvana is beyond the limitations of both earthly and heavenly existence.

Within the round of rebirths, worlds belong to one of three broad categories. The 'realm of sense-desire' comprises the worlds of hells, ghosts, animals, humans and the six lowest heavens. In all these, beings' likes and dislikes dominate and distort their perception of the world. The 'realm of (elemental) form' comprises sixteen heavens, paralleling deep states of meditative calm, which are progressively more subtle and refined, and where various sorts of Brahman deities live. Their perception is not distorted by sense-desire, but they have faults such as pride. The 'formless realm' consists of four extremely subtle realms which, being devoid of anything visible, tangible etc., are purely mental.

KARMA AND ITS EFFECTS

The movement of beings between rebirths is not seen as a haphazard process, but as ordered and governed by the law of karma. Karma (Pali kamma) literally means 'action', and the principle of the 'law of karma' is that beings are reborn according to the nature and quality of their actions. Past actions are said to 'welcome' one in a future life like a person being welcomed by kinsmen, so that:

Deeds are one's own ... beings are heir to deeds, deeds are matrix, deeds are kin, deeds are arbiters. Deeds divide a being that is to say by lowness and excellence. This is explained as referring to the karmic effect of various actions. A person's actions mould their consciousness, making them into a certain kind of person, so that when they die their outer form tends to correspond to the type of nature that has been developed. What begins as a trace in the psyche later crystallizes out as an aspect of a person and their world.

Prior to the time of the Buddha, the basic idea of karma and rebirth had been expressed in the Brahmannical (early Hindu) compositions known as Upanisads. Here, though, there was as much emphasis on karmas/actions being ritually right as on their being ethically right. In Buddhism, though, the emphasis is strongly on the ethical aspect of action as the relevant factor in causing karmic results. It is said that acts of hatred and violence tend to lead to rebirth in a hell, acts bound up with delusion and confusion tend to lead to rebirth as an animal, and acts of greed tend to lead to rebirth as a ghost.

It is also said that 'By constantly committing evil deeds we are reborn in hell, by doing many we become spirits [i.e. ghosts], and when we do only a few we are reborn as an animal'. Rebirth in a hell is also seen as particularly due to both doing evil actions and encouraging others to do them, by approving of and praising such actions. Abstaining from evil actions and encouraging others to do so leads to a heavenly rebirth. In Mahayana Buddhism, it is also held that obstructing a Bodhisattva – a heroic, compassionate being - in a good deed has terrible karmic consequences, for it hinders the welfare of many beings.

Actions can also lead to karmic fruits in a human life. This might be the present life, or a future human life, be this one's next life, or one that comes after one or more other types of rebirth. In textual descriptions of such fruits, one sees that they reflect back on a person something which is particularly appropriate to the nature of the relevant action. In the present life, killing or harming living beings conduces to being shortlived; stealing to loss of wealth; sensual misconduct to rivalry and hatred from others; lying to having to eat one's false words; backbiting to the break-up of friendships; harsh words to having to listen to unpleasant sounds; frivolous chatter to unacceptable, ineffective speech; intoxication to madness.

As regards the fruits of actions in a future human life: mercilessly killing and injuring living beings leads to being short-lived; striking living beings lead to being often ill; being easily angered leads to being ugly; being jealous and spiteful leads to being of no account; being stingy leads to being poor; being haughty and disrespectful leads to being of a lowly family; and not asking about what is morally wholesome and unwholesome leads to being weak in wisdom. The opposite good actions lead to a heavenly rebirth or the opposite kinds of human life. Poor, ill or ugly people are not to be presently blamed for their condition, however, for the actions of a past life are behind them, and the important thing is how they behave in the present and how others act towards them.

Living an ethical life is variously said to lead to: wealth, through diligence; a good reputation; joyful recollection of moral purity; selfconfidence in all types of company, without fear of reproach or punishment; easier progress in meditation; dying without anxiety, and rebirth in a heaven world. It is said that to develop generosity and moral virtue to a small degree leads to rebirth as a human of ill fortune; to develop them to a medium degree leads to being a human of good fortune; to develop them to a high degree leads to rebirth in one of the six sense-desire realm heavens. To reach the heavens of the (elemental) form realm requires meditation, which leads to the attainment of one or other jhana, lucid trances which 'tune' the mind to this level of existence.

The different affiliations of unwholesome and wholesome impulses are nicely expressed by Santideva thus:

'If I give this, what shall I (have left to) enjoy?' – Such selfish thinking is the way of ghosts; 'If I enjoy this, what shall I (have left to) give?' – Such selfless thinking is the quality of the gods.

THE STATUS AND WORKING OF THE LAW OF KARMA

The law of karma is seen as a natural law inherent in the nature of things, like a law of physics. It is not operated by a God, and indeed the gods are themselves under its sway. Good and bad rebirths are not, therefore, seen as 'rewards' and 'punishments', but as simply the natural results of certain kinds of action. Karma is often likened to a seed, and the two words for a karmic result, vipaka and phala, respectively mean 'ripening' and 'fruit'. An action is thus like a seed which will sooner or later, as part of a natural maturation process, result in certain fruits arising to the doer of the action.

What determines the nature of a karmic 'seed' is the will behind an act: 'It is will (cetana), O monks, that I call karma; having willed, one acts through body, speech or mind'. Cetana encompasses the motive for which an action is done, its immediate intention (directed at a specific objective, as part of fulfilling a motive), and the immediate mental impulse which sets it going and sustains it. 'Karma' is the overall psychological impulse behind an action, that which sets going a chain of causes culminating in a karmic fruit. Actions, then, must be intentional if they are to generate karmic fruits: accidentally treading on an insect does not have such an effect, as the Jains believed.

Nevertheless, thinking of doing some bad action is a bad mental action (karma), especially when one gives energy to such a thought, for example by jealousy or anger, rather than just letting it pass. Deliberately putting such a thought down is a good mental karma. The mind is thus seen as constantly generating good and bad karma - whether mild or heavy - by the way it attends to and responds to objects of the senses, memory or imagination. An important point to note, here, is that an action's being good does not consist in its having pleasant karmic results. Rather, it is seen as having pleasant results because it is itself good or wholesome.

It is thus said that good actions are those which are themselves 'bright' as well as being 'with bright result'. Why is the moral tone of an action seen to cause certain results? It is said that wrong view leads on to wrong thought, and this to wrong speech and thus wrong action, while right view has the opposite effect. As wrong actions thus come from the misperception of reality, they can be seen to be 'out of tune' with the real nature of things. As they thus 'go against the grain' of reality, they naturally lead to unpleasant results. Thus it is said to be impossible that wrong conduct of body, speech or mind could result in a 'fruit that was agreeable, pleasant, liked', or for right conduct to lead to a 'fruit that was disagreeable, unpleasant, not liked'.

THE KARMIC FRUITFULNESS OF ACTIONS

Good actions are said to be 'lovely' (kalyana) and to be, or have the quality of, punna, a term which can be used as an adjective or a noun. As an adjective, Cousins sees it as the 'fortune-bringing or auspicious quality of an action', while as a noun 'it is applied either to an act which brings good fortune or to the happy result in the future of such an act'. Thus we see:

Monks, do not be afraid of punnas; this, monks, is a designation for happiness, for what is pleasant, charming, dear and delightful, that is to say, punnas. I myself know that the ripening of punnas done for a long time are experienced for a long time as pleasant, charming, dear and delightful. After developing a heart of lovingkindness for seven years, for seven aeons of evolution and devolution, I did not come back to this world ... [being reborn in a delightful heaven for that time].

Punna is usually, rather limply, translated as 'meritorious' (adjective) or 'merit' (noun). However, 'meritorious' implies deservingness, but what is referred to be something with a natural power of its own to produce happy results; it does not depend on anyone to give out what is due to the 'deserving'. A punna action is 'auspicious', 'fortunate' or 'fruitful', as it purifies the mind and thus leads to future good fortune. Indeed, through other IndoEuropean languages it may be related to the English words 'boon' and 'bounty' (the Thai word for punna is bun). As the noun punna refers to the auspicious, uplifting, purifying power of good actions to produce future happy results, one might translate it as 'goodness-power', but this offers no convenient related adjective.

A better translation would be '(an act of) karmic fruitfulness', with 'karmically fruitful' as the adjective. This makes a connection with the fact that actions (karmas) are often likened to 'seeds' and their results are known as 'fruits' (phalas) or 'ripenings'. While such phalas can be the results of either good or bad actions, and punna relates only to good actions, the English word 'fruit' can also mean only edible, pleasant fruit such as apples, without referring to inedible, unpleasant ones. The link to 'fruitfulness' is also seen in the fact that the Sangha is described as the best 'field of punna', i.e. the best group of people to 'plant' a gift 'in' in terms of karmically beneficial results of the gift.

The opposite of punna is apunna, which one can accordingly see as meaning '(an act of) karmic unfruitfulness' or 'karmically unfruitful', i.e. producing no pleasant fruits, but only bitter ones. A synonym for apunna is papa, which, while often translated as 'evil', really means that which is 'infertile', 'barren', 'harmful' or 'ill-fortuned'. A good way of rendering these meanings would be to see papa as an adjective as meaning '(karmically) deadening', and as a noun as '(karmic) deadness', meaning that what is so described has a deadening effect on the psyche, making it more constricted and lifeless, rather than having an uplifting, fruitful effect.

Buddhists are keen to perform 'karmically fruitful' actions; for punna is an unlosable 'treasure', unlike physical goods. The early texts refer to three 'bases for effecting karmic fruitfulness' (punna-kiriya-vatthus): giving (dana), moral virtue (sila) and meditation, and later texts add to this list. Nevertheless, an act of giving is not such a basis if it is done 'through fear, or with hope of reciprocity, or through attachment, etc. ', rather than 'Through desire to render homage or service'.

KARMIC FRUITFULNESS AND MOTIVE

It is said that 'the mental aspiration of a moral person is effective through its purity'. That is, when such a person gives a gift to a monk or Brahmin with the hope of being reborn in a certain way, this will occur, whether the heart is set on rebirth as a rich human, or in any of the six heavens of the desire-realm, or even in the world of the Brahmans. Yet if such an aspiration is really going to work, it must not be itself the sole motive of the giving, for this is seen to affect the nature of the beneficial karmic result.

If a person gives something to a monk 'with longing, with the heart bound (to the gift), intent on a store (of karmic fruitfulness), thinking "I'll enjoy this after death" ', it is said that he will be reborn for a while in the lowest of all the heavens. A series of what seem to be meant as progressively higher motives is then outlined: giving because one feels 'it is auspicious (sahu) to give'; wishing to continue a family tradition of giving; wishing to support those who do not cook for themselves; because great sages of the past were supported by alms; because giving leads to mental calm, joy and gladness; or because giving enriches the heart and equips it for meditation.

Giving from the last of these motives is then said to lead to rebirth in the first heaven of the realm of (elemental) form, where the Brahmans dwell. Thus doing a good action simply because it is seen to have pleasant results is not the highest of motives - it is better to value goodness in itself, and the peace and wisdom that it facilitates. Accordingly, the Theravadin commentator Buddhaghosa says, on moral virtue:

That undertaken just out of desire for fame is inferior; that undertaken just out of desire for the fruits of karmically fruitful actions is medium; that undertaken for the sake of the Noble state thus, 'This is to be done', is superior.

A generous supporter of the Buddha and his monks and nuns was Anathapindika ('Feeder of the Poor'), who never showed any interest in the results of his generosity, though the Buddha often spoke of these to him. 'He just gives, joyful in the chance to do so' and 'would be less than a perfect giver if he gave for the sake of the rewards that, according to his Master, are derived from the gift'. Nevertheless, acting so as to generate karmic fruitfulness is an effective motive for getting people to begin to act in a more generous and moral way.

While Buddhists often see a large gift as generating more karmic fruitfulness than a small one, a small gift from a poor person is said to be worth as much as a large one from a rich person. Here, purity of mind makes up for the smallness of a gift, for 'where there is a joyful heart, no gift is small'. Thus, 'If you have a little, give little; if you have a middling amount, give a middling amount; if you have much, give much. It is not fitting not to give at all'. Thus it is emphasized that even the poor have the means to give, be this as little as leftover noodles as food for ants.

The karmic fruitfulness of a gift is not seen to depend on its usefulness to the recipient (which may be variable and unpredictable), but on the donor's state of mind when giving. Indeed, a person with nothing to give can do an act of karmic fruitfulness by helping someone else to give or by simply rejoicing at another person's giving, which is a good mental act in itself. This even applies to the joyful contemplation of one's own past wholesome deeds. Indeed, two types of beneficial meditation are said to be the recollection of one's own unbroken virtue and of one's liberal generosity, though the karmic fruitfulness of actions is said to dwindle if one brags about the relevant good act.

It is said that an act of karmic fruitfulness is greater than its opposite, as regretting a bad action can stop one repeating it, but one has no need to regret a karmically fruitful action, and it leads on to further spiritual progress - joy, calm, concentration and insight - which generates more karmic fruitfulness. The state of mind in which an act is done is partly a matter of motive, but also of the manner in which it is done. This is also seen as having an effect on the karmic result. It is said that to give 'disrespectfully, without due consideration, not with one's own hand, of something unwanted (by oneself), not with a view to the future (i.e., not recognizing the giving as having a karmic fruit)' leads to a karmic fruit where the mind does not incline to the enjoyment of the best of sense-pleasures (i.e. being miserly with what one has), and to one's family and workpeople not being considerate towards one.

This is how a bad man gives, a good man giving in the opposite way. More specifically, it is said: 1. Giving with faith (saddha) leads to the giver having wealth and being handsome; 2. Giving respectfully or carefully leads to the giver's wife, family and workpeople listening carefully to him and helping him in an understanding way; 3. Giving at the appropriate time leads to wealth coming at the appropriate time; 4. Giving with no reluctance in the heart leads to the mind inclining to enjoyment of the best of sensepleasures; 5. Giving without harm to self or other leads to future wealth being free from harm from fire, water, kings, thieves or unfriendly heirs.

The Mahayana tradition agrees with such passages from Theravada texts; for Santideva cites the Aksayamati Sûtra as saying that a 'gift' is no real gift if it harms someone, or is less than has been promised, or is accompanied by contempt, boasting or hostility, or causes distress, or is of what would otherwise have been thrown away, or is not given with one's own hand, or is improper, or given at the wrong time.

THE SANGHA AS THE BEST FIELD OF KARMIC FRUITFULNESS

The karmic fruitfulness of an act of giving is said to be great not only if the state of mind of the donor is pure, but also if the recipient is very virtuous or holy. Thus 'even so little as a handful of rice-beans ... bestowed with devout heart upon a person who is worthy of receiving a gift of devotion will be of great fruit of great splendour'. A gift is said to be 'purified' by the donor, the recipient, both or neither, according to whether they are virtuous and of good character or not. To be 'purified' by a donor, a gift must be 'rightfully acquired, the mind well pleased, firmly believing in the rich fruit of karma'.

Even if a gift is given by an evil person, in the opposite way, it may be 'purified' by the virtue of the recipient. While a gift to an animal yields a hundredfold, and to an unvirtuous human a thousandfold, one to an ordinary virtuous person yields a hundred thousandfold, and one to a spiritually Noble person has an immeasurable fruit. A gift of the virtuous to the virtuous has the greatest fruit, though.

A gift given to renunciants and Brahmins who are not endowed with the qualities of the path to Nirvana is of little fruit, like a seed sown on poor, ill-watered soil. The opposite applies for a gift to those endowed with the factors of the Eightfold Path, which leads to much good karma and conduces to spiritual accomplishment. The well-trained Noble Sangha (which includes some lay people) is said, in a well-known chant, to be 'worthy of respect, worthy of hospitality, worthy of gifts, worthy of salutation, an unsurpassed field of karmic fruitfulness for the world'.

For this description to apply to a monk, he should be such that objects of any of the senses do not engender attachment, elation or depression so as to disturb his calm concentration. He controls his senses, uses his robe and alms-food without greed, patiently endures unpleasant sensations or abuse, and avoids situations in which he might be suspected of misconduct, abandons lustful or cruel thoughts, and develops the seven factors of awakening, beginning with mindfulness.

He is endowed with straight for wardness, speed of understanding, gentleness, patience and restraint. One can summarize this by saying that the saintly members of the Noble Sangha, being of exemplary, inspiring character, engender much joy in those who give to them, such that the giving generates a powerful purifying effect in the givers' minds, leading to abundant karmic fruitfulness. As Noble persons are relatively few in number, the best 'field of karmic fruitfulness' normally available is the monastic Sangha, which symbolizes the Noble Sangha and is also likely to contain some members of it.

According to the Theravadin Milindapanha, even a monk of poorly developed virtue 'purifies gifts of faith' through the good effects of participating in the life of the Sangha, and associating with those more strongly intent on spiritual development. In any case, the gift of a virtuous person to a monk will always be purified by the giver. When giving to the Sangha, it is best to give without discrimination or favouritism, even if one knows that some monks are more spiritually advanced than others, and irrespective of whether a monk is a relative or friend.

It is also better to give to the Sangha of monks or nuns as a whole, or to a group specified by them, than to an individual monk or nun. As the alms-giver bestows long life, a good appearance, happiness and strength on the recipient of alms, then such qualities, in a human or heavenly rebirth, are said to be the karmic results of alms-giving. This means that the monks' virtuous way of life can be of powerful benefit to others. Accordingly, it is said that the Buddha was not uncompassionate when he went with his monks on alms-round in an area where there was famine, for giving is the source of good fortune. Nevertheless, the 'field' of giving can also be excellent when one gives to the sick or a parent or other benefactor.

KARMA AND FATALISM

While belief in the law of karma can sometimes degenerate into a form of fatalism, the Buddha emphasized that deterministic fate (niyati) and karma are very different. The idea of karma emphasizes the importance of human action and its effects: people make their own 'destiny' by their actions. Karma and fatalism differ on two scores. Firstly, humans have freedom of choice; their present actions are not the karmic results of previous actions, though karmic results may influence the type of action that a person tends to think of doing, because of the character he or she has developed. Secondly, not everything that happens to a person is seen as due to karma.

Any unpleasant feelings or illnesses that one has can arise from a variety of causes: 'originating from bile, phlegm, or wind, from union (of bodily humours), born from seasonal changes, born from disruptive circumstances, arriving suddenly [due to the action of another person], or born of the fruition of karma'. The aspects of life which are seen as the result of past karma include one's form of rebirth, social class at birth, general character, crucial good and bad things which happen to one, and even the way one experiences the world. Out of the mass of sense-data, one only ever gets 'edited highlights' of what lies around one. Some people tend to notice pleasant things, while others tend to notice unpleasant things; these differences are said to be due to karma.

As a person never knows what aspect of any situation may have been determined by karma, difficult situations are not to be passively accepted, but a person should do his or her best to improve them. Only when things happen in spite of efforts to avert them might they be put down to past karma. If the situation can be averted or changed, fine, but then any anxiety or suffering it led to may be still seen as due to past karma. As an aid to planning courses of action in a karma-influenced world, many traditionalist Buddhists use divination methods such as astrology at certain points in their lives, so as to try to gauge what their karma has in store for them.

The idea of the influence of karma, while not fatalistic, does encourage a person to live patiently with a situation. Rather than making new bad karma by getting angry with society, family, or other people, blaming them for his or her lot, he or she can view the situation as the result of his or her own past actions. This attitude arises from a person's taking responsibility for the shape of his or her life. Thus the Buddha criticized theories which saw all experiences and associated actions as due either to past karma, the diktat of a God, or pure chance. Like people of other religions, however, Buddhists sometimes have an idea of fate, in parallel with their idea of karma, or they may even use past karma as an excuse for continuing with present bad karma.

FLEXIBILITY IN THE WORKING OF KARMA

It is mostly at the human level that good and bad actions are performed. The gods are generally seen to have little scope for doing either good or evil, and most simply enjoy the results of the previous good actions which led to their existence. Animals, ghosts and hell-beings have little freedom for intentional good or bad actions, though Vasubandhu claims that hell-beings can do some good and bad actions, but any good actions will only bring fruits in a later life. Moreover, the higher animals can sometimes act virtuously, if not in a self-consciously moral way.

Beings in the lower rebirths generally just reap the results of previous bad actions. When these results come to an end, the results of some previous good actions will come to fruition and buoy up the being to some better form of life, until sooner or later the being reaches the human level again. The law of karma is not regarded as rigid and mechanical, but as the flexible, fluid and dynamic outworking of the fruits of the volition associated with actions. Thus the full details of its working out, in specific instances, are said to be 'unthinkable' (acinteyya) to all but a Buddha.

DELAYED RESULTS OF KARMA

Karma does not just bring results in the next life: an action can have effects later in the present life, the next life, and also in some subsequent ones. Only very evil or good actions are certain to bring their result in the immediately following rebirth. When King Ajatasattu became his disciple, the Buddha said (not to his face) that he was done for, with his fate sealed, as he had earlier killed his own father.

One who has deliberately killed his or her mother or father, or an Arahat, or has shed the blood of a Buddha, or caused a schism in the monastic Sangha, is said to have done an action with immediate karmic effect, leading to rebirth in a hell for the remainder of an aeon. No good actions can avert such a rebirth in the next life. Such people cannot be monks or nuns, and cannot understand Dhamma even if they try. On the other hand, those who are 'Noble persons', through some degree of experience of Nirvana, will as a result certainly be free of all sub-human rebirths, so that their insight has an invariable effect on their next rebirth.

All other actions are indeterminate as to when they will bring their results. It is thus said that the next life of one who lives a moral life and is of right view might be in a heaven or a hell. The latter will be the case if he or she did a strong evil deed in a previous life that had not yet produced its result, if he or she took to evil deeds late in life, or if he or she firmly took up a wrong view at the time of dying. That might be the case if a habitually generous person were to come to regret his generosity as worthless, and resent those who had not repayed his kindness.

In that case, he would die in a bad state of mind and make a bad transition to the next life. This accord with Itivuttaka 13–14, which says that one who dies at a time when his mind is corrupted is reborn in a hell, while one who dies while his mind is clear and calm is reborn in a heaven. In a similar way, a generally immoral person, with wrong view, might be reborn in a heaven if there were some previously unexpended strong good karma from the past, if he took to good ways late in life, or firmly took up a right view at the time of dying. Nevertheless, the results of the good or bad actions would catch up with the person sooner or later, perhaps in an attenuated form, just as a smouldering fire will burst into flames at some time in the future.

THE EFFECT OF CHARACTER

The karmic result of an action is not necessarily of precisely the same nature and magnitude as the action itself. Killing a goat does not necessarily lead to being reborn as a goat and being killed - though it may do. The Buddha says that if 'just as a man does an action, so does he experience (its fruit)' were the case, there would be no opportunity for spiritual improvement, no way of growing beyond previous unvirtuous ways. He goes on to say that, for a person whose virtue, mind and wisdom are undeveloped, a small evil deed may lead to rebirth in a hell, just as a pinch of salt in a cup of water makes it undrinkable.

For a person with developed virtue, mind and wisdom, though, the same action will produce its karmic results in the present life, with little, if any, in a future life, just as a pinch of salt does not make the river Ganges undrinkable. This seems to imply that, in a spiritually developed person, a small moral slip will have less effect, as it will be 'diluted' by his or her generally moral nature.

For a spiritually undeveloped person, described here as having a 'small self', the same act has a greater impact. It, so to speak, 'flavours' a person's character more, setting up greater reverberations within it, in tune with other such reverberations. The good person suffers less from his or her bad action, though as most of the karmic results come in this life for him or her, this may not be immediately apparent. The Mahayana Upasaka-Sila Sûtra also holds that one with selfdiscipline and spiritual effort may change some karmic effects from being serious ones in a future life into lighter ones in the present life.

REMORSE AND THE ACKNOWLEDGEMENT OF FAULT

An important way in which the karmic result of a bad action can be lessened is by a person's regretting it, thinking that 'that evil deed cannot be undone by me' and resolving not to do it again. This can be seen to lessen the psychological impact of the act, so as to reduce its karmic fruit. In the Sarvastivadin view, an action is not 'accumulated' (upacita), with a full karmic result, if it is not repeated (the number of times is dependent on the nature of the action), so as to be 'complete', or is regretted.

The notion of regret or acknowledgement of fault, as lessening the karmic fruit of an action is also affirmed in the Mahayana. It is said that a Bodhisattva who quarrels with another Bodhisattva, but who confesses this fault and promises future restraint, escapes from the consequences of that action. In a recent Tibetan account, based on canonical sources, it is said that to confess, with regret, even to the actions of killing one's father and an Arahat, will lessen - to some extent – the terrible bad karma of such actions.

The importance of regretting a bad action is seen in the refrain, 'It is a mark of progress in the discipline of the Noble Ones, if anyone recognises the nature of his transgression and makes amends as is right, restraining himself for the future.' Among monks and nuns, the acknowledgement, to another monk or nun, that one has broken a monastic rule is a vital part of monastic discipline. Likewise, in the Mahayana, Bodhisattvas, whether monastic or lay, should conceal their good points as well as acknowledge their faults.

Regret has an impact on karmic results even in the case of good actions. Thus it is said that a man who, in a past life, had given alms to an enlightened ascetic, but then regretted doing so, was born as a rich man - because of his giving - but as a miser unable to enjoy his wealth, because of his regret. The Mahayana makes much of the power of acknowledgement of past evil, particularly when done to heavenly Buddhas or Bodhisattvas. In this tradition, such actions, if sincere and devout, are seen as able to remove past bad karma.

It cites the Catur-dharmaka Sûtra as saying that, to overcome the accumulation of evil, the Bodhisattva should: 1. Practise self-reproach, by immediately regretting any bad action; 2. Follow any bad action by counteractive good ones; 3. Resolve to abstain from such bad actions and 4. Express faith in the three refuges, and not neglect the compassionate aspiration to Buddhahood (the bodhicitta). On 1, Ss. 160 cites the Suvarna-prabhasottama Sûtra's chapter on acknowledging faults, which says that one should call on all Buddhas to look on with compassion, acknowledge all the evil deeds one has done, and say:

On account of the evil done by me previously even in hundreds of aeons, I have a troubled mind oppressed with wretchedness, trouble and fear. With an unhappy mind I continually fear evil acts. Wherever I go there is no enjoyment for me anywhere. All the Buddhas are compassionate. They remove the fear of all beings. May they forgive my sin and may they deliver me from fear. May the Tathagatas [Buddhas] take away for me the defilement of impurities (and) acts. And may the Buddhas bath me with surging waters of compassion.

Counteractive good actions are seen as the development of deep insight, or clearly understanding the difference between evil and good action, with the latter stopping the effect of bad karma. It is also said that reciting a certain hundred-syllable mantra 8,000 times, while meditating on Buddhas and Bodhisattvas, makes one's evil pass away.

In one Tibetan account, it is said that, while the death of the Arahat Udrayana was due to his having killed an enlightened ascetic in a past life, his being able to become an Arahat was due to his immediate regret at this deed, followed by building a shrine to the ascetic and making offerings there, with continual confession of his evil deed. In line with the above, Eastern Buddhism contains a rite in which a person repeatedly bows before an image in a spirit of repentance for any past evil deeds that have been committed.

In the Theravada tradition, while the Buddha is generally seen as no longer contactable by humans, there is a chant from Sri Lanka in which a person, expressing reverence to the Buddha, Dhamma and Sangha, asks each to 'forgive' or 'be patient' (khamatu) if they have been wronged in any way. Likewise, a chant from Thailand asks the Buddha, Dhamma and Sangha to 'accept' (patigganhatu) any wrong actions done towards them, using the same sort of wording as used by monks when acknowledging, to another monk, monastic transgressions.

However much Buddhism may value genuine remorse, it does not – certainly in its Theravada form - encourage feelings of guilt; for such a heavy feeling, with its attendant anguish and self-dislike, is not seen as a good state of mind to develop, being unconducive to calm and clarity of mind. Indeed, it can be seen as an aspect of the fourth spiritual hindrance, of agitated 'restlessness and worry'. Such a feeling might arise as part of the natural karmic result of an action, but is not to be actively indulged in. In the Mahayana, Santideva says that a Bodhisattva should not be excessively regretful for wrong actions, citing the Upali-pariprccha as saying that a Bodhisattva retains his great virtue if he returns to the aspiration for Buddhahood not more than a few hours after doing an evil deed.

2

Rebirth, Karma and Motivation

Belief in rebirth and karma clearly has an impact on the way people view their actions: good and bad actions matter; they are of consequence, not things with any impact on life. Good actions are thus encouraged because, through their goodness, they lead to pleasant, uplifting effects for the doer. Bad actions are discouraged as their badness leads to unpleasant karmic results. Thus Melford Spiro found that, in Burma, the two most common reasons given for keeping the precepts are fear of hell and the fact that the precepts were ordained by the Buddha.

The idea of the cycle of rebirth also provides a perspective on life which is supportive of sympathy and respect for other beings. Within the round of rebirths, all beings are part of the same cycle of lives. Each human being has been an animal, ghost, hell-being and god in the past, and is likely to be so again at some time in the future. Any form of suffering one witness in another human or other being has been undergone by oneself at some time: thus one should not cling to rebirths and should have compassion for other sentient beings.

In one's innumerable past lives, the law of averages dictates that most beings one comes across, however one may dislike them now, have at some time been close relatives or friends, so that lovingkindness towards them is appropriate. Thus in Jataka story no. 68, a man and his wife address the Buddha as their son, and say that it is the duty of children to comfort their parents in old age. As the man and woman are not the Buddha's recognized parents, they explain that, in past lives, the man had been his father, uncle and grandfather 500 times each; likewise the woman had been his mother, aunt and grandmother 500 times each.

Such teachings, of course, urge a kindness and non-violence towards all forms of life. Humans are part of the same cycle of lives as other beings, and are not separated from them by a huge gulf. Nevertheless, the more complex and developed a being is, the worse it is to harm or kill it; so it is worse to kill a human than an animal.

Working with a rebirth perspective also helps sustain a long-term motivation for moral and spiritual practice. While death means that one loses all physical possessions, and is parted from one's loved ones and one's life's 'attainments', the purification of character that is developed by ethical and meditative practice is seen as something that death does not destroy. It becomes part of one's mental continuum that will 'spill over' into another life. In that life, the spiritual development of this life may be neglected or further built on: but at the very least, it can act as a positive residue of this life, to be used as a foundation for further development. The opposite applies in the case of bad character-traits.

In the Tibetan tradition, there is a series of reflections, drawing on central Buddhist principles, to help motivate spiritual practice. The first reflection concerns the rarity of human life. Given the other forms of rebirth, and the fact that there are many more animals (including birds, fish, insects etc.) than humans, being born as a human is a rare and precious opportunity for spiritual improvement. To gain a human or divine rebirth, or have two in a row, is said to be rare.

As against the number of beings born in other realms, those reborn as humans are like a pinch of sand compared to the size of the earth, or the number of India's pleasant groves compared to its rough terrain. The chance for a being in a hell to be reborn as a human is less than that of a blind turtle, surfacing once a century, to happen to put its head through a ring moved by the winds across the surface of the sea. Even if a human rebirth is attained, the person will be poor, ugly and ill, and will tend to do evil actions which will send him or her back to hell.

The Tibetan Buddhists talk of having attained a 'precious human rebirth': a marvellous opportunity for spiritual growth that should be used wisely and respected in others. As it may be cut short at any time by death, it should not be frittered away: 'So if, when having found leisure such as this, I do not attune myself to what is wholesome, there could be no greater deception, and there could be no greater folly'.

In the lower realms, there is much suffering and little freedom of action. In the heavenly realms, life is blissful in comparison with human life, but this tends to make the gods complacent, particularly those in the highest heavens, so that they may also think that they are eternal, without need of liberation. The human realm is a middle realm, in which there is enough suffering to motivate humans to seek to transcend it by spiritual development, and enough freedom to be able to act on this aspiration. It is thus the most favourable realm for spiritual development.

Not any human rebirth has this precious quality, though. The early texts say that one cannot lead the holy life of the monk at a time when Buddhism has died out, or in a region devoid of Buddhist monastics and lay followers, or if one has a wrong view which denies the efficacy of karma and the possibility of spiritual development, or is stupid or deaf and dumb.

Santideva cites the Gandavyûha Sûtra on the hard-to-attain favourable circumstances which make liberation possible: 1. rebirth as a human, 2. at a time when there has been a Buddha, 3. the perfection of one's bodily senses, 4. hearing the Dharma, 5. the company of good men, 6. a true 'good friend' (teacher), 7. the means for 'instruction in the true rule of life' and 8. the holy life (Ss. 2). Reflecting on this, he says 'If the arising of a Tathagata, faith, the attainment of a human body, and my being fit to cultivate virtue are scarce, when will they be won again?'

The second of the Tibetan reflections is on the uncertainty as to when one's life will end: no-one knows how much longer they have before they die - it might not be long. In line with this, the early texts say that human life, however long it lasts, is comparable to a line drawn on water. Those entering a hellish rebirth, moreover, are told that they have ignored the significance of the suffering of birth, ageing, sickness and death, not being motivated to do karmically fruitful deeds by the realization that they were themselves still liable to such states.

It is emphasized that death and old age come to all people, whatever their social class: 'As though huge mountains made of rock, so vast they reach up to the sky, were to advance from every side, grinding beneath them all that lives, so age and death roll over all' (S. I.2). Once the Buddha advised a good king distracted by the affairs of state that if he, King Pasenadi, were told that such mountains were advancing on him, he would of course is full of fear at such a destruction of human life, given that a human rebirth is so hard to obtain.

When asked what he could do in such circumstances, Pasenadi says he could only 'live in accord with Dhamma, live rightly, do what is wholesome and do karmically fruitful actions'.The third reflection is that, after death, one will be reborn according to one's karma - and the backlog of one's karma from this and previous lives might not be such as to lead to a human rebirth next time. The fourth reflection is that, in whatever form one is reborn, suffering will be part of that life, whether as hellish agony, human pain and worry, or the more subtle unsatisfactoriness of a heaven realm.

The fifth reflection is that such suffering can only be transcended by attaining Nirvana, and the sixth is that to attain Nirvana, one need to practise under the guidance of a spiritual preceptor. Accordingly, one should apply oneself to spiritual practice now, for the benefit that this will bring both to oneself and others: 'As from a heap of flowers many a garland is made, even so many good deeds should be done by one born mortal'.

THE FOUR NOBLE TRUTHS

In early Buddhism and in the Theravada tradition, the most central teaching is that on the Four Noble Truths. These express spiritually ennobling insights which basically assert that:

1. The processes of body and mind and the experience of life are dukkha (Pali; Skt duhkha): unsatisfactory,

frustrating and productive of suffering, whether in a gross or subtle form;

2. This situation is caused by 'craving' (Pali tanha; Skt trsna), demanding desires which lay one open to frustration and disappointment, and keep one within the round of rebirths, with its attendant ageing, sickness and death;
3. This situation can be transcended by destroying craving, and associated causes such as attachment, hatred and delusion, in the experience of Nirvana. Once this is attained during life, a person will no longer be reborn, but will pass into final Nirvana at death, beyond space, time and dukkha;
4. The way to attain this goal is the 'middle way' consisting of the Noble Eightfold Path.

The first of these 'Truths' is elaborated through an analysis of personality through five kinds of unsatisfactory processes:

1. Material form (rûpa), consisting of various physical processes;
2. Feeling (vedana), consisting of the 'taste' of any experience as pleasant, unpleasant or neutral;
3. Identification (Pali sanna; Skt samjna), consisting of the interpretative function of mind, acting so as to label sense-objects, either correctly recognizing them or misperceiving them;
4. Constructing activities (Pali sankharas; Skt samskaras), consisting of will (cetana), and various other active mental processes such as moods and emotions;
5. Discernment or discriminative consciousness (Pali vinnana; Skt vijnana), the basic awareness of there being an object of the senses or mind, and the discernment of it as having various parts or aspects, which are then labelled by identification.

These comprise the five 'groups' (Pali khandhas; Skt skandhas), or 'personality factors'. All of them are seen as mutually conditioning each other, as well as being affected by sense-objects. They are seen as in a state of constant change, whether of a subtle or more obvious kind. Consequently, they are seen as impermanent (Pali anicca; Skt anitya), so as to be unstable and not fully satisfactory (Pali dukkha; Skt duhkha), and to be all 'not-Self' (Pali anatta; Skt anatma): not a permanent, self-secure I or Self. It is emphasized, though, that normally we erroneously look on ourselves and the world as made up of permanent, desirable, substantial things. We are thus attached to aspects of ourselves and the world, and so suffer when they change or disappear.

Nevertheless, in this collection of impersonal, ever-changing and conditioned events or processes, there are relatively stable, repeated patterns of arising that account for the persistence of what one might call a person's 'character'. Moreover, the dynamic pattern which is a person, though devoid of a permanent self or essence, flows on from life to life, driven by the forces of craving and karma. This process is explained by Conditioned Arising (Pali paticca-samuppada; Skt pratitya-samutpada; Harvey, 1990a: 54–60), which at an abstract level is the principle that mental and physical phenomena only arise or exist when their appropriate conditioning factors arise or exist.

In its usual concrete application, Conditioned Arising spells out a specific sequence of twelve conditioned and conditioning states that explains the ongoing flow of personality and rebirths: 1. spiritual ignorance or misperception underlays the 2. intentions and concerns of unenlightened people - karma - so that these direct 3. consciousness into noticing certain things and into being reborn in a certain way thus 4. the sentient body is sustained in life or develops in the womb at the start of a new life. This supports the 5. senses, the basis of 6. sensory stimulation and thus 7. feeling. Thus 8. craving for and against pleasant and unpleasant feelings arises, hence 9. grasping and 10. further involvement in the stream of existence. This leads on to (11) rebirth in either a new situation or a new life, which leads on to (12) ageing and then death of these: dukkha.

SUFFERING

The emphasis that all the conditioned processes that compose a person, and all worlds of rebirth, are impermanent, dukkha and not-Self forms an important part of the philosophical basis of ethics in Buddhism. The aim of overcoming dukkha, both in oneself and others, is the central preoccupation of Buddhism, and one towards which ethical action contributes. As Buddhists come to appreciate the extent of dukkha in their own lives, and to see that they so often contribute to it by their deluded response to life's happenings, the natural human feeling of sympathy (anukampa) for others - solidarity with them in the shared situation of dukkha – is elicited and deepened.

Accordingly, the importance of 'comparing oneself with others' is stressed, for both self and other 'yearn for happiness and recoil from pain' (M. I.341). When explaining the five basic ethical precepts, the Buddha once gave the following reflection as a reason for keeping them:

For a state that is not pleasant or delightful to me must be so to him also; and a state that is not pleasing or delightful to me, how could I inflict that upon another?

In a more general context, the Buddha is also reported to have said: 'Having traversed the whole world with my thought, I never yet met with anything that was dearer to anyone than his own self. Since the self of others is dear to each one, let him who loves himself not harm another'. Thus, on finding some boys tormenting a snake and poking it with sticks, the Buddha said:

All trembles at punishment, Life is dear to all. Comparing others with oneself, one should neither kill nor cause to kill. (Dhp. 130)

Likewise:

Comparing oneself to others in such terms as 'Just as I am, so are they, just as they are so am I', one should neither kill nor cause others to kill. (Sn. 705)

These passages emphasize that other beings are just like oneself in desiring pleasure and disliking pain, so that there is no good reason to add to the common lot of suffering by inflicting it on others. Doing so, moreover, harms oneself as well as others, for:

Whoever, seeking his own happiness, Harms with sticks Pleasure-loving beings, He gets no happiness hereafter. (Dhp. 131).

The benefit of self and other are intertwined, because of the law of karma, so that concern to lessen one's own suffering goes hand-in-hand with lessening that of others. Helping others helps oneself (in terms of karmic results and good qualities of mind that are developed), and helping oneself (by purifying one's character) enables one to help others better.

IMPERMANENCE

While impermanence often leads to suffering, it also means that people, having no fixed Self, are always capable of change for the better, and should be respected accordingly, rather than dismissed as unworthy by saying, for example, 'Oh, he's a thief. ' A famous example of such change is reported in Buddhist texts, which tell of a time when the Buddha deliberately visited the haunt of the murderous ascetic-bandit Angulimala, as he saw that he needed only a little exhortation to change his ways, become a monk, and soon attain Nirvana.

Whatever a person is like on the surface, it is held that the depths of their mind are 'brightly shining' and pure. This depth purity, referred to as the 'embryo of the Truth-attained One' (Tathagata-garbha) – or 'Buddha-nature' – in the Mahayana, represents the potential for ultimate change: the attainment of enlightenment, and as such is a basis for respecting all beings.

The changes involved in the round of rebirths are also relevant to ethics, for they enable one to consider beings aside from their present roles, character and nature. No matter how 'bad' beings may be, they will have been different in previous lives, and at some point in their incalculable number of lives, they must have crossed paths with one and been good to one: 'It is not easy, monks, to find a being who has not in the past been one's mother, or one's father, brother, sister, son or daughter'.

Viewing them in such a light enables one to have a positive regard for them. Not only past, but also future changes are relevant. In advising that one should always attend to the good points of people, so as to overcome ill-will towards them, the Theravadin commentator Buddhaghosa advises that if a person is so evil as to have no apparent good points, then compassion should be had towards him or her on account of the great suffering that he or she will undergo as a karmic result of such evil.

Labelling someone as having a certain fixed nature often has a bad effect on him or her, whereas respecting him or her helps elicit change for the better. This cannot be forced, however: it is up to him or her. Nor should one passively accept negative traits in oneself as unchangeable. They need acknowledgement, but as they, like all else, are conditioned phenomena, they can be changed if their causes are understood and undermined. The same applies to wholesome states of mind: they can decay if not sustained by appropriate practice, so they are not grounds for being complacent or conceitedly looking down on others. Indeed, to do so or to treat others badly is just the way to undermine one's existing wholesome states.

From the Buddhist point of view, there are three forms of 'conceit' (mana), all based on the delusion of having a fixed 'I' as one's nature. Looking at others and comparing oneself to them, one then either sees oneself as 'superior', 'inferior' or (in a competitive or complacent way) 'equal', rather than simply calmly assessing what qualities one presently has, and how these might be strengthened or weakened.

NOT-SELF AND RESPECTING OTHERS

The teaching that no permanent Self or I exists within a person is also a support for ethics. While it does not itself support a positive regard for persons as unique entities, as the Christian emphasis on the value of individual persons does, it works in other ways. Primarily, it undermines the attachment to self - that 'I ' am a positive, self-identical entity that should be gratified, and should be able to brush aside others if they get in 'my' way - which is the basis of lack of respect for others. It undercuts selfishness by undercutting the very notion of a substantial self. Anger, for example, feeds off the notion that 'I' have been offended. The idea of not-Self does not deny that each person has an individual history and charachter, but it emphasizes that these are compounds of universal factors.

In particular, it means that 'your' suffering and 'my' suffering are not inherently different. They are just suffering and so the barrier which generally keeps us within our own 'self-interest' should be dissolved, or widened in its scope till it includes all beings. The aspect of the not-Self teaching which emphasizes that we are not as in control of our own minds as we would like to think also adds a leavening of humility and a sense of humour to our attitude to the weaknesses of ourselves and others, for it is said that all those who have not yet had any glimpse of Nirvana are 'deranged'.'Respect for persons' is in many ways a key basis of Western ethics. It may be summed up as comprising four main elements (Smart, 1972):

1. The right to 'individuation': to be treated not just as a human being, but as a particular one, with all one's personal difference;
2. The right to 'acceptance': to be taken as one is, good or bad;
3. The right to 'self-direction': to autonomy and the making of one's own choices;
4. The right to impartial treatment.

Buddhism has not traditionally expressed its ethics in terms of 'rights', but more in terms of the appropriateness and benefit of treating others well. This is partly because no unchanging 'owner' of inalienable 'rights' is accepted, and because 'demanding rights' can lead to anger and greed if one is not careful. Nevertheless, the Buddhist perspective on how one should treat others provides analogues to the above four 'rights':

1. Individuation: while there is no permanent Self, each person is seen as a particular, individual combination of changing mental and physical processes, with a particular karmic history. This means that specific spiritual advice must be adapted to a person's character, to help them evolve in a better direction. The goal may largely go beyond individual differences, but the path must take account of them.
2. Acceptance: good and bad qualities are not fixed parts of an unchanging 'Self ', so one should never tie a person down to what he or she has done or been in the past. Persons should always be addressed with regard to their present state, and openness to possible future changes. The faults that others have or have had are also something that we have or have had at some time.

3. Self-direction: any worthwhile change must come from within, by understanding and personal development. It cannot be forced from without. People can be offered opportunities to change, but it is up to them if they take them.
4. Impartial treatment: all have the potential for Nirvana, in this or a future life and all bring themselves into their situations, good or bad, by their own karma. Thus all should be viewed with equanimity and impartiality.

THE NOBLE EIGHTFOLD PATH

The Noble Eightfold Path is the Middle Way of practice that leads to the cessation of dukkha. The Path has eight factors, each described as right or perfect (Pali samma; Skt samyak): 1. right view or understanding, 2. right resolve, 3. right speech, 4. right action, 5. right livelihood, 6. right effort, 7. right mindfulness and 8. right concentration or unification. These factors are also grouped into three sections. Factors 3–5 pertain to sila (Pali; Skt Sila), moral virtue; factors 6–8 pertain to samadhi, meditative cultivation of the heart/mind (citta); factors 1–2 pertain to panna (Pali; Skt prajna), or wisdom.

The eight factors exist at two basic levels, the ordinary (Pali lokiya; Skt laukika), which leads to good rebirths, and the transcendent (Pali lokuttara; Skt lokottara) or Noble (Pali ariya; Skt arya), which builds on this preliminary development to go beyond rebirths, to Nirvana. There is thus both an ordinary and a Noble Eightfold Path. Most Buddhists seek to practise the ordinary Path, which is perfected only in those who are approaching the lead up to 'stream-entry'. At stream-entry, a person gains a first glimpse of Nirvana and the 'stream' which leads there, and enters this, the Noble Eightfold Path. Each Path-factor conditions wholesome states, and progressively wears away its opposite 'wrong' factor, until all unwholesome states are destroyed.

Ordinary 'right view' (Pali samma-ditthi; Skt samyak-drsti) relates mainly to such matters as karma and rebirth, making a person takes full responsibility for his or her actions. It also covers intellectual, and partial experiential, understanding of the Four Noble Truths. Noble right view is true wisdom, knowledge which penetrates into the nature of reality in flashes of profound insight, direct seeing of the world as a stream of changing, unsatisfactory, conditioned processes.

Right resolve concerns the emotions, with thought rightly channelled towards peaceful freedom from sensuality, and away from ill-will and cruelty to lovingkindness and compassion. At the transcendent level, it is the focused applied thought of one practising the Noble Path. Right speech, at the ordinary level, is the well-established abstaining from lying, divisive or harsh speech, and empty gossip. At the transcendent level, each of the three factors relating to 'virtue' is a person's spontaneous restraint from wrong speech, action or livelihood, or immediate acknowledgement to another person when such acts are done. Right action is abstaining from wrong bodily behaviour: onslaught on living beings, taking what is not given, and wrong conduct with regard to sense-pleasures.

Right livelihood is avoiding ways of making a living which cause suffering to others: those based on trickery and greed, or on trade in weapons, living beings, meat, alcoholic drink or poison. The three last factors of the Path are of the Noble level when they are accompanied by other factors at this level. Right effort is directed at developing the mind in a wholesome way. The first effort is to avoid the arising of unwholesome states of mind which express attachment, hatred or delusion.

The second seeks to overcome or undermine unwholesome states which nevertheless arise. The third is directed at the meditative development of wholesome states of mind, while the fourth is the effort to maintain and stabilize wholesome qualities of mind which have been generated. Right mindfulness (Pali sati; Skt smrti) is a crucial aspect of any Buddhist meditation, and is a state of keen awareness of mental and physical phenomena as they arise within and around one, and carefully bearing in mind the relationship between things. Right concentration or unification (samadhi) refers to various levels of deep calm known as jhanas (Pali; Skt dhyanas): states of inner collectedness arising from attention closely focused on a meditation object.

The order of the eight Path-factors is seen as that of a natural progression, with one factor following on from the one before it.

Right view comes first because it knows the right and wrong form of each of the eight factors; it also counteracts spiritual ignorance, the first factor in the chain of Conditioned Arising, leading to dukkha. From the cold knowing of right understanding blossoms a right way of thinking which has a balancing warmth. From this, a person's speech becomes improved, and thus his or her action.

Once he or she is working on right action, it becomes natural to incline towards a virtuous livelihood. With this as basis, there can be progress in right effort. This facilitates the development of right mindfulness, whose clarity then allows the development of the calm of meditative concentration. Neither the ordinary nor the Noble Path is to be understood as a single progression from the first to eighth factor, however. Right effort and mindfulness work with right understanding to support the development of all the Path-factors: the Path-factors mutually support each other to allow a gradual deepening of the way in which the Path is trodden.

NOBLE PERSONS

Any person not yet on the Noble Path is known as a puthujjana (Pali; Skt prthagjana), an 'ordinary person' who lacks the mental balance of those on the Noble Path, the eight kinds of spiritually 'Noble' (ariya) persons. These comprise the Noble Sangha, which with the Buddha and Dhamma are the 'three refuges' of a Buddhist. The Noble persons are those who have been permanently changed, to some degree, by insight into Dhamma: the Stream-enterer, Once-returner, Non-returner and Arahat (Pali; Skt Arhat), and those established on the specific paths which lead up to each of these states.

The Stream-enterer is one who gains a first glimpse of Nirvana, and so will be free from rebirth at anything less than a human level, and be bound to become an Arahat within seven lives at most. The Once-returner is one whose remaining lives will include only one in the 'sense-desire-realm', as a human or god in a lower heaven. The Non-returner will not be reborn again in the desire-realm, but will be reborn in one or more of the 'pure abodes', a small group of heavens in the '(elemental) form-realm'. Here, the Non-returner will go on to become an Arahat. The Arahat is one who fully experiences Nirvana during life, and who destroys the causes of any more rebirths. At death, he or she passes into final Nirvana, beyond all time, space, conditions and dukkha.

The progression through these grades of sanctity is measured by the number of the ten spiritual 'fetters' which have been destroyed. The Stream-enterer destroys the first three:

1. 'Views on the existing group', which takes a permanent Self as existing in some relation to one or all of the five personality groups;
2. Vacillation in commitment to the three refuges and the worth of morality;
3. Grasping at moral precepts and vows.

The Stream-enterer has unblemished morality (S. II.69–70), not in the sense that no unwholesome action is ever done, but in the sense that, if it is, he or she always freely acknowledges having done such a deed (Sn. 232). There is no grasping at moral precepts because, though they are carefully followed, there is no belief that these alone will lead to becoming an Arahat: meditation and wisdom are also needed. Moreover, a person keeps the precepts without thinking what he or she will gain by doing so. The Once-returner destroys the gross forms of the next two fetters:

4. Sensual desire;
5. Ill-will.

The Non-returner destroys even subtle remnants of them, so as to have great equanimity. The Arahat destroys the remaining five fetters:

6. Attachment to the (elemental) form heavenly world;
7. Attachment to the formless heavenly worlds;
8. The 'I am' conceit, perhaps now in the form of lingering spiritual pride;
9. Restlessness;
10. Spiritual ignorance.

In order for such negative traits to be eradicated from the mind, other positive ones must also be developed: the factors of the Noble Eightfold Path, and other associated ones such as the 'seven factors of awakening': mindfulness, Dhamma-investigation, vigour, joy, tranquillity, mental unification and equanimity.

THE PLACE OF ETHICS ON THE PATH

From the perspective of the Four Noble Truths, ethics is not for its own sake, but is an essential ingredient on the path to the final goal. This is well expressed in a passage which explains that 'purity of virtue' leads onward to 'purity of mind', this to 'purity of view', and this, through various stages of increasing spiritual insight, to 'utter Nirvana without attachment', 'unshakeable freedom of mind'. It is emphasized that while each stage supports the next, the 'holy life' is not lived for any of them except the final one. This is because at any lower stage of spiritual progress, there is still attachment and a person may become complacent, conceited or arrogant about his or her attainments, thus hindering further progress. The foundational importance of ethics for the rest of the Path is, however, crucial.

So you see, Ananda, wholesome virtues have freedom from remorse as object and profit; freedom from remorse has gladness; gladness has joy; joy has tranquillity; tranquillity has happiness; happiness has concentration; concentration has seeing things as they really are; seeing things as they really are has turning away and non-attachment; turning away and non-attachment have release by knowing and seeing as their object and profit. So you see, Ananda, wholesome virtues lead gradually up to the summit. In this process of development, the cultivation of one stage leads naturally on to the cultivation of the next, so that the components of the Path support one another and interact to form a harmonious whole. The basis for them all, however, like the earth for plants or a foundation for a building, is moral virtue.

In terms of the division of the Path into virtue, meditation and wisdom (always given in this order), the Path can be seen to develop as follows. Influenced and inspired by good examples, a person's first commitment will be to develop virtue, a generous and self-controlled way of life for the benefit of self and others. To motivate this, he or she will have some degree of preliminary wisdom, in the form of some acquaintance with the Buddhist outlook and an aspiration to apply it, expressed as saddha, trustful confidence or faith. With virtue as the indispensable basis for further progress, some meditation may be attempted. With appropriate application, this will lead to the mind becoming calmer, stronger and clearer.

This will allow experiential understanding of the Dhamma to develop, so that deeper wisdom arises. From this, virtue is strengthened, becoming a basis for further progress in meditation and wisdom. Accordingly, it is said that wisdom and virtue support each other like two hands washing each other (D. I.124). With each more refined development of the virtue-meditation-wisdom sequence, the Path spirals up to a higher level, until the crucial transition of stream-entry is reached. The Noble Path then spirals up to Arahatship.

Defilements such as greed, hatred and delusion exist in the form of unwholesome activities of body and speech, unwholesome thoughts, and the latent tendencies in the mind which are the root of all these. Moral virtue restrains the external expression of the defilements, meditation undermines active defilements in the mind, and liberating insight destroys defilements in the form of latent tendencies. These three levels of development can perhaps be seen in the popular verse:

Not to do any evil, to cultivate what is wholesome, to purify one's mind: This is the teaching of the Buddhas. (Dhp. 183)

WISE, SKILFUL, WHOLESOME ACTIONS

In the Pali Canon, the term punna occurs mainly in the context of giving and other aspects of lay practice, as a pan-Indian term for good, beneficial actions. However, a more frequently occurring term for good actions, with more particularly Buddhist connotations, is kusala (Pali; Skt kusala). A kusala action is a blameless one (A. I.263), which is 'wise' or 'skilful' in producing an uplifting mental state and spiritual progress in the doer (unless he or she has already attained the goal), or 'wholesome', in that it involves a healthy state of mind - stable, pure, unencumbered, ready-to-act, calm and contented (Payutto, 1993: 19). The opposite term, for a bad action, is akusala: 'unwholesome' or 'unskilful'.

L. S. Cousins traces the meaning of kusala/kuSala in pre-Buddhist and Buddhist sources and summarizes thus:

1. An original meaning of 'intelligent' 'wise';
2. Expert in magical and sacrificial ritual (in the [pre-Buddhist] Brahmannas); for Brahmins, of course, this would precisely constitute wisdom.
   A. Skilled in meditational/mystic (/ascetic?) practices (in the early Pali sources and, no doubt, in other contemporary traditions), including skilled in the kind of behaviour which supported meditation, etc., i.e. Sila [keeping moral precepts], etc.
   B. Skilled in performing dana [giving] and yanna [sacrifice], now interpreted in terms of central Buddhist ethical concerns; and associated with keeping the precepts and so on.
3. Kusala in later Buddhist and Jain sources becomes generalized to refer to something like wholesome or good states. So there is no reason to doubt that by a later period (i.e. in the commentaries and perhaps later canonical sources) kusala in non-technical contexts means something which could be translated as 'good'. (1996: 156)

Under 3, Cousins see the meaning as states 'produced by wisdom' that contribute to the development of various qualities leading to awakening (1996: 137). While this meaning often occurs in the Suttas, and is emphasized in the Canonical Abhidhamma, the Suttas also often see kusala as meaning 'blameless'. The criteria for determining whether an action is kusala or akusala will be discussed below. Before that, the somewhat ambiguous relationship between karmically fruitful actions and Nirvana will be discussed.

At the culmination of the Noble Eightfold Path stands the Arahat, who is actually said to have 'passed beyond' punna and papa and to have 'abandoned' them: 'Not clinging to karmically fruitful or deadening actions, he abandons what has been taken up, and does not fashion (anything more) here'. He or she constructs no karmically fruitful or unfruitful action. What could this mean? It certainly does not mean that an Arahat abandons moral behaviour: an Arahat is said to be fully endowed with moral virtue and insight, one with the highest wholesomeness, incapable of killing. The Buddha, himself an Arahat, is foremost in moral virtue, even though this is only part of his perfection.

The Nirvana experienced by the Arahat during life is said to be the destruction of attachment, hatred and delusion. As the Arahat is one in whom attachment/greed, hatred and delusion, the roots of unwholesome action, have been destroyed, he or she is no longer capable of morally unwholesome action, though he or she may inadvertently break a monastic rule, such as not eating after noon, through ignorance of worldly matter. His or her actions are morally wholesome, but arise spontaneously, without resistance from unwholesome traits. This is one sense in which the Arahat has 'abandoned karmic fruitfulness': he or she no longer has to deliberate about doing the 'right thing'.

A second way in which he or she is beyond karmic fruitfulness is that his or her actions no longer have either good or bad karmic fruits. It is said that karma is conditioned by craving – destroyed by the Arahat – and that only when there is greed, hatred and delusion can fruit-bearing karma originate. While non-greed, nonhatred and non-delusion are causes of action, like their opposites, the wholesome actions springing from them are said to conduce to the future cessation of (good or bad) karma, while the unwholesome actions springing from their opposites are said to conduce to the continued arising of karma in the future.

In one who still has remnants of greed, hatred and delusion, acts rooted in non-greed etc. still bring good karmic results. In one in whom they are destroyed, actions are wholesome, but do not generate future fruits. Thus the Buddha once spoke of four kinds of action:

1. That which is dark, and with dark result: harmful actions that lead to rebirths with harmful experiences in them;
2. That which is bright and with bright result: non-harming actions that lead to rebirth with non-harmful experiences in them;
3. That which is both dark and bright and with dark and bright result: a mixture of the first two;

4. That which is 'neither dark nor bright, neither dark nor bright in result, the action that conduces to the destruction of actions': the will to get rid of the first three types of action.

Elsewhere, Nirvana is said to be 'neither black nor white' (A. III.384–6), and the fourth type of action is said to be the Noble Eightfold Path. This path is also said to be 'the way leading to the stopping of karma', with the stopping of karma being 'that stopping of bodily action, verbal action and mental action by which one touches freedom'. That is, the Noble Eightfold Path leads up to a profoundly still experience, Nirvana, in which the capacity of actions to bring future karmic fruits comes to an end.

The Arahat is one for whom both unwholesome and wholesome moral conduct (sila) are said to have have 'stopped' completely. Unwholesome conduct is stopped by replacing wrong conduct with right conduct. Wholesome conduct is stopped by being 'virtuous (sila-va), but not sila-maya'. Now, 'maya' means something like 'made of' or 'consisting in'. At It. 51, there is reference to the 'basis of effecting an act of karmic fruitfulness' 'consisting in moral virtue (sila-maya)'.

The commentary (M. A. II.270) explains the term at M. II.26–7 as meaning that the Arahat has nothing further to add to his or her already developed moral virtue, and accordingly I. B. Horner translates 'and has no addition to make to moral habit'. K. N. Jayatilleke translates the term as meaning 'not virtuous through conditioning' (1972: 26), and Bhikkhus Nanamoli and Bodhi translate 'but he does not identify with his virtue', meaning that he or she is not attached to it, seeing it as not-Self, like everything else.

The upshot of these different readings is the same, though: the Arahat, standing at the culmination of the Noble Eightfold Path, has perfected all its factors, including those relating to moral virtue. He or she has nothing further to add to this moral and spiritual perfection, but his or her virtue is not constrained by ideas of what he or she ought to do: he or she just naturally acts in a virtuous way, without being attached to virtue. Thus an Arahat says that he is non-violent because of his destruction of attachment, hatred and delusion, not because of grasping at precepts and vows.

As the Noble Eightfold Path leads to rendering karmic fruitfulness ineffective, karmic fruitfulness is clearly seen to have some limitations. Thus it is sometimes said that a monk may think of returning to the lay life because he can then enjoy life's pleasures and still perform karmically fruitful acts. Also relevant is a distinction between 'ordinary' and Noble right view. The first, concerning belief in karma and rebirth, is said to have 'cankers [mental limitations holding the mind back from Nirvana], it is on the side of karmic fruitfulness, it ripens in cleaving (to another rebirth)'.

The second, wisdom or direct insight, is said to be 'Noble, cankerless, transcendent, a factor of the path [the Noble Eightfold Path to Nirvana]' (M. III.72). The point here seems to be that 'karmically fruitful' actions, while they have the beneficial result of leading to good rebirths, have limitations in that they cannot, unaided, lead to Nirvana, which transcends all rebirths - and their unsatisfactory nature - whether bad or good. To attain Nirvana, wisdom or insight is also needed. While 'karmically fruitful' actions strengthen character-traits which facilitate the development of wisdom, the latter is an extra step.

Moral virtue is said to be the 'gateway to the city of Nirvana'(Vism. 9), though not to go all the way. Karmic fruitfulness is necessary for movement towards Nirvana – thus some texts even say the latter is attainable by karmic fruitfulness (Khp. 7) – but not itself sufficient. Nevertheless, it is incorrect to see actions orientated to karmic fruitfulness and actions of the Noble Path as radically different, as King (1964) and Spiro (1971) have in their analyses of Burmese Theravada Buddhism. They see the former kind of actions as the sphere of the laity and the latter as the sphere of the monks.

That this is a false dichotomy has been well argued by Keown (1992: 83–105), Aronson (1980: 78–96) and Katz (1982: 175–80). Both monks and laity can and do practise both types of action, and the first type is the very foundation - and continued sustainer - of the second. It is not the case that moral virtue (a prime source of karmic fruitfulness) is a mere instrumental means towards a goal consisting only of insight. One standing at the goal of Buddhism has both moral virtue and deep insight, for he or she has perfected all factors of the Noble Eightfold Path, covering moral virtue and meditation as well as wisdom.

PHILOSOPHY OF ACTION

CRITERIA FOR DIFFERENTIATING GOOD AND BAD ACTIONS

The criteria for deciding what action is 'wholesome' (kusala) and what 'unwholesome' (akusala) is are of three kinds:

1. The motivation of the action;
2. The direct effects of the action in terms of causing suffering or happiness;
3. The action's contribution to spiritual development, culminating in Nirvana.

The three possible motivating 'roots' of 'unwholesome' action (M. I.47) are:

1. Greed (lobha), which covers a range of states from mild longing up to full-blown lust, avarice, fame-seeking and dogmatic clinging to ideas;
2. Hatred (Pali dosa; Skt dvesa), which covers mild irritation through to burning resentment and wrath;
3. Delusion or spiritual misorientation (moha), the veiling of truth from oneself, as in dull, foggy states of mind through to specious doubt on moral and spiritual matters, distorting the truth or turning away from it, and misconceptions, such as that it is acceptable to kill animals as a religious sacrifice or to eat, or to kill criminals (AKB. IV.68d).

The opposites of these are the three 'roots' of wholesome action:

1. Non-greed, covering states from small generous impulses through to a strong urge for renunciation of worldly pleasures;
2. Non-hatred, covering friendliness through to forbearance in the face of great provocation, and deep lovingkindness for all beings;
3. Non-delusion, covering clarity of mind through to the deepest insight into reality.

While phrased negatively, these three are nevertheless seen as positive states. The importance of seeing the harmfulness of the unwholesome roots and the benefit of the wholesome ones is emphasized in the Kalama Sutta. The three roots of the unwholesome are intertwined. Greed and hatred are grounded in delusion, and greed may lead to hatred. It is said that greed is a lesser fault, but fades slowly, hatred is a great fault, but fades quickly, and delusion is a great fault and fades slowly (A. I.200). This gives a clear indication of Buddhist values, especially the need to develop wisdom, so as to overcome delusion. It is also said that common motives for evil deeds are partiality, enmity, stupidity and fear, and that greed, hatred and delusion can each lead a person to abuse others with the thought 'I am powerful'.

An action is also assessed in terms of its direct effect in terms of causing suffering or happiness. This is shown by a passage where the Buddha advises that one should reflect before, during and after any action of body, speech or mind, to consider whether it might conduce to the harm of oneself, others or both, so that it is unwholesome and results in dukkha. If one sees that it will, one should desist from the action. If one sees that the action conduces to the harm of neither oneself nor others, nor both, it can be seen to be wholesome, with a happy result.

The 'harm' to oneself which is relevant here is spiritual harm, or material harm if this arises from self-hatred (for example by harsh asceticism, M. I.342–9): an act which benefits others at the expense of material harm to oneself is not unwholesome. Harm to oneself is also seen to arise as an immediate result of unwholesome action: 'One who is thus caught up, whose mind is thus infected, in the karmically deadening, unwholesome states born of greed …of hatred …of delusion, experiences suffering, stress, agitation and anxiety in this present life'.

An action is also assessed in terms of its contribution to spiritual development, culminating in Nirvana, which criterion is seen to lead on from the one just described above. Thus it is said that unwholesome conduct is that which causes injury that is, having dukkha as fruit, because it leads to the torment of oneself, others or both, and conduces to the arising of further unwholesome states and the diminution of wholesome ones: that is, having unhealthy effects on the psyche. Wholesome actions are of the opposite kind. Moreover, 'wrong resolve', for example, is said not only to conduce to the harm of self and other but to be 'destructive of intuitive wisdom, associated with distress, not conducive to Nirvana', while 'right resolve' has the opposite effect.

Overall, one can say that an 'unwholesome' action is one that arises from greed, hatred or delusion, leads to immediate suffering in others and/or oneself - and thus to further karmic suffering for oneself in the future - and contributes to more unwholesome states arising and liberating wisdom being weakened. 'Wholesome' actions have the opposite characteristics. They arise from a virtuous motive, are free of all direct harm to self and other, contribute to the improvement of the character of the person who performs them, and thus assist in moving a person along the Path to Nirvana.

While saying that an action is 'karmically fruitful' refers to its potency to produce happiness as a karmic result, saying that it is 'wholesome' has a different emphasis. Any karmically fruitful action is also wholesome, but there is a range of mental states which are referred to as wholesome, but are not specifically said to be karmically fruitful.

Using the above criteria, one list of what is unwholesome is: 1. Onslaught on living beings, 2. Taking what is not given, 3. Sensual misconduct, 4. Lying speech, 5. Divisive speech, 6. Harsh speech, 7. Gossip, 8. Covetousness, 9. Ill-will and 10. Wrong view. That is, it is wrong action of body (1–3), speech (4–7) and mind (8-10). What is wholesome is restraint from each of these (M. I.47). Such actions are said to be 'of unwholesome will (akusala-sancetanika), yielding dukkha, ripening in dukkha'.

Of these actions, only those relating to body and speech would normally be seen as coming under the purview of the English words 'morality' or 'ethics'; indeed, the Pali word sila, or 'moral virtue', has a similar range. That which is 'wholesome' or 'unwholesome' then, goes beyond the purely moral/immoral to include states of mind which may have no direct effect on other people. All the factors of the Eightfold Path, for example, are seen as 'wholesome'.

COMPARISONS WITH WESTERN ETHICAL SYSTEMS

Various scholars have reflected on the question of what is the nearest analogy to Buddhist ethics in Western ethical theory. One theory it is commonly likened to is Utilitarianism, which holds that a specific act (Act Utilitarianism) or a general type of action (Rule Utilitarianism) is right if, and only if, it results in a greater amount of happiness, or a reduction in unhappiness, for anyone affected by it. That is, the rightness of an action consists in the nature of its effects. However, in Buddhism, while good actions are seen as leading to future happiness as a karmic fruit, they do so because they are right; they are not right because they happen to lead to happy karmic fruits.

Those good actions are seen as having happy karmic fruits for the agent will be one factor relevant to his or her motivation for doing such acts:

> Buddhism says that, if one wants to attain prosperity, amicable social relationships or a good reputation, self-confidence or calm and joy, a good rebirth or progress towards Nibbana, then act in such and such a way: for this is how such things are fostered. If one behaves otherwise, then one will suffer in this and subsequent lives, as a natural (karmic) result of unwholesome actions.

Nevertheless, happy fruits are not what make good actions good. Motive and intention are crucial, though when simple joy is observed to arise from an action, it is often a sign that it is a good action, and the immediate effect of an action on the happiness of others is one factor in assessing it.

A danger in Utilitarianism (particularly Act Utilitarianism) is that it tends to a perspective of 'the end justifies the means', so a means which one might want to say is evil might be 'justified' by the goal it is seen to lead to. In Buddhism, certainly in its Theravada form, this is not possible: only wholesome means have the ability to conduce to truly wholesome ends. Admittedly, the goal of Buddhism, Nirvana, is equivalent to the end of dukkha, the end of suffering, a goal which a Utilitarian would share.

But Nirvana is also the destruction of attachment, hatred and delusion (Itivuttaka. 38–9), and the Path to this is good or wholesome because it is intrinsically related to this goal, not contingently so: it is not the Path which just happens to conduce to it. As it consists of actions rooted in non-greed, non-hatred and non-delusion, the Path has natural affinities to Nirvana, the destruction of the opposites of these. Moreover, it is not that Nirvana, the absence of greed, hatred and delusion, is (arbitrarily) chosen as the ultimate goal, and then actions seen as 'good' if they happen to conduce to this. Actions rooted in non-greed etc. can be recognized as good or wholesome whether or not one is a Buddhist with Nirvana as one's ultimate goal.

This shows that a better broad Western analogue to Buddhist ethics is Aristotelian ethics, as argued by Keown, supported by Tatz (1986: 1) and Shaner (1989: 175) for Mahayana ethics and Mahayana-shaped Japanese ethics respectively. For Aristotle, ethics is about developing one's ethos or 'character' by the cultivation of virtues – wholesome dispositions and inclinations - which conduce to the goal of eudaimonia. This goal involves true happiness and a human flourishing in which the psyche is marked by excellencies of both reason and character.

Both Aristotle and Buddhism aim at human perfection by developing a person's knowledge and character, his or her 'head' and 'heart'. In Buddhist terminology, this is done by eliminating both spiritual ignorance and craving, which feed off each other, by cultivating intellectual, emotional and moral virtues sharing something of the qualities of the goal towards which they move. In both Aristotelian and Buddhist ethics, an action is right because it embodies a virtue which conduces to and 'participates' in the goal of human perfection. Both are 'teleological' in that they advocate action which moves towards a telos or goal/end with which they have an intrinsic relationship.

This is as opposed to being simply 'consequentialist', like Utilitarianism: judging an act by the effects it happens to have – though some Utilitarians would dispute this distinction. Another possible Western analogue for Buddhist ethics is Kantian ethics, which sees what is good as residing in a good will, which respects other people as ends in themselves rather than as means to one's own ends. While there are clearly some similarities with Buddhist ethics, Buddhism does not ignore the actual results of action on others as opposed to the will or motive behind it.

More importantly, Kantian ethics is deontological, or based on duty. For Buddhism, though, moral constraints are not imposed on people without regard to their own good, and the Buddha said that he gladly taught others out of compassion and sympathy, not because he felt that this was a burdensome duty. A moral life is not seen as a bald 'ought', but as an uplifting source of happiness, in which the sacrifice of lesser pleasures facilitates the experiencing of those which are more enriching and satisfying, for both oneself and others. Nevertheless, duty is not a concept foreign to Buddhism; it is simply that what one should do is also seen as what is enriching and rewarding.

Overall, the rich field of Buddhist ethics would be narrowed by wholly collapsing it into any single one of the Kantian, Aristotelian or Utilitarian models, though Buddhism agrees with each in respectively acknowledging the importance of 1. A good motivating will, 2. Cultivation of character and 3. The reduction of suffering in others and oneself. This is because the first two of these are seen as crucial causes of the third of them, while aiming at the third, in a way which does not ignore aspects of the full karmic situation, is a key feature of the first two.

A key aspect of Western ethical systems is that moral prescriptions should be universally applicable to all people who can understand them. Buddhism, though, is generally gradualist in approach, so while it has ethical norms which all should follow from a sense of sympathy with fellow beings (such as not killing living beings), others only apply to those who are ready for them, as their commitment to moral and spiritual training deepens. This most obviously applies to the monastic level of commitment as compared with that of an ordinary lay person. A monk or nun vows to follow over 200 precepts or training rules, as compared with the usual five of a lay person.

Many of these relate to behaviour which does not directly harm other beings - and thus do not come under the scope of ethics, as such - but are simply part of a training system to help a person overcome his or her greed, hatred and delusion: the roots of any behaviour which does harm others. The level of morality and general conduct of a monk or nun is expected to be of a higher level than that of a lay person, because he or she has made the commitment to be ordained. Actions which would be totally unacceptable for a monk or nun, such as sexual intercourse, are acceptable (within certain limits) for a lay person.

INTENTION, KNOWLEDGE AND DEGREES OF UNWHOLESOMENESS IN ACTIONS

The degree of unwholesomeness of an action is seen to vary according to the degree and nature of the volition/intention behind the action, and the degree of knowledge (of various kinds) relating to it. A bad action becomes more unwholesome as the force of the volition behind it increases, for this leaves a greater karmic 'trace' on the mind. The Theravadin commentator Buddhaghosa discusses the unwholesome act of 'onslaught on breathing (i.e. living) beings' as follows:

> 'Onslaught on breathing beings' is, as regards a breathing being that one perceives as living, the will to kill it, expressed through body or speech, occasioning an attack which cuts off its life-faculty. That action, in regard to those without good qualities (guna-) – animals etc. – is of lesser fault when they are small, greater fault when they have a large physical frame. Why? Because of the greater effort involved. Where the effort is the same, (it is greater) because of the object (vatthu-) (of the act) being greater. In regard to those with good qualities – humans, etc. – the action is of lesser fault when they are of few good qualities, greater fault when they are of many good qualities.
>
> But when size or good qualities are equal, the fault of the action is lesser due to the (relative) mildness of the mental defilements and of the attack, and greater due to their intensity. Five factors are involved: a living being, the actual perceiving of a living being, a thought of killing, the attack, and death as a result of it. There are six methods: with one's own hand, by instigation, by missiles, by contrivance (trap or poison), by sorcery, by psychic power.

Here, one can see that an act is made worse by a stronger or more perverse volition motivating and accompanying it. To kill a virtuous human, or one deserving respect such as a parent, is particularly perverse, just as giving to a virtuous person is particularly good.

That killing in a state of intense defilement is worse would mean that premeditated killing, from a mix of greed, resentment and also delusion, would be very bad. Other aspects of the above quotation will be discussed in later chapters, as appropriate. One can see similar principles at work, though, in the Mahayana Upasaka-Sila Sûtra, which holds that the object of the act of killing can be heavy (such as a parent) or light (an animal), and the thought behind it heavy or light dependent upon the degree of viciousness in it.

In such an act, there is the motivating root, the means, and sometimes the thoughts and actions which come after it as its completion, such as eating an animal one has killed. Of these, just the means, just the completion, the root and means, or the means and completion may be heavy. 'If the object is the same, it is the thought that makes the difference of heavy or light retribution'.One can also outline a five-fold gradation of types of bad action according to the degree of both intention and knowledge involved:

1. An action performed without intending to do that particular action, for example accidentally treading on an insect, without any thought of harming.

Such an action is not blameworthy and generates no bad karmic results. There is no offence for a monk if he kills a living being unintentionally, not realizing that his actions would harm a living being. Likewise, in regard to the case of the monastic offence - entailing defeat in the monastic life - of deliberately killing a human, there is no actual offence entailing defeat 'if it was unintentional, if he did not know, if he were not meaning death, if he was out of his mind, the first offender (who caused the rule to be made)'. It is also said that to crush worms accidentally while crushing sugar-cane for its juice is not blameable, nor was the Buddha blameable when, after a certain sermon of his, monks of wrong view vomited blood.

Again, Udana 28–9 says that a certain monk was not to be blamed for addressing other monks as if they were outcastes, for it was merely a habit arising from his last 500 lives, in which he had been a member of the Brahmin class, who were accustomed to speak in such a harsh manner. The text explains that the monk had no hatred in his heart when saying this, and its commentary, which actually sees him as an Arahat, says that his harsh speech was not something that he himself desired. In the Jatakas is another story on non-intentional action. A captured partridge is hit by a hunter so that its cry attracts other birds to their deaths.

As it has no bad intention, and only plays a passive part in the hunter's actions, it is not blameworthy. What, though, of an act which is not intended to harm any being, but is such that one knows, or has strong reasons to expect, that a being or beings will be harmed? For example, crushing the sugar-cane when one knows, or strongly suspects, that it contains worms? Or driving a car on a hot day when it is very likely that many insects will be killed? Are these cases of (a) culpable carelessness, or (b) simply a lack of extra-mile altruism? In the Vinaya, certain forms of careless behaviour, such as throwing a stone off acliff, are small offences.

Nevertheless, the Kurudhamma Jataka, of which Andrew Huxley gives a good analysis (1995c), emphasizes the idea that unintended harm to others should not be counted against one, and that it is not wise to agonize over such matters.

2. If one knows that a certain kind of action is evil, but does it when one is not in full control of oneself, for example when impassioned.

This is a lesser evil than doing it with full knowledge of what one was doing, and with full intention. The Milindapanha discusses the case of a Jataka story in which the Bodhisattva, as an ascetic, sacrifices (or almost does?) many animals when a king says that he can marry his beautiful daughter if he does so. The Miln says that this was an action done when he was 'out of his mind (visannina) with passion, not when he was thinking of what he was doing (sancetanena)'.

The action was not in accordance with his nature, for he was 'unhinged, impassioned. It was when he was out of his mind, thoroughly confused and agitated, with thoughts confused, in a turmoil and disturbed', like a madman. Thus it is said that 'Evil done by one who is unhinged is not of great blame here and now, nor is it so in respect of its ripening in a future state. 'Indeed, if an actual madman kills, his action is pardonable. Likewise, a monk who breaks a monastic rule when mad does not commit an offence. Here, one can say that the actions of a madman are blameless (as at 1. above), while actions done when impassioned are of little blame - though getting into such a state can be held to be blameworthy. Actions done when drunk can perhaps be assessed in a similar way.

3. If one does an evil action when one is unclear or mistaken about the object affected by the action.

This is moderately blameable. Thus, while it is an offence requiring expiation for a monk to kill a non-human living being intentionally, it is a lesser offence, of 'wrong-doing', if (a) he is in doubt whether it is a living being, or (b) if he tries to damage a non-living thing that he thinks is, or might be, living, for example by shooting an arrow at it. There is no offence, though, if he fires an arrow at a living being not knowing that it is a living being.

An attempt to use such reasoning to lessen the evil of an action can be seen in the actions of the Buddhists of Zanskar, a Kashmiri valley bordering Tibet, who feel that they have to kill predatory wolves. The killing is done as indirectly as possible: after the wolves have been lured into high-walled stone traps, large stones are thrown over the wall by a group of people - consequently nobody knows for sure whether their stones are among those that kill a wolf. In this way, the people seek to put a distance between themselves and what they see as a practically necessary evil. This is comparable to the way in which, in the West, only some of the rifles used in a firing squad are loaded with live bullets, so that nobody knows whether they have fired one of the fatal shots.

1. An evil action done where one intends to do the act, fully knows what one is doing, and knows that the action is evil.

This is the most obvious kind of wrong action, with bad karmic results, particularly if it is premeditated. Thus Buddhaghosa states, at the start of this section, that in the case of killing a living being, the precept against this is only broken if five factors are present: 'a living being, the perception of a living being, a thought of killing, the action of carrying it out, and death as a result of it'. If any of these factors is absent, as when death results from a person striking something that he does not realize is living, the precept is not broken.

4. An evil action done where one intends to do the act, fully knows what one is doing (as in 4.), but do not recognize that one is doing wrong.

This is seen as the worst kind of action. Such an action is discussed at Miln. 84, which says that if an evil action is done 'unknowingly (ajanato)', it has a worse karmic effect than if it is done 'knowingly'. This is illustrated by saying that a person taking hold of a red-hot iron ball is more severely burnt if he does so unknowingly. This suggests that an evil action - such as an onslaught on a living being – is worse if it is done without hesitation, restraint or compunction. This will be the case if an action is not seen to be wrong, as there will be no holding back on the volitional force put into the action. On the face of it, this may seem unjust; but perhaps not on further reflection.

In an English court of law, the 'ringleader' of a crime is often punished more harshly than those who had been led on, half-reluctantly. The leader may well be held to see no wrong in the action, but the others have some compunction. Relevant to this is the case of doing a so-called 'necessary evil', for example killing an enemy to prevent one's country being invaded. Here, recognition that such an act is still evil is preferable to a glorying in the act. Indeed, some of the worst crimes of the twentieth century have been carried out under the banner of an ideology which saw them as 'right' actions: Hitler's Holocaust, Stalin's purges and the Khmer Rouge's murder of many Cambodians.

If one has the wrong view, for example that one belongs to the 'master race' and that Jews are 'vermin' who should be killed, one is not likely to hold back in one's evil actions. Here, wrong physical action is both accompanied by and strengthened by wrong view. In all the above, intention, knowledge and ignorance are crucial factors, though there are different kinds of 'ignorance', only some of which excuse an action. If one knows that sentient beings should not be harmed, but not that one's action is actually harming one, this 'ignorance' of a matter of ordinary fact excuses one. The spiritual ignorance which leads one to deny that harming living beings is wrong is no excuse, however, but compounds a wrong action.

Of course, lesser degrees of spiritual ignorance - lack of spiritual insight - are seen to affect all beings until they are enlightened. This forms a background to all unenlightened actions, good or bad, though it specifically feeds into wrong actions when they are 'rooted' in, that is, motivated by, delusion (and associated greed and hatred): 'whatever unwholesome states there are, all are rooted in spiritual ignorance ... are fixed together in spiritual ignorance', like rafters in a roof-top. Among other things, spiritual ignorance feeds the 'I am conceit': the conviction that one has a permanent Self to protect and bolster up: the root of selfishness.

It is no coincidence that the Buddha's criticism of people is not couched in terms of their being evil or sinful, but usually in terms of their being 'fools'; thus, when dismissing a person, he always did so without anger. It is said that a person is known as a 'fool' by immoral conduct of body, speech and mind, just as a wise person is known by moral conduct. Moreover, a fool neither recognizes a transgression for what it is nor accepts another person's acknowledgement of having committed a transgression.

That is, it is good to see one's own faults and pardon those of others. Indeed, 'a fool who knows he is a fool is to that extent a wise person; the fool who thinks he is wise is called a fool indeed'. Given this, it is clear that one is, for example, doing a slaughterer a favour if one tries to get him to see that what he is doing is wrong (though to do so in an aggressive manner is unwholesome as it is an expression of ill-will). Even if he carries on in his trade, he is better off if he is at least uneasy about what he is doing, and starting to have some compunction about his actions. The unease might unsettle whatever calm he had, but the Buddha, at least, was willing to tell people things that they found unpleasant if it would be of spiritual benefit to them.

Of course, this assumes that there is such a thing as objectively wrong action. Only then does it make sense to say that one could be mistaken in holding something not to be wrong.

Given Buddhism's clear criteria of what is unwholesome action, it is quite happy to agree to this, with an action's 'wrongness' subsisting in a combination of the action itself and the state of mind in which it is done. It is not a matter of what a person happens to like or dislike (emotivism), or of what his or her society happens to approve or disapprove of (cultural relativism).

Parallel things to the above could mostly be said for good actions: 1. an unintentionally beneficial action is not to one's credit; 2. a beneficial action done when one was in a disturbed state is only of little credit; 3. an action done when one is unsure that there is someone to benefit from it is moderately good; 4. an intentional good action is straightforwardly good. The straightforward parallel breaks down at 5. though: if one thinks that a right action is a wrong one but still does it, one will do it with compunction, so that it is a less good action than it would otherwise be.

This perhaps shows the wholesome potency of 'right view'. Indeed, it is said that the thing which is the greatest cause of the arising or increase of unwholesome states, and the non-arising or decrease of wholesome states, is wrong view. It is likewise the greatest cause of rebirth in hell. For one of wrong, evil view, whatever deeds of body, speech or mind 'undertaken in complete accord with (that) view, whatever volitions, aspirations, resolves, activities, all those states conduce to ...suffering'. The opposite is said of right view. As a wholesome mental action, right view is defined as holding that good and bad actions do have results beyond this life, and that spiritually developed people have knowledge of such things, wrong view being to deny this.

On the other hand, one who holds the false view that there are no good or bad actions, and no karmic results of these, have their 'roots of wholesomeness' (kuSala-mûlas) cut off (AKB. IV.79a–c), though they return if they start to doubt this view or come to see that it is wrong. A partial 'good' parallel to 5 would be doing a truly good action even though others say that it is a bad one. Here, great determination is needed, so the action can be seen as a very good one.

Another partial parallel is the case of a young child doing a good action even though he or she has not been told that it is 'good', as at Asl. 103, where a young boy is told to catch a hare to provide healing food for his sick mother; he cannot do so, though, for he intuitively recognises that it is wrong to kill; here natural right view enhances the action.If the child did kill the hare, or he or an adult stole to feed a starving parent, this would be seen as an act which is a mixture of bad and good, in which the good aspect counterbalances the bad to an extent, especially if the act is done with recognition of its wrongness. Indeed, Buddhism acknowledges that poverty in a society makes theft more likely. It is thus less blameable in such circumstances, though still not unblameworthy.

The above perspective thus views morality as part of a spiritual path which largely consists of cultivating a more wholesome character by undermining moral/spiritual defilements and cultivating counteractive virtues. This process of - generally gradual - transformation is seen to culminate in a state of liberation from all traces of greed/attachment, hatred and delusion, and their consequent suffering, through the experience of Nirvana. Such a vision assumes that people have no fixed, unchanging Self, but are capable of radical transformation, brought about by attention to the nature of the mind and actions.Attention is given to actions out of a concern for:

a. Their motivating root;
b. The happiness/unhappiness that actions directly bring to the agent and others;
c. Moral praise and blame, or sanctions within a monastic community;
d. Contribution to spiritual development, or its opposite;
e. The natural karmic effects that are seen to arise, in the future, for the agent.

All of this entails that what one does, and how and why one does it, is of great import: for one's actions both express and shape one's character, and contribute to one's destiny. Much emphasis is put on the state of mind, and intention, lying behind any action; yet some actions are identified as always unwholesome to some degree, dependent on precise motivation. Consequently, it is good not only to seek to avoid such actions, but to vow formally to avoid them.

Criteria are spelt out to identify, in as objective a way as possible, which action-intentions should be recognized as morally unwholesome or wholesome. In this, ignorance of ordinary matters of fact is seen as excusing what might otherwise be seen as an unwholesome action, but moral/spiritual ignorance is seen as compounding an action's unwholesomeness. That is, to perform an unwholesome action while regarding it as acceptable or wholesome is seen to be particularly perverse. In other words, it is held that some action-intentions - primarily those that deliberately cause harm to a sentient being - are wrong, and that it is wrong to deny this and to act on this denial or from moral blindness.Such moral objectivism is derived from:

a. The notion that we all have a natural sympathy for the plight of others, however much we try to ignore or bury it;
b. Acting in accord with, and strengthening, this sympathy naturally leads to more happiness and less suffering for oneself and those one interacts with;
c. No substantial, permanent Self or I exist, and actions selfishly rooted in the I-view or -attitudes are out of accord with reality, so as to be both morally unwholesome and naturally productive of unpleasant karmic result.

Of course, for Buddhism, an act is seen to have unpleasant karmic results because it is wrong; it is not seen as 'wrong' because it happens to produce bad karmic results. Reference to karmic fruits acts simply as a way to help motivate good actions and to emphasize that they are in harmony with and registered by the basic structure of reality.

A final point is that it is better to do a wrong action with compunction than without it (though subsequent guilt-trips are not encouraged, as they lead to an agitated, beclouded mind-state). Moreover, a key aid to moral development is the formal avowal of moral precepts, which are seen to strengthen one's moral vision and help to increase the momentum of moral development. In other words, it helps to have some moral 'aims and objectives' that one agrees with and can happily affirm, even if one is not always so good at achieving them.

3

Factions and Fortitude

There has been little recent research on the history of Buddhism in Bengal and the area we now call Bangladesh; women there, in particular, have received little or no attention. Address this lack by introducing the Buddhist women of Bangladesh, presenting selected portraits of their lives, exploring the formation of their cultural identity as Buddhists and members of distinctive ethnic groups, and speculating on the future of women in Bangladesh. My research is based upon written sources, conversations and correspondence with members of the Bangladesh Buddhist Women's Association since 1986, and observations gathered during a three-week stay in Bangladesh in 1998.

This narrative examines the relationship between gender and religious identity among Bangladeshi Buddhist women, and their strategies for coping with cultural endangerment and rapid social change. My travels in Bangladesh took me to homes and temples in cities, villages, and rural "tribal" areas. As a fellow Buddhist practitioner, had the opportunity to closely observe the role that Buddhist beliefs and practices play in ordinary women's lives and also the variety of roles that Buddhist women play in society. As a bhikkhuni (fully ordained nun) in a country with few nuns and no lineage of full ordination for women, I had a unique opportunity not only to observe monastic practice of monks in Bangladesh, but also to assess the prospects for developing an order of nuns there in the future.

Based on my experiences in Buddhist cultures over the past 30 years with the assumption that an order of Buddhist nuns is beneficial for preserving Buddhist practice and cultural identity. I reasoned that capable leadership is essential to preserving traditional Buddhist cultures and, because monastic life provides an environment for intensive education and training, it is valuable for nurturing capable Buddhist leaders. Men in Buddhist cultures currently have many opportunities for religious education and training, but they also have many options in the worldly sphere, including secular education, business opportunities, international travel, and professional advancement. As a result, men who become monks do not always maintain a lifelong commitment to monastic life and do not always fully utilize their religious training.

Women in Buddhist cultures typically do maintain their lifelong commitment to celibacy and monastic practice. When their leadership potential is tapped and they have opportunities for education and training, they can become effective teachers, translators, and organizers of Buddhist activities. It follows that investments in the monastic training of women are well-placed. Therefore an order of nuns is an asset to a group or country wishing to preserve Buddhist culture. I was interested to see whether this thesis would apply in the case of minority Buddhist cultures in Bangladesh.

First contact with Bangladeshi Buddhist women occurred when officers and members of the Bangladesh Buddhist Women's Association attended the first Skyadhita International Conference on Buddhist Women in Bodhgaya, India, in February 1987. Since those meetings and renewed acquaintance with these women at subsequent Skyadhita conferences and through correspondence. In 1987, they established a national branch of Skyadhita in Chittagong and since that time have contributed ideas and essays to Skyadhita publications.

The three-week period between the fifth Skyadhita Conference in Cambodia and the International Full Ordination Ceremony in Bodhgaya in February 1998 was a perfect opportunity to undertake the trip. A group of Bangladeshi student monks at Wat Mahathat enthusiastically encouraged me to visit their country and stay at their home monastery,

Dhammarajika Vihar, in Kamalapur, Dhaka. Over the years, the monastery has housed, educated, and trained thousands of Buddhist children and monks. Although the monastery has now fallen on difficult times, staying there gave me an opportunity to meet monks and students from not only the majority Barua community, and also from the Chakma, Marma, and other tribal communities.

In addition to large temples such as Nobopandit Vihar and Bodha Vihar in Chittagong and visited smaller temples in the villages, many staffed by active young monks. As an American bhikkhuni in Tibetan robes something of an anomaly, but was nevertheless welcomed as a fellow Buddhist. Every day we met dozens of Buddhist women and men who spoke candidly about their lives, problems, and hopes for the future. It was a unique opportunity to learn more about their lives and hear stories of their cultural survival.

THE BUDDHIST HERITAGE OF BANGLADESH

Between the fourth and eleventh centuries, Bangladesh was a powerful and thoroughly Buddhist land where thousands of monks in hundreds of monasteries studied the Dharma, taught, meditated, and gained realization. Historical sites abound. In the north is Mahasthan, one of several sites where, according to believers, the Buddha himself walked. Other ruins of the Pala Dynasty of Bengal (circa 750-1150 C.E.), such as Paharpur and Mainamati, dot the countryside, and only a tiny fraction of those that exist have been unearthed.

The Mahayana teachings flourished throughout the land, producing such luminaries as AtiSa Dipankara Srijnnana, the revered scholar-practitioner who initiated a revival of Buddhism in 11th-century Tibet. Reading the accounts of Chinese pilgrims and observing the surviving ruins of ancient cities, it is easy to imagine the power and prosperity of these ancient kingdoms - part of a vast Buddhist cultural diaspora extending east from Magadha, where the Buddha achieved enlightenment. This Buddhist heritage is thought to have had a salutary effect on the people's national temperament; their non-martial nature was noted by the British as they attempted to fill the ranks of their armies.

Many theories have been advanced to explain the inroads of Brahmannism and subsequent Muslim domination of Bangladesh. Aggressive conversion tactics, military conquest, proximity to ports where Muslim traders docked, promises of a blissful afterlife, and other theories have been advanced. Whatever the reasons, we know that for over 1200 years the people of Bengal were strongly influenced by Buddhist teachings and cultural norms. We also know that they strongly resisted the caste system and attempts to Sanskritize their language. Although today Buddhists number less than one percent in a Muslim population of 120,000,000, there are more than 800 monks in 500 temples and aramas in the country. As a result of Arakanese influence, Buddhists in Bangladesh today follow the Theravada tradition.

BUDDHIST MINORITIES IN A MUSLIM LAND

All Buddhist cultures in contemporary Bangladesh are cultures at risk. They are threatened not only by majority Muslim cultural domination and increasing Islamic fundamentalism, but also by secular influences, particularly consumer trends and the impact of Western culture via modern media. International sports, Hindi films, and Star TV (a tamer, South Asian version of MTV) beam daily into many homes among the country's 800,000 Buddhists. The images and values these programs convey do little to bolster Buddhist values or cultural identity. Women attempting to raise their children along traditional Buddhist lines are up against formidable competition.

The Buddhists of Bangladesh come from a broad range of ethnic and cultural backgrounds. The people distinguish themselves as belonging to either the Barua ("plains") Buddhist community or one of the tribal ("hilly") groups: Chakma, Marma, Tripura, Tongchengya, Mong, Cak, Kheang, Khumi, Murang, Moro, Lusai, Boam, Pangko, Banjogi, and so on. Although the origins of these diverse cultural identities are largely lost to us, historical records explain at least some of their background. Physically, the Barua Buddhists resemble the peoples of the northern Indian plains from which their ancestors are said to have migrated.

Most identify themselves as members of the Briji clan of the Licchavi people who immigrated from Vaisali, Magadha (now Bihar) as early as the time of the Buddha. According to their oral histories, these Briji migrants zigzagged along the paths in the hills of Assam, eventually settling in the plains around Chittagong with the help of local rulers. The term "Barua," currently used as an ethnic designation as well as a surname by the majority, is explained by the people themselves to derive from "bara," meaning "big, great," and "arya," meaning "noble."

Some believe that the title was applied to the migrants as they passed through Assam as a mark of respect, possibly associating them with the land of the Buddha's enlightenment. Barua Buddhists themselves are quite confident, even adamant, about this ancestral link with Magadha. In appearance, Barua Buddhists are difficult to differentiate from the majority Muslim population in modern-day Bangladesh. Often the presence of women in their midst is the primary clue that they are Buddhists. Members of the Barua community have distinguished themselves in many fields: business, education, law, medicine, literature, and also on the battlefield, in the struggle for freedom from the British and more recently from Pakistan.

Baruas are dominant in Buddhist activities in urban areas and have also dominated Bangladesh's Buddhist representation abroad, a point that has led to considerable controversy and resentment among other Buddhist groups. Although both plains and hill tribe Buddhists belong to the Theravada tradition, intermarriage is not considered desirable from either side. "We do not mix socially," is an oft-heard phrase. Although members of the hill tribes share certain characteristics and the cultural categories that distinguish them are not indelibly fixed, the sense of a shared identity among the hill tribes is a relatively recent phenomenon, developed primarily in response to attempts at domination from outside.

Subtle ethnic tensions still exist among the groups, as they negotiate complex issues of cultural and economic survival in the face of massive in-migration, political disenfranchisement, social dislocation, and economic change. Buddhist women of all these groups, regardless of their ethnic identities, face similar challenges in their attempts to preserve traditional culture and promote Buddhist values among the youth. As their children become influenced by the popular media, it becomes increasingly difficult to interest them in visiting the temple rather than the sports field or cinema.

PRATIVA MUTSOODY OF TANGAIL

Ms. Prativa Mutsoody, a prominent Buddhist educator who taught at the Homes for decades and now serves as headmistress. In her youth, Prativa was a student leader at prestigious Dhaka University. When Mahatma Gandhi was assassinated, she and three close friends felt that, rather than tears and lamentation, the best way to express their grief was to follow the principles that the great being (mahatma) had taught.

Therefore, the four young women made a lifelong pact to be vegetarians, abstain from taking an evening meal on Fridays, and devote themselves wholeheartedly to the benefit of society. Her friends eventually married and were not able to fulfill their aspirations, but Prativa has remained unmarried and vegetarian since 1949. She is highly respected, not only among the Buddhist community, but also by the members of other religious communities.

The personal shrine that Prativa keeps in her bedroom is neatly tended. In addition to pictures and a statue of Buddha Sakyamuni, she has arranged photographs of Sri Ramakrishna, Sri Aurobindo, and Swami Vivekananda. She finds this eclectic approach in keeping with the social and spiritual ideals of Mahatma Gandhi. She explained that on the full moon, new moon, and quarter moon days, she and Buddhist women living at the Homes gather to take the eight precepts. The ritual serves to mark and maintain their spiritual companionship.

Prativa finds time for her religious devotions amid a busy professional schedule overseeing the educational development of 800 young women. The students in residence do not all come from Buddhist backgrounds; the majorities are Muslim or Hindu. The Homes offers a secular curriculum of both primary and secondary education to both residents and day students, with classes in world religions and a choice of vegetarian or nonvegetarian meals. Bharateswari Homes is not a charity institution, but is financially self-supporting.

The resident tuition of 7,000 takas per year makes Bharateswari Homes beyond the reach of ordinary families, but the school serves a valuable function in the community by providing girls and young women a solid academic curriculum, character education, and safety under Prativa's care. During our meeting at Prativa's home, an engineer from the Barua Buddhist community, a resident of Dhaka, arrived to confirm the admission of his nine-year-old daughter to the Homes.

After he and his daughter paid their respects to Prativa in the traditional manner, bowing to the floor and touching both their hands to her feet, he expressed complete confidence that his daughter would be "100 percent safe" at the Homes. Similar declarations by officials of Agrasara Girl's College and Agrasara Orphanage, Buddhist institutions in Raozan ("Parents who admit their daughters here need have no fears for their safety"), implied that there are dangers to young women in other institutions.

Two teachers at Bharateswar Homes came to prepare lunch for my two monk companions and me before our meeting with Prativa. Because there were few Buddhists living in the area of Tangail, the opportunity to create merit by offering food to monastics was regarded as a joyous occasion. My companion bhikkhus, one Barua and one Marma, were seated on a raised platform in the place of honor (farthest from the door).

After the meal and the recitation of a short sutta by the monks, the women and children of the house and neighborhood gathered and, as often happened during my visit to Bangladesh, requested meditation instruction. After giving them basic instructions on mindfulness of breathing (anapanasati), the women and children sat quietly in meditation for 20 minutes. It seemed as if they would have continued indefinitely had not ended the meditation session.

Among the small crowd that gathered for meditation were two teachers from the Homes: Paisanu Marma, the daughter of a devout Marma Buddhist family, and Ananya Barua, an orphan who belonged to the "plains" Buddhist community. Although there had been no prior discussion of ordination, the two teachers suddenly declared, "Now we are convinced. We want to become nuns. Take us with you." Amused and somewhat taken aback and asked how they had come to this decision.

Ananya told me that, because she was an orphan, she was free to become a nun if she wished, without any hindrances from her family. Paisanu said that, because her family members are all devout Buddhists, she would not face any objections or obstacles in becoming a nun either. Referring to Paisanu, our host, Mr. M. K. Barua, engineer, commented, "She is very pious. She gives her entire salary to needy persons."

The two teachers discussed their aspirations to devote themselves wholeheartedly to Buddhist practice and regretted that there was nowhere they could go to become nuns. Since there is as yet no Buddhist studies program or training center available for women in Bangladesh, I suggested developing a daily study program of readings on Buddhism and short morning and evening meditation sessions each day. I expressed the hope that eventually Buddhist institutes for women could be developed both in India and Bangladesh. Everyone in the room agreed that if opportunities were available, many women would want to become nuns, and if pious, educated women like these two teachers became nuns, it would be an excellent beginning for a bhikkhuni order in Bangladesh.

MIRA BARUA OF UKHIYA

The simple temple, located on a small wooded hill, has several shrines, a bodhi tree, and a large reclining Buddha image that was brought from Thailand. Like many temples in Bangladesh, Ananda Bhavan Vihar also houses an orphanage, situated at the edge of the temple grounds, to care for some of the estimated one million children orphaned in the floods and other natural disasters that devastate the country annually. After wandering the grounds for a short time, we were ushered up a wooden staircase to a spacious room to meet the temple's abbot in the large wooden main hall of the temple. Demurely to the side stood a young woman named Mira Barua.

Mira Barua was born into a devoutly Buddhist family in Ukhiya and has been active in the life of the temple since childhood. Her family home is located amidst the gleaming paddy fields just five minutes away. Since she was a small girl, Mira has had a close relationship with Bhikkhu Rebato, the head monk of the temple, who is now 49. There are four bhikkhus and four samanòeras at the temple, but no nuns. At 23, Mira is confident, capable, and an indispensable component of the temple's activities.

As she served lunch to the resident monks and guests, the abbot described her approvingly as "very religious." After completing high school in Ukhiya, Mira pursued a degree in religious studies at Ukhiya College, taking classes in Pali, Buddhism, and Islamic history. She now teaches Pali, Buddhism, and Bengali at Ukhiya High School and to the 42 boys at the temple's orphanage school. When asked whether she would consider becoming a nun, her eyes sparkled with delight.

An altar with a Buddha image, simple offerings, and a string of prayer beads was clearly the focal point of the immaculate earthen home. As we entered the drawing room, her family members spread a mat on the floor and bowed to the monastics from a kneeling position, in Theravada style. Except for a few posters of natural scenery sent by a brother working in Saudi Arabia, all the pictures decorating the room are religious in nature.

Her parents are faithful Buddhist practitioners, familiar with vipassana meditation, and devoted to the bhikkhus, but when the question of Mira's future came up; they timidly admitted they would not agree to her becoming a nun. Although she would be living only five minutes away, it was hard for them to conceive of their daughter as a nun. Monks are revered in Bangladeshi Buddhist society, but nuns have no status and are virtually invisible.

TRIBAL BUDDHIST NUNS

At the time of my visit, the district of Bandarban technically was restricted territory due to ethnic tensions and the prospect of a peace accord, but there was no one at the check post, so we drove right through. A short drive through the gently rolling hills brought us to the township of Bandarban. On the right was a newly constructed cultural center, part of the government's efforts at restitution to the tribal people who have suffered years of attacks by settlers from the plains encroaching upon their lands.

Just a few minutes further down the road, we arrived at a peaceful temple constructed of wood, with a large open Buddha hall in the center. After ascending the stairs and honoring the Buddha images in two small decorative shrines, we approached U Sumangala Mahathero, the temple's abbot. As we paid our respects to him in a reception area arranged in one corner of the hall, we noticed a slight Marma nun watching us intently.

Ma Chan Daw Wadi was born in the village of Murongkyo in 1925 and grew up in Bandarban. When she was 29 years old, she received the ten precepts from U Sumangala, the abbot. Now 74, she has lived at the temple since then, serving the abbot and devoting her time to vipassana meditation practice. She learned the technique of vipassana from the abbot, who learned it during a stay in Burma.

In the hut that Ma Chan Daw Wadi shares with another woman at the back of the temple, her possessions consist of a change of clothes, a mosquito net, and a few empty tins. The only valuable possession is a meditation text that rests on a makeshift table. Her carefully shaved head and disciplined demeanor convey the intensity of her meditation practice. She has never traveled outside the area, nor cared to, but her eyes lit up as we spoke of Bodhgaya, sacred site of the Buddha's enlightenment.

Her companion Apuma has been staying at the temple for the last seven years. Apuma's father and brother are monks at the temple, and the abbot, U Sumangala, is her uncle. Apuma's husband suddenly left her about 30 years ago, and the suffering she experienced at that time convinced her of the truth of the Buddha's teachings. Now 60, she works in the temple and takes care of her father and uncle. She is deeply committed to meditation practice and plans to become a nun once her father has passed away.

At another temple nearby three micchela (Burmese: Mae Sila, female precept-holders) from the culturally endangered Murong tribe. One is a 77-year-old nun who shaved her head and took precepts six years ago when a highly respected sayadatv (teacher) visited the temple. The other two women (64 and 52) received eight precepts and began living in the temple at the same time. One told me that she will shave her head as soon as her daughter grows up, and the other woman said she will also shave her head then.

All three women are from Kaptai and said they get what food they need from the temple. Two of the women speak only their tribal language, but we were able to communicate through their companion, who speaks Marma. The way these micchela live, work, and practice quietly in the temple, without Sangha status or privileges, is typical of the few nuns to be found in Bangladesh. Even without recognition from society, they feel fortunate to be able to stay in the temple, serve the monks, create merit, recite suttas, and meditate for the rest of their lives. Their simple needs are met by the monks they serve and, living in the temple, they are protected from the woes of worldly life.

Although we have no records to prove it, nuns and female practitioners have probably practiced quietly and unnoticed like this for centuries. Changes are afoot, however, that may open up new directions for Buddhist women in Bangladesh. The primary initiator of the innovations is U Paa Jotha Thero. Popularly known as Uchala Bhante, he is a young bhikkhu from the Marma royal family who was trained as an attorney. After becoming renowned as a judge, considered an outstanding accomplishment for a hill tribe member, he suddenly resigned his position, received ordination, and went to practice meditation in Burma for six years. Inspired by the large number of nuns (tila shin) he saw in Burma, he began organizing temporary ordinations for nuns after his return to Bandarban.

In December 1994, he arranged an ordination for 62 monks and invited respected mahatheros from Burma to officiate. The following year, he invited both monks and nuns to officiate, also giving girls and young women the opportunity to shave their heads, don the robes, receive nine precepts, and temporarily experience monastic life as micchela. Two ordinations have been held so far: 65 nuns were ordained in December 1995 and 68 were ordained in January 1997.

The ordinations have attracted candidates from all over Bangladesh and from a variety of ethnic groups: Marma, Chakma, Barua, Tripura, Tongchengya, and Rakkhaine, in addition to three from Burma. Ordinarily a girl's mother or sister accompanies her to the ordination, helps cut her hair, and assists as she goes for alms. In some cases, like Tipu and Nobodita (two women I met at a wedding in Chittagong), both mother and daughter took precepts. Most of the nuns who participated in these two ordinations, like 14-year old Au Mei Thowai, whom I met in Bandarban, disrobed after a month to continue their studies at school. However, seven of the newly ordained nuns, four Marma and three Barua, decided to remain as nuns and have gone to Burma to pursue studies in Pali, Vinaya, and Abhidharma at temples in Rangoon (Yangon).

The ordinations organized by Uchala Bhante represent a bold new step and have had a powerful social impact on Buddhist society in Bangladesh. People told me that before these ordinations were held, the public was not aware that there was such a thing as micchela. Bhante had hoped to make the ordinations an annual event, but politics intervened.

Now that a peace accord has been signed, hopefully putting an end to 15 years of hostilities in the hill tribe areas, he plans to continue the ordinations, establish a monastery for nuns, and build a Buddhist institute in Bandarban where both monks and nuns can get an education in Buddhist studies and temple management. On the topic of full ordination for women, he told me, "We have no problem with making the nuns bhikkhunis. It is only a question of who will make them bhikkhunis." After some initial resistance, he admitted that it may be possible to establish a bhikkhuni lineage in Bangladesh by inviting nuns from the Chinese tradition.

BANGLADESHI LAYWOMEN'S LIVES

When Bhikkhu Visuddhananda's (the founder of Dhammarajika Monastery in Dhaka) mother died, the ample courtyard of their traditional-style home was too small to contain all those who came to pay their respects. The reason for this fanfare was that the woman had been the mother of a well-known bhikkhu. Her body was placed in the courtyard for several hours, during which time aggrieved friends and relations cried and expressed their sorrow. The body was then washed and covered with a single length of white cloth. After some time, the droves of people who crowded into the courtyard made it necessary to remove the body to the temple of Agrasara complex, five minutes away. There the body stayed for several days so that the villagers could come to pay their respects. At last it was cremated at a cremation ground a short distance from the village.

The crowds of hundreds of villagers surrounding the body as it lay in state in the courtyard of Agrasara Temple before the cremation. As is customary, a huge sanghadana (an offering of food and gifts to a gathering of bhikkhus, 60 in this case) was held on the seventh day after her passing, and again on the 15th and 30th, then monthly for six months, and annually thereafter. On these occasions, males in the family wear a white square of cloth pinned diagonally over the left shoulder and under the right arm "in tribute to their dead ancestors."

Women in the family wear no special cloth, yet they are in charge of all the food preparation and cleanup. Offerings of fruits and vegetables, artistically carved and arranged, are placed on the altar. The men spoke with volunteered that women are essential to men's ability to practice generosity (dana), a central Buddhist virtue. Men, they say, are able to earn money, but they depend entirely on the women in their family to prepare and arrange offerings of food and provide hospitality to guests and the Sangha. Significantly, although women ordinarily serve guests in the home, both ordained and lay, only men serve bhikkhus at a Sanghadana. Men are therefore most visible in merit-making activities, even though behind the scenes it is women who make these activities possible.

Although it is rare at present, there is no restriction against women teaching Buddhism in Bangladesh. Priti Kana Barua, President of the Bangladesh Buddhist Women's Association, told me the story of her Aunt Babuillarma (lit., "Babul's mother"), a woman who became a well-known meditation teacher. Babuillarma grew up in Aburkhil, a large Buddhist village a half hour's drive from Chittagong, and studied meditation with a variety of teachers, including a monk at the old Jamitjuri Meditation Center. At the age of 55, she left family life and trained to become a teacher. Wearing a white sari, she gave meditation training to women and men at various meditation centers, conducting courses at least ten days long, until her death in 1997 at the age of 78.

Especially in contrast to the sequestering of women common among the Muslims, Buddhist women appear to enjoy a large measure of social equality and freedom of movement. Although there is no functioning order of nuns, "Women are comparatively more religious than men in our country." One further informed me, "Mother Theresa, the most famous person in the world, is a woman." Indeed, women's presence in large numbers at Buddhist activities was very noticeable in Bangladesh. Women take their children to the temples to listen to Dhamma talks, especially on Buddhist festival days.

The most important days, celebrated in temples all over the country, are Buddha Purnima (Vesak), Ashwini Purnima (the conclusion of the monks' rains retreat), Katòhina Chibar Dana (the ceremony of offering robes to monks), and Falguni Purnima (the ceremony of the "wish-fulfilling tree"). During Kanhina Chibar Dana season, at the conclusion of the Safigha's rainy season retreat (vassa), robe-offering ceremonies are held at different temples on different days to give people more opportunities to accumulate merit. Women are lauded as the most conscientious donors.

Many women observe precepts on new and full-moon days, and periodically invite monks to their homes for dana. In addition to public devotional activities, many women told me that they meditate daily in their homes, chant suttas, tell Buddhist stories to their children, and attend meditation retreats whenever they get the chance.

THE GENDER LITMUS TEST

Although Bangladesh has very few nuns and no tradition of bhikkhunis although this may not surprise the casual observer, such respectful treatment is not always the case for a nun, either in Asia or in the West. For a nun to be welcomed on a par with monks in a social situation is unusual and significant. The skill with which protocol was handled in a new and complex situation - coping with a foreign bhikkbuni - reflects the open-mindedness and flexibility of Bangladeshi Buddhists.

The relative absence of gender discrimination was notable. Although bhikkhunis do not exist in Bangladesh, many Buddhists bowed in the traditional manner without hesitation and with the same respect they would show to a bhikkhu. Some hesitated for a moment, but quickly computing bhikkhuni to be the feminine of bhikkhu, then paid their respects. Others, after running through the same computation, concluded it was inappropriate or unnecessary to bow to a nun. A few, visibly perplexed, quickly busied themselves with other duties to avoid having to deal with the unaccustomed situation.

These different reactions suggest a complex admixture of factors affecting religious attitudes and behaviors. In addition to social constructions of gender, they were influenced by social status, age (older people generally being more devout), depth of Buddhist commitment, attitudes toward the ordained Safigha, personal patterns of observing traditional protocol, and, perhaps, uncertainty about foreigners' responses to traditional protocol, such as bowing.

More than 150 monks were served lunch in a huge tent decorated with colorful banners and streamers. Monks had been invited from towns and villages far and wide for the occasion, and the high-ranking monks were seated inside a building, chatting and catching up with the news, before the meal was served. After lunch, when the official program began, over a thousand people gathered under a huge awning for several hours of speeches. Somehow they had all been fed after the monks were served. Despite their demanding family responsibilities, women attended the function in far greater numbers than men, in a ratio of about four to one. The speeches tended toward the polemic, with very little Dhamma content, repeatedly emphasizing the achievements of the Buddhist community and the need for even greater achievements.

As time wore on not fail to notice the exemplary behavior of the women; they sat quietly in neat rows, listening with full attention to the interminable windy speeches, while the men got up, sat down, talked, slept, smoked, and shuffled about remarked that the mindfulness and discipline the women displayed are vital qualities in Buddhist practice, and that women and men are equally responsible for creating and preserving Buddhist cultural identity. Women want to be active as teachers and leaders; all they lack is Buddhist education.

BUDDHIST FUTURES IN BANGLADESH

On the one hand, the lack of attention given to religious training for Buddhist women indicates a huge blind spot. On the other hand, Bangladeshi Buddhists are struggling for economic, social, and cultural survival with so very few resources available that it is a continual challenge even to support the monks. Buddhists in Bangladesh appreciate the freedom that their women enjoy in relation to Muslims and many take full advantage of whatever educational opportunities they have.

The question of women's future prospects within Buddhism in Bangladesh therefore cannot be addressed without addressing the question of Bangladeshi Buddhism as a whole; that is, the health of half the religious body politic cannot be considered in isolation from the health of the whole. As an example, Buddhist studies programs at present are inadequate even for monks, much less for women. Of course it is possible to study Pali and Buddhism at some government colleges and universities in Bangladesh. But although women and men are equally free to take these classes, comprehensive Buddhist studies programs are not available, either to women or to men.

To ensure a healthy future for Buddhist women, Buddhism as a whole needs dedicated effort, vision, and support. Buddhists in Bangladesh are proud of their cultural heritage and keen to maintain it, particularly in the face of Muslim domination and a growing Islamic nationalism. Buddhist women and men already work conscientiously to sponsor Buddhist events, observe traditional marriage and funeral customs, celebrate all the Buddhist holy days, organize teachings and vipassana meditation courses, reinforce Buddhist values in the family and community, maintain the temples, and support the monks' communities.

They persevere in these efforts despite continual natural disasters, economic woes, extortion, ethnic and religious discrimination, the wooing of young Buddhist women by Muslim suitors, Christian and Muslim attempts at conversion, communal and family dislocation associated with outmigration of Buddhist youths seeking opportunities abroad, and myriad other social problems.

Nevertheless the situation is potentially very positive for Buddhist women's development in Bangladesh for a number of reasons. First, in their beleaguered situation, Buddhists in Bangladesh clearly need to activate every conceivable resource to ensure their cultural survival. Second, women's capabilities are already recognized; Bangladeshi Buddhist men are proud of the accomplishments that Bangladeshi women have already demonstrated. Third, Buddhist women enjoy a large measure of social freedom. Unlike their Muslim sisters, they are not veiled.

They have access to secondary and higher education, and enjoy considerable freedom in their choice of lifestyles. They have a strong voice in family decisions, including those related to their reproductive health. Although divorce is not common, there is no bar to divorce among Buddhists. Literacy is high, widow remarriage is permitted, and the incidence of domestic violence is relatively low. Buddhist women are free to frequent temples and to pursue Buddhist studies at the university level, if they so desire. All of these factors augur well for Buddhist women's future. If monastic facilities were available, many parents would no doubt allow their daughters to pursue a Buddhist vocation if they wished.

Considering all these factors, it is difficult to explain the absence of an effective order of nuns in Bangladesh. Yet in reconfiguring the gender landscape, this lack may be used to advantage. Without the precedent of an unrecognized order of nuns of ambiguous status, such as exists in other Theravada countries, women in Bangladesh may be at liberty to create a viable, socially acknowledged order after their own vision. As an endangered minority facing cultural degradation and possible extinction, women in Bangladesh may have greater freedom to create an effective bhikkhuni Sangha.

In the face of this urgent cultural imperative, educated Bangladeshi Buddhists may be able to discard the gender baggage, cut through patriarchal tradition, and support women in their efforts to establish an erudite and active order of Buddhist nuns. It is too early to determine exactly how the goal of creating a Bhikkhuni Sangha can be accomplished, but four elements are essential. First, women need access to Buddhist education. Systematic, comprehensive Buddhist studies programs to train women and men as translators, researchers, and educators are essential for the future of Buddhism in Bangladesh. Second, women need to cultivate allies among the established Buddhist hierarchy.

A few highly placed bhikkhus have already traveled outside Bangladesh and witnessed the phenomenal achievements of bhikkhunis active in Taiwan, Korea, and other countries. With encouragement, this exposure, combined with open-minded gender attitudes among Bangladeshi Buddhists as a whole, may convince these respected monks to become advocates of women's religious advancement. Third, Buddhist women from disparate ethnic groups need to consolidate their power and develop a sense of solidarity with other women.

In their beleaguered situation, Buddhists in Bangladesh have no option but to overcome communal factionalism and rivalries. In this regard, a unified multi-ethnic coalition of women could be a powerful example. Fourth and the most critical of all for the gender restructuring of Buddhist institutions in Bangladesh is motivating Buddhist women themselves to work for women's advancement. With these four crucial factors in place, women could not only create a bhikkhuni Sangha, they could also take leadership roles in restoring and revitalizing their cherished Buddhist heritage.

4

Ordination and Legitimacy

In February 1998, a momentous international full ordination ceremony was held in the religious metropolis of Bodhgaya, India, site of the Buddha's enlightenment. Among the newly ordained were 134 female practitioners from various Buddhist traditions, most of which had long since lost their own bhiksunòi lineages. Chinese Buddhists claim that their nuns are ordained according to a lineage introduced from India to Sri Lanka in the fourth century B.C.E. and subsequently to China in 432 C.E. Unfortunately, the bhiksunòi lineage disappeared in Sri Lanka as a result of the 11th-century Colòa invasions, and apparently never reached Tibet. Buddhist monks from these traditions joined the 1998 ceremony, conferring blessings and lending support to the nuns.

Their participation effectively restored the lineage of full ordination to these traditions, a milestone in Buddhist history. The current movement to introduce full ordination for Buddhist nuns involves a significant reconstruction of religious traditions. The process of gaining legitimation for their own nuns in the eyes of the global Buddhist community is effecting changes in attitudes and institutions in various monastic communities. The historical tension among the Buddha's ordination of women, textual ambiguity, and de facto exclusion of women from full ordination in certain traditions, may soon be replaced by the principle of universal equality, from which a vital new tradition can emerge.

The impetus to establish an order of fully ordained nuns is fueled by three primary factors. First, monastic organizations attempting to expand in the West require many dedicated nuns for their success. Some competition for Western nuns has already surfaced between Tibetan and Taiwanese institutions. Second, there is competition between the traditions to demonstrate their commitment to social equality by recognizing women's equal right to full ordination. This competition is most evident between Tibetan and Theravadin institutions in the West. Third, there is competition between the bhiksunòi orders in Taiwan and the People's Republic of China to prove their legitimacy and pedigree.

This competition, involving Tibetans in exile, the PRC, and Taiwan, is closely tied to political concerns that may be far removed from Buddhist doctrines and ideals. Given the extremely complex nature of the controversy over full ordination for women in the international Buddhist community today, the ceremony in Bodhgaya provides a vantage point from which to view gender issues within Buddhist communities worldwide: the construction of Buddhist women's identity, Buddhist nuns' struggle to improve their status within the monastic framework, and the role of women in reforming monastic regulations. From this vantage point, I shall discuss the full ordination in Bodhgaya, the process of becoming a bhiksunòi, the crucial role of nuns in Taiwanese Buddhist monasteries, and the gender issues that are emerging globally in Buddhist communities.

THE FULL ORDINATION IN BODHGAYA

The exiled Tibetan authorities had permitted Western nuns of the Tibetan tradition to receive full ordination in Taiwan. After that, I had many opportunities to discuss the bhiksunòi issue with leading Taiwanese nuns, during both the Dalai Lama's first visit to Taiwan in March 1997 and the November 1997 visit of Bhiksu Tashi Tsering, representative of the Tibetan Government-in-Exile's Ministry of Religious and Cultural Affairs.

When members of Foguangshan, Taiwan's largest monastery, told me about their plans to conduct an international full ordination ceremony in Bodhgaya in February 1998, a team of organizers and workers from Foguangshan had already proceeded to Bodhgaya a week earlier. Traveling with them was a large group of Taiwanese lay Buddhists participating in a pilgrimage arranged by Foguangshan.

It was election time, and all local vehicles had already been commandeered by the local government. The nuns and prosperous Taiwanese pilgrims were very visible as they boarded their designated buses in this impoverished, crime-prone town.

The organizers carefully maintained boundaries between the ordination candidates and the laity to make sure that the candidates, already exhausted by their busy schedule, could concentrate on the ordination, a crucial turning point in their lives. The village of Bodhgaya became crowded with the arrival of 1,200 Taiwanese pilgrims and 300 Buddhist monks and nuns participating in events connected with the ordination. This was one of the few times in history that Buddhist women in the Indian, Sri Lankan, and Tibetan traditions have had an opportunity to take full ordination. Out of more than 300 applicants, only 148 (134 nuns and 14 monks) were selected to participate. From February 15 to 23, candidates were ordained at three levels: novice monk or nun (ròramanòera/ròramanòerika), fully ordained monk or nun (bhiksu/bhiksunòi), and bodhisattva. Meanwhile, lay applicants received the five precepts at the Mahabodhi Stupa.

The daily schedule of the ordination candidates was very similar to monastic life in Taiwan: waking at dawn, morning prayers from 5:00 to 6:00, meals at 6:00 and 11:10 a.m., evening prayers from 5:00 to 6:30 pm, and retiring at 10:00 p.m. Ceremonial training, lessons on the Bhiksu and Bhiksuni Pratimoksa Sûtras, and the actual ordination ceremonies occupied most of the candidates' time. They were only allowed short breaks for resting at noon and for bathing in the evening.

The first stage of the full ordination (upasanipada) for bhiksunòis was conducted by ten bhiksu precept masters on the evening of February 20. Candidates entered the ordination hall after 11:00 p.m., and the ceremony lasted until nearly 4:30 the next morning. After a very brief rest, the newly ordained bhiksunòis then went to request the next stage of the upasampada ordination, conducted by ten bhiksu precept masters at 7:00 a.m. The process of ordination was very intensive, with intermittent kneeling, bowing, and recitations, but sincere in their determination, the exhausted ordination candidates concentrated their attention on the training and ordination procedures.

Following Chinese custom, the ordination was divided into five sections: 1. ceremonial training in small groups, 2. lessons on the Pratimoksa precepts, 3. repentance rituals, 4. the formal ordination procedures, and 5. a large sanghadana (meal offering to the monastic community). The Chinese method of conducting the ordination differs from the Tibetan and Theravadin traditions, in which ordination is completed in a single day. By contrast, a Chinese ordination ceremony can take up to 90 days. During this time, the ordination candidates are not only taught the precepts, but also acquainted with monastic regulations and protocol, culminating in the ordination ceremony toward the end. Tashi Tsering commented that the Chinese style of ordination is more complex and ritualized than in Tibet.

For example, in Bodhgaya the ordination hall was elaborately decorated with colorful flags and fabrics, and Buddhist music was broadcast loudly. In contrast, a Tibetan ordination ceremony is relatively simple and quiet. The highly decorative style of the Chinese ordination ceremony seems directed toward the lay devotees and guests rather than the candidates, who are required to be silent and stay in restricted areas during the ordination. The laity including the family and friends of ordinands was permitted to attend certain activities - to serve at the sanghadana, participate in repentance ceremonies, and receive the lay precepts - but were strictly excluded from the ordination procedures.

Taiwanese lay followers believe that by participating in these activities, they share the great merit accumulated by the ordination masters and candidates. Often they contribute the ordination fee for the candidates and contribute toward the organizing expenses. For instance, each Taiwanese layperson who received the five precepts in Bodhgaya not only paid an ordination fee and her own pilgrimage expenses, but also donated a certain amount for a nun at the ordination. One Taiwanese woman referred to her support for the newly ordained monks and nuns as "making a Buddha." In this way, a strong sense of religious community and reciprocal relationship is created between the monastics and the laity.

Another characteristic that distinguishes the Chinese system of ordination from the Tibetan and Theravadin is incorporating novice (Sramanòera/ Sramanòerika), full (bhiksu/lbhiksunòi), and bodhisattva ordinations in sequence, in what is known as a Triple Platform Ordination. Until 1987, Taiwan had a centralized ordination system in which only ordinations sanctioned by a national committee of Buddhist representatives and verified by an official ordination certificate were permitted. A probationary training period in a monastery, equivalent in some ways to the Ssikaamanòa (probationer) idea in early India, precedes the Triple Platform Ordination. Some novices may need more than six months to adjust to their new religious identity. Others might spend several years in a monastery waiting to get their parents' permission to be ordained. Some monastic groups have their novices delay their ordination until their tonsure master is invited to serve as the Sala-upadhyaya at the national ordination ceremony.

Incorporating the bodhisattva precept ceremony into the Triple Platform Ordination procedure illustrates how Chinese Buddhism integrates Mahayana doctrine and Dharmagupta Vinaya into the ordination. The Pratimoksa ordinations (Sramanòerika and bhiksunòi) demonstrate that the Chinese Safigha maintains the orthodox monastic lineage as descendants of Sakyamuni Buddha. Incorporating the bodhisattva ordination as an integral part of the Triple Platform Ordination Ceremony demonstrates the importance of the bodhisattva ideal for their Mahayana identity.

The sectarian implications of this ideal and its centrality in the ordination procedure were not lost on the Theravadin participants. Indeed, once the ordination candidates had received the bhiksunòi ordination, the Theravadin acaryas pointedly led all of their disciples out of the ordination hall and only returned for the closing ceremony two days later. They clearly had no intention of becoming Mahayana Buddhists.

ORDINATION MASTERS AND WITNESSES

The Bodhgaya ordination brought together bhiksus and bhiksunòis from diverse Buddhist traditions. Since transmission of the bhiksuni lineage to the Tibetan and Theravadin traditions can only come via the Chinese tradition, preceptors and recipients of all these traditions must come to terms. In some ways, recognition of the ordination as valid and legitimate is as important as full ordination itself, because the future survival of the newly ordained bhiksunòis rests on continual support from their local monastic communities, and this will only be forthcoming if their ordination is recognized as valid.

Three main bhiksus precept masters officiate at a full ordination ceremony: the Sila-upadhyaya, the dharma-acarya, and the instructing acarya. At the ordination in Bodhgaya, all three were from the Chinese tradition: the Sila-upadhyaya was Foguangshan's founder, Xingyun; the dharnia-acarya was Wuqian; and the instructing acarya was Yongxing. The ordination in Bodhgaya was largely driven by the personal charisma of Xingyun. He is one of the most renowned, if controversial, Buddhist teachers in Taiwan, with a high international profile.

He has been a leading proponent of bhikssunòi ordination internationally since at least 1988. In Calcutta, just before the ordination in Bodhgaya, he pointed out that to exclude women from bhiksunòi ordination was to waste half of the Buddhists' potential energy worldwide. Despite historical and social differences between the different Buddhist schools, he argued, the Bodhgaya ordination would demonstrate that international cooperation on this issue is possible.

In addition to the three principal bhiksu acaryas already mentioned, 22 witnessing acaryas also attended the Bodhgaya ordination. They came from Malaysia, Sri Lanka, Nepal, Thailand, India, Great Britain, Cambodia, and Tibet, thereby representing both the Tibetan and Theravadin traditions. Many of these monks live and promulgate Buddhism abroad. Bhiksu witnesses served four distinct roles at the Bodhgaya ordination. The first group of five monks - Tep Vong (Supreme Patriarch of Maha Nikaya, Cambodia) and four monks from Thailand - served as witnesses rather than participants because the ordination of women is illegal in their own monastic communities.

The second group of acaryas consisted of monks active in the Bodhgaya Buddhist community: Dhammananda Maha Thero (the Chief High Priest of Malaysia), Dr. Mapalagama Wipulasara

Maha Thero (President of the Maha Bodhi Society in India), Dr. Rastrapala Mahathera (Founder and President of the International Meditation Center), and Nyaneinda Mahathera (Abbot of the Burmese Temple).

Also participating were Ashvaghosh Mahathera (Editor-in-Chief of Dharmakirti, a Nepalese Buddhist monthly) and Inamaluwe Sumangala Nayaka Thera (Chief Secretary of Rangiri Dambulla Chapter, Sri Lanka). All of these monks are influential in the important movement to revive Buddhism in India. They come from different countries and wear different styles of robes, but their mission to revitalize Buddhism in the place of its birth has joined them in longterm cooperation.

The third group of acaryas consisted of ten Sri Lankan monks, a meaningful number considering that ten bhiksus are required to perform the full ordination. This group of respected senior bhiksus was arguably the most important for re-establishing the Theravadin bhiksunòi lineage; some of the monks had devoted themselves to the advancement of Buddhist women for a long time. Most had participated in the ordination of ten Sri Lankan nuns in Sarnath, India, in October 1996. They conducted a Theravadin ordination ceremony for the 20 Sri Lankan nun candidates the morning before they received Sramanòerika precepts from the Chinese monks in Bodhgaya.

In a special meeting with Xingyun in Bodhgaya these ten acaryas invited Foguangshan to conduct a bhiksunòi ordination in Sri Lanka in January 1999. This demonstrated their strong commitment to full ordination and established a connection between them and Foguangshan toward this goal. They expressed their belief that the re-establishment of bhiksunòi ordination would provide women greater access to Buddhism, both in Sri Lanka and in the West. Subsequently, however, rather than wait until January 1999, they went ahead and organized three ordinations in Dambulla, Sri Lanka, on their own: in March, July, and December 1998.

The fourth group of monks included just one acarya, Lama Yeshe Losal Rinpoche, Abbot of Kagyu Samye Ling, Scotland, who brought eleven Western nuns from this center to Bodhgaya to receive full ordination. In comparison to other Western nuns, who often have to struggle to earn their living by working at jobs unrelated to spiritual practice, these nuns were privileged. They had received monastic training in an institutional setting and were able to settle down for longterm retreats. Satisfied with their situation in Scotland, they had not been particularly concerned about receiving full ordination. Their motivation for receiving it was discussed in general terms: personal satisfaction, the welfare of all sentient beings, the transmission of the Buddha's lineage to others, and the importance of correct monastic discipline.

On the one hand, they regarded spiritual cultivation as primarily dependent on individual effort, regardless of ordination status. On the other hand, one told me that she understood the meaning that this international ordination held for her center (although if her master had told her there was no need to come, she would have followed his advice). In this case, the institutional advantages and protection of living in a monastic community become clear. It is significant that even a Dharma master as well-established as Lama Yeshe, with a relatively strong institutional base, considered full ordination an important direction for the development of Buddhism in the West.

The ten bhiksunòi acaryas who assembled in Bodhgaya reflected the contemporary development of the bhiksunòi lineage in the various Buddhist traditions. Three senior bhiksunòi from Foguangshan assumed the positions of Sila-upadhyaya, dharma-acarya, and instructing acarya, indicating the important role that the Taiwanese Bhiksunòi Sangha played in the Bodhgaya ordination. Kuang Woo, head of Bhiksunòi Affairs of the Chogye order in Korea, represented the next largest bhiksunòi lineage in the world, lending its approval to the ordination.

The appointment of Karma Lekshe Tsomo and Thubten Chodron as witnessing acaryas demonstrates the emergence of the Western BhikBhiksunòi Sangha. Tsomo and Chodron are American bhiksunòis practicing in the Tibetan tradition; both are active internationally. The combination of the three components - Taiwanese, Korean, and American - among the ten bhiksunòi acaryas reveals the important emerging links between the various bhiksunòi groups.

THE ORDINATION CANDIDATES

Of the 134 nuns who arrived in Bodhgaya to receive ordination, all but three - one Korean, one Indian, and one Spanish - fulfilled their aspirations to receive bhiksunòi ordination. Candidates were selected from among roughly 300 nuns who had applied, on the basis of health examinations, personal recommendations, and interviews. According to a Taiwanese male candidate, the competition to participate in the ordination was keen and Bhiksu Xinding, abbot of Foguangshan, conducted the interviews quite strictly. First, the applicants had to provide evidence that their own Dharma masters and communities approved of their participation.

Then, during interviews conducted by Xinding, the applicants were evaluated on the basis of their monastic experience and responses to questions about their motivation, their subsequent plans, and so on. Foguangshan insisted upon accepting only those applicants whose participation in the ordination was approved by their monastic communities, reasoning that this approval was crucial for validating the Bodhgaya ordination.

The Taiwan group consisted of 25 members of Foguangshan and eleven Taiwanese nuns from other Taiwanese Buddhist institutes. The Foguangshan group included not only ethnic Taiwanese, but also four Ladakhi novices of the Tibetan tradition, two Chinese Australians, one Chinese American, and one Singaporean, most of whom had studied at Foguangshan. The ages of the nuns in the Foguangshan group ranged from 20 to 42, with an average age of 25 - relatively young in comparison to other groups.

The ages of the eleven other nuns from Taiwan ranged from 28 to 54, with an average age 41, representing a difference of 16 years from the Foguangshan group. Although these nuns were older than the Foguangshan candidates, they had been nuns for about the same length of time. Except for one who had been a nun for more than ten years, the Taiwan nuns had all taken vows within the last five years.

The religious identities of the Taiwan group were complex. They represented different practice lineages: Chinese, Tibetan, and Theravadin. The Ladakhi nuns and three non-Foguangshan nuns from Taiwan belonged to the Tibetan lineage, while two others identified themselves as Theravadins. In private interviews, they expressed the view that the Bodhgaya ordination was "more appropriate" for them than the annual ordination in Taiwan, conducted in a school to which their masters generally did not belong. Their explanation indicates a significant current phenomenon in Taiwan. Both the Tibetan and Theravadin traditions have been attracting more and more women followers, yet these traditions do not offer women bhiksunòi status. The absence of bhiksunòi ordination may eventually become problematic for these nuns as they conduct their activities in Taiwanese society, where people take the availability of bhiksunòi ordination for granted.

The second category of female candidates consisted of 18 Western nuns - 17 practicing in the Tibetan tradition and one German nun practicing in the Theravadin tradition. Of these nuns, seven were from the United Kingdom, three from the United States, two from Denmark, two from Belgium, two from Canada, one from Germany, and one from Spain. The educational backgrounds of the Western candidates included one Ph.D., eight M.A.s, three B.A.s, and four who had completed post-secondary vocational training. Their ages ranged from 28 to 59. Almost all of them had been nuns for more than ten years.

The third category included 66 South Asian candidates, ranging in age from 19 to 80. Their educational backgrounds included five M.A.s, six B.A.s, and five who had completed post-secondary vocational training. Some had been nuns for as long as 30 years, while others had been nuns for only four years. This relatively high level of education indicates a recent shift in the status of nuns.

TRANSLATING THE DHARMA

During the ordination proceedings, most monks relied on interpreters to communicate their ideas, and most of the interpreters were nuns. Whenever invited scholars explained the proceedings to monks and journalists from various countries, and whenever the senior monks of the various Buddhist traditions sat down for discussions - whether on monastic regulations, the establishment of the bhiksunòi lineage, or the future of the newly ordained nuns - communications were almost always facilitated by interpreters who were nuns or laywomen. All ideas needed to be expressed in at least six different languages: Hindi, Nepali, Tibetan, Sinhalese, Mandarin, and English.

At times, Burmese, Malaysian, Japanese, Hakka, Taiwanese, Cantonese, Cambodian, and Thai were also used. As more and more Asian nuns receive Western educations and assume important monastic positions, they become indispensable in organizing and administering international Buddhist events. Because the nuns who translated had access to key discussions and planning meetings, they generally had a more complete picture of the proceedings than other participants. In addition, because of their more cosmopolitan training and experience, these nuns understood the concerns of different groups more fully than some of their monolingual superiors.

Nevertheless, when the leading monks met to decide the future of the bhiksunòi lineage in their countries, the nuns were remarkably reticent and were not encouraged to express their views. On the surface at least, they seemed to place their fate in the hands of monks. The authority of leading monks at the conference was never questioned; it was assumed that monks would decide the future of nuns. Yet indirectly, nuns played key roles and gained insights into the issues at stake, insights that they can pass on to other nuns.

The importance of nuns as translators and international administrators was not lost on their male counterparts. Far from feeling threatened by the nuns' competence, the monks seemed proud of their female disciples' qualifications and capabilities. Obviously, a command of English provides greater access to resources, and more nuns than monks in this generation seem to have recognized the urgency of this. Some Western Buddhist nuns even earn their living by teaching English at Asian Buddhist monasteries. In Asia, more and more college-educated women have entered the Buddhist order. To many of these nuns, English represents a practical tool for promoting both Buddhism and their own religious careers. More than simply a tool for communicating traditional ideas, English also brings a new worldview, a new sense of community with nuns from other cultures, and a new self-identity for Buddhist women.

THE VITALITY OF TAIWANESE NUNS

To organize and administer an event as large and complex as the ordination ceremony in Bodhgaya, Foguangshan asked a working team of 30 Taiwanese nuns to take the main administrative responsibilities. Although many non-Chinese nuns came to help out periodically, in a location so far from modern conveniences it was still a challenge for the core group of nuns to arrange all the details of the ordination, including accommodations for two weeks for 50 masters, 160 novices, and countless journalists and pilgrims. These nuns woke up early, retired late, and held daily meetings to evaluate the day's events and delegate responsibilities for the next day.

The main office was a frenetic hub: attending to medical needs, travel arrangements, public relations, and the daily schedule of events. A sign on the wall that read, "Speak in a Friendly Voice with a Gentle Mind"," reflected the nuns' determination to keep their composure. The nuns of Foguangshan are generally very capable administrators and skilled at communicating with the laity. They excel in teamwork and financial management. Because of their educational qualifications, their ability to work in groups, and their numbers, the nuns are essential for administering large international events and monastic life in Taiwan.

The nuns' capabilities and solidarity may even make the monks uncertain of their role. Foguangshan monks are charged with important liturgical and spiritual responsibilities, of course, but are far less active than the nuns. The popular monks at Foguangshan are kind and considerate listeners and, outnumbered by the nuns, are willing to be almost invisible.

NUNS AS A COMMUNITY OF WOMEN

In addition to the pivotal role of nuns in formal, public settings at the ordination, nuns also related to each other in more informal, private settings, establishing and strengthening their identity as Buddhist women. Eight people gathered, including nuns from Taiwan, Burma, the United States, and Nepal. In addition to celebrating a birthday, these nuns were celebrating a reunion, since most of them had received full ordination together at Xilai Temple in Los Angeles in 1988.

Ten years later, they were together again as part of an efficient work team to help other nuns receive ordination. In their various languages, they discussed the Bodhgaya ordination and reminisced about their own ordination at Xilai Temple. These nuns agreed that one of the most significant events of the ordination was the appearance of nine Indian nuns who suddenly arrived for the ordination without previous registration. These nuns belong to a large community of over six million people from scheduled castes, primarily ex-"untouchables," who have converted to Buddhism since 1965 under the influence of B. R. Ambedkar.

The nuns explained that they had walked for five days, all the way from central India, and would rather die than leave Bodhgaya unordained. In the beginning, no one understood their language (Marathi), but the nuns conveyed their sincerity through gestures. Although their robes were tattered and some did not even have shoes, their sincerity impressed the Taiwanese abbot in charge. After much discussion on women's limitations in India and their potential to help revive Buddhism, the nine nuns were admitted. At the birthday party, the nuns discussed with great appreciation the hardships these Indian nuns had endured. Indeed, the oldest, a nun over 80, became very popular, even though she was hardly able to communicate a word.

At the party, the nuns mentioned their masters, colleagues, mothers, and friends. At one point they tried imitating the different styles of chanting practiced in the various Buddhist traditions. They reflected on the joys and challenges of the ordination, too, especially the frustrating communication difficulties. One Taiwanese nun even said she found her Ph.D. useless in taking care of the candidates. The cultural differences, often brokered by gestures and nods, had been a learning experience for all, now recalled with good humor. This final gathering was a warm, relaxed, and enjoyable way of creating and maintaining their strong sense of shared identity as Buddhist nuns.

FOCUS OF INTERNATIONAL COMPETITION

Nuns play a crucial role in communicating Buddhist teachings and attracting female followers, but their importance to Buddhist institutions goes beyond this. Although most influential Buddhist intellectuals are still elderly monks, young nuns are increasingly the most educated and sophisticated members of the Buddhist community, especially in Taiwan. This trend was well-illustrated by events in Bodhgaya.

There is an integral relationship between ordination, discipline, monastic administration, and financial support. Full ordination for women has become a focal point in the Buddhist women's movement because it provides women with full membership in the monastic community, entitling them to monastic training and support. It also allows them to participate in monastic procedures such as ordinations, bi-monthly confession ceremonies, and other rituals. Ordination therefore provides not only a means to individual spiritual cultivation, but also access to the benefits of a collective administrative system.

Buddhist nuns without full ordination are excluded from the core of power, including the right to manage their own spiritual training. Unfortunately, at present this is the case for most Buddhist nuns of the Tibetan and Theravadin monastic communities. By contrast, in the Chinese tradition currently flourishing in China, Hong Kong, and Taiwan, Buddhist nuns have access to bhiksunòi ordination and enjoy the full benefits of monastic life. The vitality of Taiwanese nuns, in particular, has created a paradigm for Buddhist women. Many Tibetan and Theravadin Buddhist nuns attribute the success of the Taiwanese nuns' community to the fact that they are able to receive full ordination.

Recent efforts by traditional Buddhists to spread Buddhism in Western countries and in India have highlighted the urgency of establishing full ordination for women. This enthusiasm is complicated by the cultural contradictions nuns encounter as they attempt to disseminate Buddhism abroad. For instance, the dilemma of preserving their own cultural heritage from Westernization is unavoidably complex in the area of gendered division of religious labor. On the one hand, Buddhist woman raised in Western countries represent valuable human resources for international propagation activities.

On the other hand, these "foreigners" with their feminist ideas often challenge the male-dominated ecclesiastic power structures of Asian Buddhist traditions. The competition for followers among the various Buddhist traditions makes full ordination for women an urgent concern; if one tradition does not attract female followers, a rival tradition will. Buddhists from Taiwan have used their well-established bhiksunòi lineage to advantage in promoting and revitalizing their traditions in other parts of the world.

The establishment of the bhiksunòi lineage among Tibetan and Theravadin Buddhists has become a focus of much Buddhist activity today. With the current Chinese Buddhist revitalization, particularly as institutionalized by Foguangshan, four major international full ordination ceremonies for women have been conducted in the past decade. In 1988, 250 female ordination candidates from 16 countries gathered in Los Angeles to receive full ordination under the auspices of Xilai Temple, the American headquarters of Foguangshan.

The ordination was organized to coincide with the opening of Xilai Temple to demonstrate that Buddhism had arrived in the West with both a large monastery and a bhiksunòi lineage. Foguangshan claimed that this was the first dual ordination held in the West and, as such, represented the revival of Sakyamuni Buddha's tradition of full ordination for women. Even before the bhiksunòi ordination was held at Xilai Temple, many nuns of the Tibetan tradition had pursued full ordination in the Chinese Buddhist tradition.

For instance, in 1982 four Western women received bhiksunòi ordination at the annual ordination ceremony hosted by Ven. Wuming vat Hae Ming Temple in Taiwan. In 1983, four Tibetan nuns from Karma Drubgyu Targye Ling, India, received full ordination at a 45-day ceremony in Hong Kong. Other nuns of the Tibetan tradition, both Westerners and Tibetans, have been ordained in Hong Kong and Taiwan, both before and since.

The Korean tradition provided some competition in the race to establish a bhiksinò lineage by arranging the full ordination of ten Sri Lankan nuns in Sarnath, India, in October 1996. The next year, after the Dalai Lama publicly expressed his continuing interest in the Taiwanese bhiksunòi lineage during his first visit to Taiwan, Buddhist authorities in mainland China conducted an international ordination for 400 monks and nuns, including both nuns from the Theravadin tradition and Himalayan nuns of the Tibetan tradition.

THE ROLE OF FOGUANGSHAN

Foguangshan organized the ordination of 134 Buddhist nuns from 19 countries in Bodhgaya in response to a suggestion made at the 4th International Monastic Seminar held at Foguangshan in 1997. Xingyun maintains that the bhiksunòi community in Taiwan is the most legitimate institution to conduct full ordination for nuns of the Tibetan and Theravadin traditions because it has inherited and transmitted the Chinese bhiksunòi lineage of dual ordination since 1953.

In addition, Foguangshan has the financial resources and a remarkable team of nuns with the administrative skills to organize such a huge event. Of course, the success of an ordination depends on more than inspiration; social and economic factors also play a significant role. The presence of Thai, Cambodian, Indian, British, American, Tibetan, Korean, Sri Lankan, Indian, and Taiwanese ordination masters was arranged to lend credibility to the proceedings. As mentioned, the Sri Lankan representatives who attended reached an agreement with Foguangshan to hold a full ordination for nuns in Sri Lanka in January 1999. Meanwhile, in March 1998 in Dharamsala, the Tibetan government-inexile organized a conference designed to conclude its 13-year investigation of the bhiksunòi ordination. To understand the historical significance of these events for gender studies, first we must unravel some fairly complex issues of Buddhist monastic law.

THE UPASAMPADA RITUAL FOR NUNS

The bhiksunòi upasampada is the ritual that transforms a female practitioner into a bhiksunòi or fully ordained nun - the highest status a woman can achieve in the Buddhist monastic framework. The first step in the ritual is to gather the precept masters and candidates. If the monastic community agrees, the number of ordination masters and teachers may be adjusted under certain conditions. For instance, in border areas of the Buddhist world, Sakyamuni Buddha allowed the number of both male and female ordination masters to be reduced from ten to five.

After assembling the participants, the teachers define the ritual arena (sima) by means of a purification ceremony. In the Chinese tradition, the sima is generally an ordination platform or altar. Setting the boundaries of the ordination altar not only protects the participants, but also symbolizes the boundaries of the monastic community. Once these boundaries are set, the ordination becomes recognized as having been approved by the monastic community.

However, in most Buddhist countries, including Burma, Cambodia, Sri Lanka, Thailand, and Tibet, the bhiksunòi order died out long ago or was never established. The lineage survives only in China, Korea, Taiwan, and Vietnam. According to monastic regulations, a bhiksunòi should be ordained in the presence of other bhiksunòi, in what is termed a "dual ordination procedure." Therefore the re-establishment of an order of bhiksunòis ideally should involve the participation of bhiksunòis ordained in an existing lineage. This inevitably gives rise to two questions: which nuns from which traditions are best qualified to carry out these ordinations, and whether or not bhiksunòi ordinations should be carried out at all.

For some traditional ecclesiastics, the idea of reintroducing full ordination for women is as absurd as changing the Buddha's gender from male to female. Full ordination has been a male-exclusive privilege in the Tibetan and Theravadin Buddhist traditions for centuries. It is widely believed and stated in some canonical texts that women are incapable of achieving Buddhahood. This belief has had the effect of keeping women in subordinate positions and away from monastic resources. However, even the staunchest critics of the ordination of nuns admit that Sakyamuni Buddha himself ordained women and made contributions to social equality.

When confronted by a bhiksu opposed to the ordination of nuns, one Sri Lankan nun recently replied, "How can you [monks] take vows of serving all sentient beings, but turn your backs on your own Dharma sisters?" Such contradictions leave much room for debate, and the controversy is greatly compounded by complex power relations and vested interests within and between the Buddhist traditions. Nevertheless, as the constraints placed upon women have come to light in recent years, the need to rectify the situation has created substantial cooperation between Buddhist nuns of the various traditions. International associations of Buddhist women, notably Sakyadhita ("Daughters of the Buddha"), have emerged to promote full ordination.

Buddha Sakyamuni's purported words and the account of his establishment of the bhiksunòi order, which are preserved in the canon, provide an external authority validating women's right to ordination. Ranking in the monastic hierarchy depended not on gender, but on the status of its members as determined by the number of years they had been ordained. Men go through two stages: Sramanòera (novice monk) and bhiksu (fully ordained monk). Women go through three stages: Sramanòerika (novice nun), Sksamanòa (a two-year probationary period created to exclude pregnant women), and bhiksunòi (fully ordained nun).

The lineage and format of Sakyamuni Buddha's monastic community have been transmitted for generations, up to modern times. The existence of the bhiksunòi lineage is certain, but the circumstances of its establishment have always been somewhat controversial. The early texts portray Sakyamuni as reluctant to allow women into the order and state that he predicted that their admission would shorten the life of the teachings (sasana). On the other hand, some early Buddhist groups believed that the bhiksunòi community would bring prosperity to Buddhism. Today, at least, many view the benefits of having both male and female monastic lineages as more important than the potential dangers.

Significantly for the history of nuns, after the Buddha ordained Mahaprajapati, it was stipulated that the full ordination of women requires the presence of both bhiksunòis and bhiksus, implying that monks or nuns alone should not ordain nuns. In

India, the order of nuns died out along with the order of monks and Buddhism in general in the 11th century. The order of nuns also disappeared in Sri Lanka when the Buddhist monastic community was destroyed there around the same time.

Although the Sinhalese reestablished their bhiksu order by inviting Siamese and Burmese monks to carry out ordinations, it was impossible to revive the bhiksunòi lineage because there were no bhiksunòis available to perform the ordination. These events were later interpreted in light of the Buddha's earlier prediction of the decline of the sasana. The presumption was that the suppression of Buddhism under the Muslim invaders was related to the decline of the Dharma, which in line with the Buddha's prophecy was hastened by the admission of women into the order. Even today, some Buddhists claim that the order of fully ordained nuns will not reappear until the arrival of Maitreya, the future Buddha.

The order of nuns did survive in China, however, and eventually made its way to Taiwan, Korea, and Vietnam. In Taiwan, before a woman makes the decision to enter the order, she usually lives in a monastic community for quite some time and is referred to as jinfanyu. Next, she requests the tonsure, a ceremony that involves shaving the head and entering into a disciple relationship with her master. After receiving the tonsure, she undergoes a probationary period to adjust to monastic life, during which her master and colleagues observe her character and depth of commitment. After a period of six months to two years, her master sends her to receive full ordination in a Triple Platform Ordination.

The full ordination ceremony is the highlight of the whole procedure. Many Taiwanese nuns refer to full ordination as "a rite of rebirth." Just as bhiksunòi ordination is received, the master announces the specific time of the ordination, down to the second, symbolizing the beginning of a new life. Thus, after a long period of intensive training and scrutiny, the nun finally becomes a full-fledged member of the monastic order - an "offspring of the Buddha." Unlike tonsure, which is performed by individual masters and monasteries, full ordination usually involves an array of important ecclesiastic leaders and representatives. Full ordination for nuns requires ten bhiksunòis in addition to ten bhiksus; the three central precept masters of each category must have been ordained for twelve years or more.

THE DUAL ORDINATION CONTROVERSY

The controversy over bhiksunòi ordination usually centers on the necessity of dual ordination. According to the Vinaya (Buddhist monastic texts), full ordination for nuns requires 20 qualified precept masters: ten bhiksus as well as ten bhiksunòis, or at least five of each in remote areas. The purpose of this requirement is to make sure the nuns are well prepared for ordination and to avoid embarrassment when certain personal questions are asked. Throughout history, Buddhist communities have encountered difficulty finding qualified bhiksunòis to perform the dual ordination.

This difficulty stems in part from prevailing social conditions, which confined most women to the family. Among the accounts of hundreds of Indian teachers who traveled to the East Asia to spread Buddhism, there are no records of nuns. Importantly, the two documented incidents of dispatching nuns abroad - from India to Sri Lanka in the fourth century B.C.E. and from Sri Lanka to China in 432 C.E. - were state-sponsored missions for the specific purpose of transmitting the Bhiksunò Sangha abroad.

When members of the Bhiksu Sangha were not available to conduct the ordination, nuns were often ordained by monks alone. For instance, before the Sri Lankan bhiksunòis arrived in China, the monastic community allowed women to be ordained by bhiksus alone. This ordination procedure was considered legitimate, as a passage in the Biographies of Bhiksunòis attests. Huimin explains:

> According to the biography of Gunòavarman in the Biographies of Eminent Monks, monks initiated the bhiksunòi ordination. If a nun did not receive dual ordination, her ordination by monks was also valid. Although the ordination masters commit a misdemeanor, the ordination is valid. This ordination has never been proclaimed invalid because the monastic regulations do not discuss the lack of dual ordination in the procedures.

Baochang, author of the Biographies of Bhiksunòis, traces the origins of the Chinese bhiksunòi Sangha to Mahaprajapati. By the fifth century, the Chinese Sangha recognized Jingjian as the first Chinese bhiksunòi, ordained by a procedure similar to Mahaprajapati's, that is, by bhiksus alone. This type of ordination is not necessarily invalid, for although the Vinaya literature explains the dual ordination procedure as the ideal, nowhere does it declare a single ordination procedure invalid.

In fact, many contend that it is the bhiksus, rather than bhiksunòis, who constitute the final authority on the ordination of nuns. Although feminists might dispute the reasoning behind this contention, the fact remains that when members of a particular monastic order endorse Buddhist nuns ordained by bhiksus alone, the ordination is considered valid. In other words, the legitimacy of monastic ordination is dependent upon decisions reached by local Bhiksunòi Sangha communities. Therefore, as the Taiwanese bhiksunòi Zhaohui has stated, if it is monks who are authorized to conduct bhiksunòi ordinations, and then it is monks who must be held accountable for the absence of a lineage of full ordination for women, not the nuns.

The deep concern for receiving ordination according to the orthodox dual ordination procedure expressed by authorities in the Theravadin and Tibetan traditions may indicate their intention to establish a core group of nuns capable of ordaining others in the future. The same concern for orthodoxy was in evidence at the ordination held at Xilai Temple in 1988. Originally ten Sri Lankan nuns applied to receive full ordination, but were unable to get their passports in time. Among the twelve Sri Lankan nuns who eventually made the trip to Los Angeles, only five candidates successfully received ordination.

Some speculate that the lack of support these five new bhiksunòis received after they returned to Sri Lanka was an indication that the Buddhist community preferred to have a full quorum of ten nuns ordained, instead of just five. The promotion of the bhiksunòi ordination at present is a result of efforts by international Buddhist associations, primarily initiated by Western nuns. The most important of these is Sakyadhita: International Association of Buddhist Women, which has encouraged research and publications on the topic of ordination through conferences and seminars since 1987.

These endeavors are a reflection of the significant role women are playing in the dissemination of Buddhism in the global community. For instance, about 80 percent of Tibetan Dharma centers in the West are maintained, and sometimes led, by women. Women, especially nuns, are also the strongest force propelling Chinese Buddhist activities abroad.

Tibetan and Taiwanese Buddhist nuns receive very different treatment in their endeavors, however. The Foguangshan authorities already know how productive Buddhist women can be. Gender equality is one of the most important dimensions of what Master Xingyun calls "humanistic Buddhism." Taiwanese and overseas Chinese women who enter the monastic order at Foguangshan become skilled in social service activities and qualified to create a sense of cultural identity among women in overseas, particularly immigrant, Chinese communities.

Recognizing this, Foguangshan offers free education for foreign students and monastic positions after their graduation. Graduates of these programs enhance Foguangshan's competitive edge in Buddhist propagation activities due to their language abilities and personal connections. For many Buddhist nuns, Foguangshan provides opportunities for education and career advancement that few, if any, other Buddhist organizations can match.

In Taiwan, Buddhist masters are generally very careful to select reliable representatives to ordain their disciples. They contribute time and financial support to ordination ceremonies; some even accompany their disciples to the temple and stay throughout. The relationship between a novice and her tonsure and ordination masters is likened to the relationship between a child, her parents, and the clan patriarchs. The tonsure master brings his "children" to the ordination master to solicit their admission into the larger monastic family. In this way, traditional monastic structures replicate familiar family structures and traditional patterns of behavior.

In contrast, there is hardly any institutional support for Western female monastics in the Tibetan tradition. This is due both to a lack of resources and to the lack of full ordination which traditionally provides recognition. The monastic role of nuns is usually limited to a supportive function, both in exile Tibetan and Western settings. Although their abilities as English teachers, fundraisers, and translators are socially acknowledged, there is no financial support, and these volunteer activities often conflict with these nuns' personal commitment to spiritual practice.

Their lack of full ordination status means that the monastic community places the nuns' needs behind those of male monastics, and sometimes even behind the laity. For instance, a layman who is interested in monastic discipline will be encouraged and supported to study in Dharamsala, while a Western nun has to pay her own expenses and usually finds no monastic facilities available at all.

The structure of Tibetan and Taiwanese Buddhist communities in the West is also quite different. Taiwanese Buddhist temples serve as important social institutions for maintaining cultural continuity. Although Taiwanese nuns may not be as active as Western nuns in teaching, they are wellintegrated into overseas Chinese communities and are appreciated for the traditional ritual services they provide. Economic dependence may have its drawbacks, but the ethnic integrity of these communities and the respect traditionally accorded to monastics in Chinese Buddhist societies ensure that nuns are appreciated and protected from financial difficulties.

In contrast, Tibetan Buddhists in the West offer very little support for monastics individually or for the establishment of monastic institutions. The Tibetan tradition has expanded rapidly in the West over the last two decades owing to the accessibility and flexibility of its spiritual training, particularly meditation. Tibetan Buddhism is very open to lay practitioners, but has not yet given sufficient support to developing monastic communities in the West. What support is available is generally channeled to refugee monasteries in India and Nepal, mostly to monks.

In Tibet, although monasteries for nuns and monks were established separately, both communities were considered part of local society, and supported at least at subsistence level. At this stage, however, Western nuns of the Tibetan tradition benefit neither from the Western notion of religious community, nor do they find an appropriate place in the Tibetan religious community. As Tibetan Buddhism becomes better established in the West, it is important that the Tibetan Buddhist authorities help integrate Western nuns into their monastic systems. Endorsing the bhiksunòi ordination is one of the most effective strategies the Tibetan Buddhist authorities could use to accomplish this task.

DHARMA AND GENDER POLITICS

The competition to gain recognition and support for bhiksunòis among Buddhists in the West is only one aspect of the ordination controversy, however. Another aspect is the competition to establish the bhiksunòi lineage that has emerged among Tibetan Buddhists in exile and Theravadin Buddhists from Sri Lanka, Thailand, and Burma. In addition, there is competition surrounding the bhiksunòi lineage within Chinese Buddhism itself.

Following the Cultural Revolution, the survival and revitalization of Chinese Buddhism relied heavily on financial support from Buddhist followers in the Chinese diaspora and Taiwan. Buddhists in China lack the resources to compete with Taiwanese efforts to spread Buddhism abroad, yet they were anxious to assert their legitimacy and orthodoxy. During the tumultuous years of the Cultural Revolution, Buddhism in the People's Republic suffered many setbacks. Buddhists in Taiwan rose to the task of representing Chinese Buddhism at conferences abroad, often supported by the government of the Republic of China. Buddhists in China have struggled valiantly to restore their traditions in the aftermath of the Cultural Revolution, but it will take decades to recover from the devastating losses of Buddhist literary, architectural, and human resources.

Although it may be impossible to replace the Taiwanese as representatives of Chinese Buddhism internationally, mainland Chinese Buddhists can claim that their bhiksunòi lineage is more orthodox than Taiwan's. Buddhist authorities in China have therefore shifted their focus to claims of historical orthodoxy for their monastic traditions and their "sovereign right" over all bhiksunòi lineages.

Political issues are also involved. The Tibetan Buddhist authorities in exile are aware that claims to religious sovereignty may affect their claim to political sovereignty, the key factor in maintaining ethnic, religious, and cultural identity in the Tibetan exile community. In the past, Tibetan authorities have avoided any type of formal association with the Taiwanese authorities, and the Guomindang government in Taiwan has also been very sensitive about the issue of Tibetan independence.

Coincidentally, however, during the Buddhist revival in Taiwan over the last two decades, so many Taiwanese Buddhists have become attracted to Tibetan Buddhism that the Tibetan Government-in-Exile has altered its stance and cautiously begun relations with the Taiwanese Buddhist authorities. If the Tibetans intend to continue cultural communications with Chinese Buddhists, the Tibetan leadership will eventually have to choose between the Chinese and Taiwanese Buddhist orders. If this choice carries weighty political implications, however, it may be simpler to reject them both.

In the present bid to reestablish the bhiksunòi order in Sri Lanka, the Buddhist leadership there has the option of cooperating with Buddhists in either China or Taiwan, with potential advantages either way. Apart from the bhiksunòi issue, however, because Theravadin Buddhist practice is popular in the West its future is inextricably linked with Tibetan Buddhist activities there. Although communications with other Buddhist traditions have been minimal in the past, since settling in India the Tibetan Government-in-Exile has also established relations with Theravadin Buddhists there.

Earlier certain bhiksunòi were concerned that Tibetan Buddhist recognition of the bhiksunòi lineage might attract censure from Theravadin Buddhists, who are generally considered more conservative, particularly on women's issues. Now the tables have turned somewhat; if the Tibetan authorities do not respond appropriately to demands for full ordination for women in its monastic system, the Theravadins will gain recognition as being more socially enlightened on the international scene.

His Holiness the Dalai Lama's first visit to Taiwan in March 1997 shows that the Tibetan Government-in-Exile has gradually realized the urgency and influence of bhiksunòi ordination. In fact, His Holiness has expressed interest in the bhiksunòi lineage publicly many times. Although he has stopped short of officially recognizing the bhiksunòi lineage, he has consistently affirmed the benefits of full ordination for women and the right of nuns in the Tibetan tradition to receive it. During his trip to Taiwan, he specifically requested a meeting with Taiwanese bhiksunòis to discuss this issue and, moreover, declared that this was one of his purposes in making the trip.

Procedures for decision-making in the Tibetan ecclesiastic system are cumbersome, however; decisions concerning monastic law require formal consultations among senior Bhiksu Safigha members. For this reason, the Dalai Lama has said that it is not within his power, as a single bhikssu, to formally recognize the Chinese bhiksunòi lineage. This may explain why he did not respond immediately to Foguangshan's suggestion of a full ordination ceremony in Bodhgaya, as proposed at the May 1997 International Federation of Buddhist Sangha Conference.

In November 1997, His Holiness sent Bhiksu Tashi Tsering to Taiwan to investigate the Chinese bhiksunòi lineage. During this visit, Taiwanese scholars frankly informed Tashi Tsering about the potential competition between the Buddhist authorities in China and Taiwan to establish the bhiksunòi lineage in the Tibetan tradition. However, it seems that the Tibetan authorities were unable to make a decision at that time. On December 20, 1997, just 36 days later, the Chinese Buddhist authorities in mainland China held their first international ordination, which was attended by nuns of both the Tibetan and Nepalese traditions. The timing suggests a conscious effort by the mainland Chinese authorities to demonstrate their stature on the international Buddhist front.

NUNS AND BUDDHIST MONASTIC LEGITIMACY

Ordination reproduces the monastic continuity. The traditional notion of monastic community, requiring three principal precept masters (acaryas) and at least seven witnesses to officiate, provides legal recognition and legitimacy to ordinations. In this way, the ordination ritual repeatedly integrates the community and guarantees its continuity. Traditionally, precept masters who performed ordinations belonged to the same monastic community, or at least the same Vinaya lineage. The traditional system is designed to establish ties and lines of authority between monastics and their own communities by maintaining sectarian boundaries.

The model used by Foguangshan at the Bodhgaya ordination - inviting instructors and witnesses from different monastic communities to preside together at the ordination of nuns from different monastic communities and Vinaya lineages - is something new, initiated only in the last two decades by monasteries in the West. From the perspective of Buddhist nuns today, however, the notion of community is unified and globalized by the full ordination itself.

Monks of the various Vinaya traditions also have a historical connectedness. For example, Tibetan monastics sew a blue cord on their vests to remember their indebtedness to the Chinese masters who assisted them in reviving their own bhiksunòi lineage in the tenth century in northeast Tibet (Amdo). This sense of mutual connectedness may be expanded upon to create a more broadminded and flexible international monastic community.

The full ordination of women may promote cooperation among ordination masters of different monastic communities, yet taking full ordination in the Chinese tradition may also alienate women from their own monastic communities. For this reason, it is necessary to develop relations with sympathetic elements in each country to help sustain newly ordained nuns and help them reintegrate into their local communities.

As more and more Buddhist nuns devote themselves to full ordination, they acquire a broader sense of monastic community, one which is unified rather than divided by sectarian identities.

In this sense, they function to reaffirm the underlying unity of the Buddhist traditions and exemplify the Dharma taught by Sakyamuni Buddha, a doctrine of universal salvation and social equality.

The Bodhgaya ordination demonstrated that most monastic groups recognize the urgency of establishing full ordination in terms of Buddhist dissemination activities rather than the gender issue per se. In the context of expanding Buddhism internationally, nuns are a valuable resource, representing not only a powerful pool of talent for spreading the Buddha's teachings, but also a key to modernizing different Buddhist groups. The bhiksunòi ordination creates a common dilemma for all monastic orders, however: how to regulate these nuns' membership and how to transmit the bhiksunòi lineage from one Buddhist tradition to another. The present strategy of Foguangshan is to assemble monks of various Buddhist traditions and schools. This is why the appointment of the three central ordination masters is important in the current international competition for bhiksunòi ordination.

Particularly owing to political conflicts, it is possible that some groups attempt to maintain their religious sovereignty by claiming orthodoxy for their bhiksunòi lineages. The movement to reestablish full ordination for women in the Tibetan and Theravadin traditions is one that requires mutual cooperation among various Buddhist traditions and schools. The establishment of the Bhiksunòi Sangha therefore necessitates crossing sectarian boundaries. Moreover, if monks are recognized as the legitimate authorities for validating bhiksunòi ordinations, the movement relies on mutual recognition among the male-dominated ecclesiastic hierarchies.

Ecclesiastic authority usually represents the institutionalized legitimacy of its founder and canon. Therefore, the discourse on full ordination for women is complicated by ambiguities intrinsic in the Buddha's attitude toward women (first hesitating, and then agreeing to ordain bhiksunòis) and in the canon (which both supports and denigrates women). Moreover, there are various interpretations of the historical events surrounding the creation and transmission of the bhiksunòi lineage. The procedures used to ordain women in the various Buddhist traditions shed light on how Buddhists traditionally dealt with notions of membership and legitimacy in the monastic community, but these procedures can be applied and interpreted differently, depending on circumstances and ideology.

For instance, ecclesiastical authorities in Tibet traditionally insisted upon the dual procedure for ordaining bhiksunòis. A 15th-century Tibetan monk's attempt to conduct a bhiksunòi ordination with bhiksus alone was an anomaly and never gained official acceptance. Nevertheless, his efforts to ordain bhiksunòis demonstrate his commitment to equal religious rights for women. Even though there apparently were no bhiksunòis available to conduct an ordination by the orthodox procedure, this monk was willing to take personal and political risks to help nuns get fully ordained.

The reluctance of Tibetan ecclesiastical authorities to recognize full ordination for women in modern times, then, naturally raises questions. When the acceptance of Buddhism in the modern world requires an egalitarian approach, what explains their hesitation? If the Tibetan monastic community wishes to avoid interference by Chinese Buddhist authorities in their internal ecclesiastic affairs, why insist on dual ordination?

The case of Sri Lanka also indicates the crucial role of historical connections. Despite canonical regulations, the lack of a Bhiksunòi Sangha since the 11th century, and vocal opposition on the part of some monks, the Sri Lankan monastic community is discussing how to regain its lost heritage by restoring the bhiksunòi lineage. Many Sri Lankans are committed to reviving this lost lineage of 'akyamuni Buddha and are ready to back an international ordination conducted by Foguangshan and its well-established bhiksunòi order.

In the process of organizing the Bodhgaya ordination, Foguangshan transcended traditional boundaries posed by canonical and historical differences. In the name of revitalization, Foguangshan is creating a new tradition by aligning internationally with traditional authorities. The ordination in Bodhgaya was not the first time a Buddhist monastery in Taiwan had exported Vinaya. In the last three decades, there have been many activities related to ordination led by Taiwanese Buddhist organizations.

For instance, the annual ordination ceremonies organized by the Chinese Buddhist Association of the Republic of China and held at monasteries throughout Taiwan have attracted both overseas Chinese and Western candidates from a range of countries since 1970. Bhiksunòi Wuyin of Xiangguangsi (Luminary Buddhist Society) in Chiayi, Taiwan, was a featured lecturer on Bhiksunòi Vinaya at a three-week monastic training seminar for 100 nuns and laywomen in Bodhgaya in 1996. It is noteworthy that all these activities focused on full ordination for women. Quite clearly, Taiwanese Buddhist monasteries are earnest about reintroducing the bhiksunòi lineage into other traditions.

As representatives of the Tibetan tradition challenge the validity of the Chinese bhiksunòi lineage, the question that arises is whether the bhiksunòi community in Taiwan legitimately represents the Chinese bhiksunòi lineage. Xingyun claims orthodoxy for the Taiwanese bhiksunòi lineage by counting the beginning of the Taiwanese bhiksunòi lineage from the ordination reforms introduced by Chinese monks in post-war Taiwan.

However, Xingyun's stance, which represents the popular perspective of Chinese refugee monks, takes the legitimacy of the Chinese lineage for granted and also ignores ordination ties between mainland Chinese and Taiwanese Buddhists from before the war. Prior to 1949 some Taiwanese Buddhist nuns received full ordination in China, but the post-war ordination system controlled by the Chinese Buddhist Association in Taiwan has consciously or unconsciously ignored this historical connection, hoping to legitimize its status as the only official Buddhist representative on the international scene.

Moreover, there is clearly more than one interpretation of the concept of lineage in the creation of Buddhist monastic identity. The Chinese system of ordination needs to be understood in the context of a particular Mahayana country's adaptation of pre-Mahayana monastic regulations in establishing its Buddhist identity. By performing dual ordination for bhiksunòis and by maintaining the monastic format initiated by Sakyamuni Buddha, the Chinese monastic community feels that it has authentically preserved the lineage. Moreover, the Dharmagupta Vinaya which the Chinese Sanha uses to conduct ordination rites is very similar in structure both to the Mûlasarvastivadin Vinaya followed by the Tibetans and to the Theravadin Vinaya followed in Burma, Cambodia, Laos, Thailand, and Sri Lanka.

Taiwanese scholars such as Bhiksunòi Hengqing, Bhiksunòi Zhaohui, and Bhiksunòi Huimin have compared the Chinese Dharmagupta and the Tibetan Molasarvfistivfidin renditions of the Bhiksunòi Pratimoksa Sûtra and discussed the close resemblance between them with Bhiksu Tashi Tsering. Comparative analysis shows that, despite small differences in monastic regulations, these two Vinaya systems are extremely similar. It is the historical and cultural differences reflected in the format of ordination that distinguish the various systems of ordination far more than the monastic regulations or textual narratives explaining them.

Although monks have traditionally been in charge of presiding at ordinations, this does not mean that Buddhist nuns have been passive in the movement to establish bhiksunòi ordination. On the contrary, since Mahaprajapati initiated the bhiksunòi movement two and a half millennia ago, the lineage has continued by virtue of women's commitment to ordination and to the Dharma.

The process of dual ordination entails the transmission of the lineage from senior bhiksunòis to novices, confirming a sense of shared identity and commitment among women from generation to generation. Because the bhiksunòi lineage is absent in the Tibetan and Theravadin traditions, however, these Buddhist nuns need to borrow, or recover, the lineage from the Chinese Buddhist tradition. This creates a special situation - a potential space for intra-Buddhist communications and an urgent need for Buddhist nuns to network internationally.

The current discourse on bhiksunòi ordination is unprecedented in Buddhist history. It may be the first and only time that Buddhist women have transcended sectarian identities to form a distinctive group. The issue of ordination therefore represents a unique opportunity for encouraging sectarian cooperation. Bhiksunòi ordination not only represents full membership in the Buddhist family, it establishes Buddhist nuns as a distinctive social and religious circle. It symbolizes nuns striving to gain legitimacy for them and it is also a visible banner uniting Buddhist nuns of the various schools.

The Buddhist nuns involved in this movement are markedly different from previous generations because of their experience in manipulating new knowledge and creating an international sisterhood. In this situation, the capacity to speak English not only opens the way to new realms of experience for Buddhist nuns and teaches them the importance of access to information, but also opens new channels for community development and the cross-fertilization of ideas.

In the process of promoting full ordination, nuns are expanding their horizons through exposure to diverse Buddhist traditions and to feminist ideas. In the process, they are consciously or unconsciously re-evaluating their traditions and their own religious, ethnic, and gender identity. For Buddhist nuns in traditions without bhiksunòi status, the vital and confident order of Taiwanese nuns serves as a rare and inspiring role model which holds promise for their own future.

Reintroducing full ordination for women has its irony, however. The emphasis on bhiksunòi status and dual ordination as the key to legitimizing Buddhist nuns oversimplifies the problem of nuns in the various Buddhist traditions. For one thing, no canonical statement specifically pronounces the single ordination invalid. In fact, there is a clear statement allowing this procedure: "Bhikus, I permit you to confer full ordination on bhiksunòis." Second, male ecclesiastics in Sri Lanka, Thailand, and Tibet have long ignored the absence of a bhiksunòi order in their traditions.

Therefore, introducing dual ordination in these traditions is not simply a matter of creating something new, but entails institutionalizing and according official recognition to an order of nuns that is already functioning outside their own traditions. This potentially complicates not only Safigha relationships in their own countries, but also patriarchal international Buddhist relationships. Third, if dual ordination is advanced as the only valid method of ordination for bhiksunòis, it calls into question those ordinations already authorized by bhiksus alone. Ordination procedures vary in the different Buddhist traditions, and each assumes it is orthodox, so to pronounce as invalid the bhiksunòi lineages that currently exist in East Asia, as some conservative bhiksus do, raises significant questions about different notions of monastic lineage and legitimacy among the various Buddhist traditions.

In addition, there are power dynamics at work that must be taken into account. Conducting ordinations may be symbolic of privilege and status for the tradition that assumes leadership. Underlying the peaceful, festival atmosphere of the full ordination activities in Bodhgaya, therefore, a symbolic international struggle for power, prestige, and legitimacy was taking place.

Regardless of political nuances, because of their strong economic and institutional base, Taiwanese Buddhists have been able to create a strong international movement for the full ordination of women. This is due primarily to the commitment and determination of the nuns themselves. It demonstrates that the more economically independent Buddhist nuns are, the more autonomy and power they have to transform attitudes and institutions. In comparison to the nuns of Thailand (mae chi), whose survival depends on the largess of monks' monasteries, and the tenprecept nuns of Sri Lanka (dasasilmata), who live independently and administer their own nunneries but are nonetheless financially constrained, nuns in Taiwan are economically independent and powerful.

In Taiwanese Buddhist circles, it is an open secret that Buddhist nuns are generally better at raising and administering finances than monks. Coincidentally, it is these relatively self-sufficient nuns, rather than nuns in economic straits, who confidently pursue a more appropriate religious status for themselves. The vitality of Taiwanese nuns, therefore, has been a significant force in the endeavor to introduce full ordination to nuns of the Tibetan and Theravadin traditions.

The bhiksunòi community is well-established in Taiwanese society. Even though the division of religious labor and leadership reflects the conventional, patriarchal expectations of Chinese society, the religious identity and relatively equal status of nuns and monks is recognized both in the monastic community and society at large. Both the ritual and economic autonomy of Taiwanese nuns are solidly institutionalized. In Taiwan, Buddhist nuns virtually control monastic education, and they wield a powerful influence on lay education as well.

The success of the Ziji Foundation, a Buddhist charity organization with 3,500,000 members, has established Bhiksunòi Zhengyan as the most influential Buddhist leader in Taiwan. Also in the top ten are Bhiksunòis Xiaoyun (Shig Hiu Wan), Zhaohui, and Hengqing - all leading Buddhist educators. The remarkable achievements and institutional success of Buddhist nuns in Taiwan make them logical role models for modern Buddhist women.

Based on their experience of a monastic culture in which nuns function at least as effectively as monks, Taiwanese society regards Buddhist education and full ordination for women as axiomatic. The Taiwanese, both lay and ordained, thus naturally support education and ordination for women in the Tibetan and Theravadin Buddhist traditions. Against this background, Foguangshan has been able to motivate Taiwanese Buddhists to donate time, energy, and money to support their international ordination activities. One might assume that Taiwan's sound economic system is the primary ingredient for success, but this explanation ignores the religious motivation of Taiwanese Buddhists.

Although many Taiwanese Buddhists may be oblivious to the complex issues of gender equality and monastic law behind the bhiksunòi ordination movement they support, most interpret their generosity as religious merit accumulated by "making a (future) Buddha." They make no gender distinctions in their religiosity, acquiring merit through supporting the ordination of monks and nuns equally, implying that the Bhiksu and Bhiksunòi Sanghas are equally respected and equally capable of achieving Buddhahood. This unbiased social support for the Safigha has been a key factor in promoting full ordination for women and the advancement of Buddhist women as a whole.

The vitality of Buddhism in Taiwan, the dedication and competence of Taiwanese bhiksunòis, and the religious commitment of Taiwanese Buddhists in supporting the establishment of a recognized bhiksunòi lineage beyond the boundaries of their own tradition combine to make the Taiwanese Buddhists pioneers in establishing full ordination for women.

The nuns of Taiwan who have benefited from the unbiased support of their lay followers have returned manifold benefits to the laity and the Dharma, becoming examples of the tremendous potential the bhiksunòi order holds for Buddhism globally. Whether they are aware of it or not, their success represents a major restructuring of Buddhist institutions that has profound significance for hundreds of millions of women.

5

Philosophies East and West

Three times during the past twenty-five centuries, process philosophies have challenged the established intellectual and cultural membrane that interprets the meaning of human experience and value. Three times these philosophies have failed to rise to dominance, submerged by the prevailing ideas of the time and place. The first process philosophy to appear is associated with the teachings of Gautama Buddha in the sixth century B.C. Strictly speaking, Buddhism is neither a philosophy nor a religion in the ordinary Western meanings of these terms; it is, however, a method of awakening to what is really real in the world, a fact that could make it fit both Western categories, broadly defined.

The second process philosophy is found in the so-called fragments of Heraclitus (536-475 B.C.), "the weeping philosopher of Ephesus," the first of the precocious Greeks to place himself at the center of the social revolution of his time, just prior to the Peloponnesian War. The "fragments" are actually self-contained sayings designed for memorization in a community in which most people were unable to read. We should not think, therefore, that we have only the odds and ends of his larger work of continuous unfragmented prose; we have Heraclitus in a style derived from oral forms of communication, a style aimed at inducing people to accept a new way of life.

The third appearance of process philosophy, this time in a fully rounded-out and systematic form, came during what Max H. Fisch calls "the classical age of American thought," beginning about 1880 with William James and Charles Peirce and continuing to the eve of World War II in the work of Josiah Royce, John Dewey, and the Anglo-American Alfred North Whitehead.

At all three points where process thought was emerging, certain cultural dislocations were moving sensitive and perceptive individuals to shake off the ways their communities had sought to rationalize and justify the established order of life. At all three points, a universal problem that is not well understood even today came into focus: men and women everywhere live with a largely unrecognized tension, anxiety, and conflict between what is concretely and directly disclosed in immediate experience and the abstract constructions of reason and science.

In every cultureworld we know anything about, people are induced by the forms of custom and convention to turn away from their own feelings and aesthetic sensibilities. In their relatively underdeveloped stage of human evolution, people are easily persuaded that they must live by other people's notions, notions that everyone is pressured to believe, but as Zen has been shouting from the housetops for centuries, those who cling to words, letters, rules, conventions, and linguistic systems will never comprehend what any speaker is trying to communicate.

The philosophies of Buddhism, Heraclitus, and the American "classical age" philosophers all seek to reverse the claims of the linguistic and cultural superstructure and return individuals to their own deeper-than-cultural awareness of life's rich qualitative flow. All three philosophies remind us that even the most ingenious works of intelligence, once they have been institutionalized, have meaning that is microscopic and meager in comparison with the qualities found in the experiences of everyday life.

All three focus attention upon the subliminal levels of experience, upon Whitehead's "tacit dimension" of the "deep experiences of organic existence," the fountainhead from which all the ingenuity and creativity of the human world are constantly watered. All three open the gates of quality flowing from the aesthetic foundations of the world. Rationality is, of course, defined differently in different cultureworlds, and, indeed, even in the same culture-world at different times and places.

From the vantage point of process thinking, a fundamental irrationalism infects the life-styles of humankind wherever the indefinite complexity of what is intuited and felt is forced into the procrustean beds of existing forms of understanding. Employed in ways indicated by process philosophy, conceptual form is a searchlight deepening understanding, probing the limits of awareness, opening experience to more of the variety and unspeakable qualitative richness of the world. As Kitarô Nishida puts it for the Japanese, "The merely conceptual is not the real; the world of actuality is the world of self-creation, a creative world which goes on forming itself; we are all creative elements of a creative world."

The problem all three process philosophies bring into focus is the problem of how to interpret events that are deeper in human experience than any rational system can take into account, events that sweep over the physiological organism, shaking and dislodging old perceptual anchorages and bearing witness to feelings that are filtered out and lost when distilled through modes of interpretation presently in place.

The fundamental stumbling block of life looms before us when these rules of logic and dominant forms of interpretation insist upon determining how and what we shall feel. This is the chief source of suffering in the human world. Individuals suffer and come face-to-face with nihilistic conclusions when no signs and symbols succeed in communicating the soft underside of the mind in the richness of its momentary now.

Process thinking, however, bears witness to the capacity of human experience to be moved by a creativity that is deeper than the limited conceptual systems and cultural metaphors of a time and place. Not our thinking but "our experience," Whitehead writes, "sounds the utmost depths of reality." As he explains elsewhere, "Our lives are passed in the experience of disclosure. As we lose this sense of disclosure, we are descending to mere conformity with the average of the past. Complete conformity means loss of life. There remains the barren existence of inorganic nature."

More fundamental than individual persons, social classes, linguistic systems, social institutions, and cultural metaphors is the succession of momentary nows, self-creative feelings that are emasculated and exploited by large-scale social organizations to keep human behavior within parochial and predictable bounds. Every social structure commits what Whitehead calls the "fallacy of misplaced concreteness," as each seeks to appropriate the concreteness of individualized experience for its own ends, fixing the attention of its members upon goals that, in the last analysis, generate the alienation from which the modern world for several centuries has been struggling, amid great suffering, to be free.

"Buddhist thought," Herbert Guenther declares, "has always been process-oriented thinking. It is out of such a process-oriented view that Buddhism formulated its concern of being-with-others, suggesting a personal spontaneous experience in which we create ourselves and participate with our fellow-creatures in the creativity of the process we calls life."

Historically speaking, process philosophy first appeared with the Buddhist perception that everything is abstract but the present moment, the fulfilled now where we encounter life face-to- face as events coming into being and passing away to become part of the permanent past. Human suffering has its source in our compulsive clinging to each fulfilled moment as it passes, placing the obstacle of our compulsive drives before the creativity of life. The Buddha's teaching appropriates the traditional concept of "rebirth" to point to the forced transformation required for each fulfilled now to be followed by the next.

Our proprietary attachment makes us prisoners of each present occasion, which we wish at times would last forever. Disoriented in this way, we are forcibly reborn from one moment to the next; in the interstices we stand outside what is really real. Individuals overcome this compulsive clinging through meditation and become part of the creativity of the world. Their identity from this point on is with the flow of quality in their experience, undergoing creatively what Rudolf Bultmann called "the eschatology of the moment," (thus giving Christian concepts of atonement and resurrection a new existential meaning).

Buddhism has taught for centuries that every moment has its own totality of conditions and causes owing to which it exists. These actual individualized moments are the final real things in relation to which everything else-persons, concepts, plans, purposes, and things-is a high-level abstraction. These moments are the happenings that constitute nature at large. In human experience each moment is, in Whitehead's words, "that portion of our past lying between a tenth of a second and a half second ago; it is gone, and yet it is here; it is our indubitable self, the foundation of our present existence."

Out of these moments, as Hartshorne says, "we are creating something additional, however slight, in the mass of memories and bodily habits that make up character." These momentary nows are what William James calls "the living individualized feelings" in comparison with which the world of generalized objects is without solidity or life. We live forward in a risky and uncertain world, producing novel forms of togetherness as we move in the concreteness of a creativity which characterizes all matters of fact. The Russian scholar T. I. Stcherbatsky spoke directly on the issue elaborated in Whiteheadian thought: "A plurality of subtle, ultimate elements, technically called dharmas, creatively synthesize the past into the novel present, making the past an ingredient in the process of 'relational origination' forevermore."

These passing moments, while the source of all motion through their creative synthesis of past and present, are part of the interrelatedness of existence Buddhism calls Sanyata or pratityasamutpada. "The elements," Stcherbatsky writes, "co-operate and are in dialogue with one another; this co-operating activity is controlled by the laws of causation (pratitya-samutpada)." This process of interrelated moments, producing novel forms of togetherness, is given a more detailed formulation in process philosophy today, but it is only in Buddhism that human suffering is understood as having its source in an individual's inability to stay in touch with these original concrete events given in the passing now.

Beginning in the sixth century B.C., Buddhism has perceived reality as the inexhaustible process of energy flowing out of the depths of things, quite apart from any conscious effort to bring the process about. Behind the first conscious moment of life, the human organism has its own amplifying awareness of reality as a dynamic, holistic process functioning mysteriously as life's pervasive ground.

The process is infinitely creative. "It comes," Herbert Guenther writes, "and is there, eliciting a response precisely by its being there.""A fundamental property of this inexhaustible energy," Guenther says, "is what is termed in Tibetan records its communicative thrust (sngags), functioning as a coherent, unified process." The real point in Buddhism is not to endeavor to grasp this "thrust of the unthought" in a categorial system; the point is to awaken to more of the vividness and vastness of experience itself.

Kitarô Nishida, the first systematic Buddhist philosopher of modern Japan and the most demanding thinker Japan has produced, is in fundamental agreement with the Tibetan point Guenther has made. "Pure experience," as Nishida calls it, is the root dimension in which reality presents itself prior to the intervention of sense experience or thought. It is this "pure experience" to which philosophy should be open, instead of imitating the methods of mathematics and natural science. It is the fundamental fact that forms the immediacy of human experience; it is the experience in which all others originate; it is reality creatively forming it; it is the world of life.

The ultimate facts in human experience are the concrete qualities or flashes of energy, the pure breath of our direct encounter with life. These moments of the experienced now, according to A. K. Warder, "are the elementary qualities which are not analyzable into anything else." This is something, Warder says, "that anyone can verify for himself." A recent translator of Nagarjuna argues that even the poorest individual has an enormous unexplored capacity for awakening to these incommunicable qualities streaming through our everyday lives: "There is in every individual," Ramanan writes, "a sense of existence, a feeling for the qualitative reality of events, a sense of the ultimacy of the undivided being."

A leading work on Zen philosophy, furthermore, defines reality as the dimension of experience before it is analytically grasped through articulate words, as does "The Secret Oral Teachings in Tibet": "What has to be understood is that theories and doctrines of all kinds are the fabrications of our mind." Everything in the Buddhist glossary is explained in terms of what is directly given in our original individualized experience, which is essentially "a revelation of our immediate contact with the world of dynamic flow and change."

The one thing in the Buddhist orientation that is good without qualification, good everywhere under all circumstances, is the individual's awakening to the vividness of the passing now. The point of life is to increase, not our speed, but our responsiveness, our ability to be moved before any specialized zone of sense perception or anonymous routine can induce us to feel in socially mandatory or psychologically compulsive ways. Buddhism is thus an effort to relate us to the essenceless, selfless spontaneous stream of experience, to awaken us to what is always being disclosed in the momentary now.

The primary task of Buddhism is to make it impossible for people to turn their backs upon this direct encounter with what is deepest in the human spirit. Other philosophies, to be sure, have had similar intentions, but they make our individualized experience more incomprehensible than ever by appealing to Platonic archetypes, Kantian transcendental egos, Hebraic-Christian souls, the emanations of a Neo-Platonic One, or other intellectualizations in the classical metaphysical traditions of the West. When we win a measure of freedom from the compulsive drive and the culture-encapsulated self, however, we discover the uncluttered, selfless, deeper-than-linguistic flow of individualized experience, drawing us into its concreteness, the mark of the reality in things.

In Buddhism even the gods one meets in the sutras are not deities in the Western objective sense, but represent mental states evoked by meditation, which may suggest new possibilities for a deepening and widening of our appreciation for the enormity and mystery of worlds beyond our ken. We are told by the new Encyclopedia of Buddhism that "Siddhartha Gautama became the Buddha, the Enlightened One, as a result of a profound spiritual experience, an abrupt knowledge of Reality, which he realised under the famous Bodhi Tree near Gaya in northern India. This knowledge, being ineffable, could never be put into words; and all the verbal teaching of the Buddha was simply an indication or suggestion of its nature, a mere device for awakening men to real insight." "There is nothing in the teaching of Buddhism," Guenther says, "which our immediate experience does not contain."

Unlike other creatures, the human individual is not confined to a biologically and socially determined nature: "He is not bound forever to his fragmentariness. He has a thirst to regain the dynamic, organic relatedness of which richness of life consists." The ability to regain this organic relatedness is, however, the most underdeveloped feature of distinctively twentieth-century life. Only the rarest individual seems able to distinguish the raw, unformed flow of quality from the communal stereotypes in which he or she has been reared.

The result is an almost totally subdued sense of conflict and tension between experience as concretely ours and the impact of cultural form, the tension and reality of this natural conflict being further concealed by an exaggerated fear of unshareable experience and a need to live with people who think and act as though they came from the same mold. In their voracious appetite for "belonging," people disorient one another from what is really going on. They satisfy one another's hungers, develop new industry, build cities of identical skyscrapers the world over, and never notice that all of it might strike a visitor from another planet as ultimately reducible to taking in one another's laundry.

Buddhism, however, has been functioning as a self-corrective method for almost twenty-five hundred years, freeing individuals one at a time from the deceits and disguises of the self-interested, class-oriented, culture-encapsulated self. Participating in disciplines of meditation and meditative thought, men and women become more creative respondents in the life they share with the speechless world's fellow-creatures. They learn that the universe is stranger and more beautiful than parochial stereotypes give anyone reason to believe. Following these meditations, people are liberated from the time-bound, authoritarian public models whose powers of control over human behavior now threaten the species with extinction.

By teaching individuals to doubt everything they have been reared to believe, Buddhism fosters that higher form of reasonableness that enables them to translate what people are "saying" into the actual world of everyday life, rejecting what cannot be so translated. As David-Neel and Yongden quote from the Vajracchedika Sutra: "It is when one no longer believes in the beliefs of the self-interested and culture-bound self that the time has come to distribute gifts." And further: "It is the ideas which we hold, and not our material activity in itself, which constructs the chains that bind us."

Out of the ancient Buddhist Way we are told, "No one can guide thee but thyself.""Do not put faith in traditions," the Aaguttara Nikaya says, even though they have been accepted for long generations and in many countries. Do not believe a thing because many repeat it. Do not accept a thing on the authority of one or another of the Sages of old, nor on the ground that a statement is found in the books. Never believe anything because probability is in its favour. Do not believe in that which you have yourselves imagined, thinking that a god has inspired it. Believe nothing merely on the authority of your teachers or of the priests. After examination, believe that which you have tested for yourselves and found reasonable, which is in conformity with your well-being and that of others."

Nothing in the Buddhist orientation, therefore, has ever been an "article of faith" in the Western sense. Everything is to be analyzed and tested. It is only as we begin to doubt the validity of established institutions that we become capable of appreciating the ancestral order of life, valuing its achievements and perceiving its shortcomings in the long struggle of an evolving species. All the moral, political, and religious achievements of the past then become valuable resources to be used as probes for discovering more of the fullness and richness in the novel forms of togetherness in everyday life.

We are thus opened outward in the Buddhist perspective to a world that is wider than civilized form. What the conscious mind is fitted by cultural rearing to understand is the one-ninth of the iceberg in comparison with the eight-ninths submerged beneath the surface of life. An anthropologist appears inadvertently to be urging upon humanity the very recognition that Buddhism asks us to address: "One of the most significant facts about us," Clifford Geertz writes, "may finally be that we all begin with the natural equipment to live a thousand kinds of life, but end in the end having lived only one."

Human beings breed across ethnic and linguistic lines because everyone carries the conditions for birthing. Individuals can understand one another across cultural barriers because everyone has the capacity to become open to what is individually felt; even the most pathological conditions of anger, terror, and fear can bring people back to the common experiences of everyday life. People can become aware in apparently inexhaustible degrees; the capacity for being moved by others, and for responding to others, is inherent in awareness as such.

Buddhism seeks to return the live creature, whatever his or her state of feeling and mind, from the dominant structures of conscious thought and institutional behavior to the concreteness that is forever nurturing human life. As Christmas Humphreys writes, "Buddhism lays stress on the individual and tends to attract all those who regard as evil the attempt of the State or any organization within it to shackle the minds of its members with dogma of any kind."

Experience in its concrete presentness, in that vast background barely touched by conscious form, has always appeared to be of superior validity when compared with any concept or institutional form. As W. Howard Wriggins comments from Sri Lanka, Buddhists there have a predisposition "to be wary of the vested interests, the ambitions, and the presumptions of authority of man over men that are the inescapable accompaniments of human organizations."

Individual Buddhists in general do not seek their fulfillment in social institutions and social movements, all of which are viewed as monuments to the ego-trips of the disoriented few, because Buddhism has always struggled to keep experience in its individualized forms from becoming enveloped, Gulliver-fashion, in those ideological, metaphysical, and ecclesiastical structures that reduce awareness to the limits of the tribe, the social class, peer group, or profession. The Buddhist influence has always required the high abstractions of large-scale social organizations to be answerable to the living individualized now.

HERACLITUS

Amid the faulting of the institutional crust of ancient Greece, Heraclitus advanced what has been called a "terrifying perspective, resembling an earthquake in which everything seems to sway." For the second time in the history of the human world a process philosophy emerged on the continental divide where experience in its inexhaustible creativity and richness was being overlaid by, as Nietzsche says, "the customary, the small, and the common, filling up all the crannies of the world like a heavy atmosphere everyone is condemned to breathe."

Nietzsche can think of no one who more fully embodied this individualized experience of the vastness of a more-than-human world than Heraclitus. Among prose masters of Greece, Heraclitus is Plato's only equal, Nietzsche believes, a philosopher of unsurpassed power and originality, "like a star without an atmosphere.""As a man among men," Nietzsche adds, "Heraclitus was incredible, refusing to believe that people have an incurable need to receive from an outside, more reliable source the clues regarding the meaning of their own experience. Though an aristocrat by birth, accustomed to a society that ruled by intimidation, Heraclitus scoffed at the suggestion that people live better when they submit their individualized experience to be molded and subsumed under the conceptual metaphors dominant at the time. "To live successfully," he writes, "the world one thinks must be one's own, sharable but not borrowed from others."

It is the greatness of Heraclitus, according to Heidegger, that he includes the "unthought" and thinks of being as "the process of disclosure." Every new insight that reaches conscious awareness originates in this unthought, often remaining in the soft underside of the mind for long periods, without being able to break through the barrier set up by the organized structures of conscious thought. Heraclitus realizes that, as Kenneth Maly says, "thinking's thought has a fundamental and originary bond to the unthought; the unthought demands to be heard and dealt with, thrusting it upon us; the thrust of the unthought is then the issue for thinking."

Process philosophy is not just a different way of thinking about our experience in the world, nor is it, in Marx's sense, primarily a way of changing the world. For Heraclitu s, James Wayne Dye argues, "it is the way we are led to think about our experience when we see the way the world presents itself for thought, for perception, and for feeling." The "weeping philosopher" grumbled that people "turn their backs to that with which they have to deal continually, and most of all, that which they encounter daily appears strange to them." A kind of blindness is thus acquired, preventing people from seeing that, according to Maly, "the main issue is to wake up and teach wakefulness to one another." Every human being when healthy and whole lives with openness to what is being forever disclosed, because, Maly argues, "man cannot remain hidden (how could he?) from the unthought."

In Heraclitus, experience is freed from the intellectual and institutional lock and key. Experience is interpreted by him in its own natural rhythms, as Dye believes, "rather than in terms of pure forms given to a consciousness supposedly capable of disinterested spectatorship.""In the most concrete sense," Dye continues, "there are no independent non-changing entities. All things are in process, and nothing stays as it was. Objects conventionally identified by a single name are really always changing." Heraclitus also visualizes the world, according to Karl Popper, "not as an edifice, but rather as the totality of all events." And the experiencer is within the process, part of the universal change, rather than outside as a neutral observer. "The greatness of this discovery," Popper says, "can hardly be overrated."

Process philosophy, however, died out in ancient Greece when the social turbulence mounted to intolerable levels, culminating in the Peloponnesian War, which lasted twenty-eight years, to be followed by the puppet government of the Thirty Tyrants in Athens, during whose eight-month rule as many citizens were killed as during the final ten years of the war. The Heraclitean vision of a universe of dynamic creative forces working as a selfexplanatory ground of change failed to resolve the cultural conflicts that were carrying the Greeks beyond the intellectual and social horizons of the traditional city-state. It was one among many efforts of brilliant philosophers constituting what has been called the Golden Age, an effort "to wake up and teach wakefulness" to fellow-citizens whose expanded trade with the whole Mediterranean world was bringing not only new commodities but new ideas and values that called into question the old parochialisms and taboos.

Following Heraclitus, those Karl Popper refers to as "the Great Generation" created the fountain from which Western civilization has continued to draw its ruling ideas, but several centuries of social and political turmoil followed, thrusting rational argument from the center of the Athenian stage. The cosmopolitan world of Alexander the Great tossed three continents of radically different culture-worlds into a single community in which citizens, resident aliens, and strangers from abroad would dwell together on equal footing and view one another as citizens of one world.

The ideal was too new and too lacking in broad social support to become deeply rooted in the Mediterranean world. The voice of Plato was extinguished even within his Academy; Skepticism prevailed almost immediately following his death in the very place where the claims of the Patterns and Archetypes had been the topic of the day. The successors to Aristotle in the Lyceum forgot his original teachings almost in their entirety; his famous manuscripts were hidden to keep them from "barbarian" hands, until Sulla in 86 B.C. confiscated the entire library and took it to Rome.

In some circles mysticism came to the fore and new religions and philosophies were born: "Materialistic and positivistic attitudes toward life lost ground, and Platonism came into its own again with the appearance of the Neo-Platonic system of Plotinus - monistic, transcendent, emanative, with a theory of knowledge, ethics, and aesthetics based on ecstasy. But most fruitful of all in its consequences was the rise of the Christian religion." A new period in the history of the Mediterranean world had begun.

AMERICAN MODE

After centuries of philosophical activity within the limits of the substance- and being-centered Greek tradition, Western philosophy, in the form of those Max Fisch designates "philosophers of America's classical period," has given many of the central perspectives of process thinking, including Buddhist process thinking, their clearest and most systematic formulation.

Charles Hartshorne, the major representative of these philosophers in the contemporary world, has, for example, related the corpus of this American tradition to what he calls "the oldest of the great international systems" in the most specific ways. Historians of the future, freed from the parochialisms that obstruct our view, will probably see that Hartshorne's major accomplishment has been his weaving of his own realization that experiencing is in principle creative together with Dewey's "logic of qualitative thinking," William James's radical empiricism and pluralistic universe, Royce's beloved community of interpretation (in The Problem of Christianity), Peirce's analysis of nature into events rather than things, and Whitehead's actual entities, prehensions, and creativity to arrive at a systematic formulation remarkably expressive of Buddhist thought.

In Buddhism and in American philosophy, as summarized by Hartshorne, one finds the same emphasis upon the infinite fertility of human experience in a world whose creativity is its most universal feature, upon the centrality of dynamic change and the consequent inconclusiveness of all knowledge and speculation, and upon the diversity of ways in which individuals experience what is most real and the danger of imposing abstract categorial systems on the individualized and original experience of everyday life.

On numerous occasions Hartshorne has expressed our need to break free from the astigmatisms of Western thought. "I think it is time," he writes, "that at least the Buddhist tradition should be taken seriously into account. I have argued for years that there are indeed non-European ideas that can serve our European purposes better. It is notable that one (somewhat Americanized) European philosopher, Whitehead, has arrived, probably independently, at some central Buddhist insights, and that two Americans, James and Peirce, partly anticipated him in this."

Buddhism is, Hartshorne says, "the greatest international alternative to our Judeo-Christian tradition; we can no longer ignore it." And further: "Our provincial neglect of this great tradition is out of keeping with the global responsibilities of our time." Throughout his long career he has been endeavoring to make Buddhism a factor in American thinking.

There is no major Hartshorne writing that does not relate some idea or concept at the core of his philosophy to what Buddhism has taught in all of its divisions and "schools." Illustrations abound:

Ancient Buddhism and Whitehead agree, against Aristotle, and also against Bergson, but in nearer agreement with Plato's Timaeus, that concrete reality consists of momentary actualities that successively become; this succession being what we call change.

If we are looking for concrete definite unitary wholes of reality, we should recognize that the individual-now is always a new such whole. The Buddhists, whom Peirce admired, saw this.

The momentary experiences are the primary realities and these do not change, they simply become. The "soul" or the self-identical ego is merely the relatedness of experiences to their predecessors through memory and the persistence of various qualities or personality traits. The first great metaphysician in the West to hold this view clearly was Whitehead, in the present century. To see this is the beginning of wisdom in the theory of selfhood.... The Buddhists saw it long ago. There are profound ethical and religious implications of this view which Buddhism appreciated and Whitehead also emphasizes. Egocentric motivations essentially consist in metaphysical confusion. This is why a Buddhist termed the egocentric view "writhing in delusion."

One should admire the genius of Buddhism in seeing into the complexity of this matter so long ago. It is not the everidentical self that thinks or feels, now in this way and now in that; this self never thinks or feels at all, for it is an abstraction, and what actually has thoughts or feelings must be concrete.

As a college sophomore [in 1916] I learned from Royce's great essay on "Community" the most essential metaphysical lesson of all, perhaps, a lesson the Buddhists had learned long before.

This was to detect the element of illusion (or, if youprefer, confusion) in the idea of a plurality of selves mutually external to each other.

In the light of illustrations such as these, it is now possible to see Hartshorne as the great connective link between Buddhism and a group of American philosophers who are not surpassed in any nation during the past century, if, indeed, they have been equaled in the history of philosophy taken as a whole. No one but Hartshorne in the West has ever matched Buddhism in its emphasis upon the chiefly evocative role of reason in sharpening our focus on the soft underside of the mind, whose fugitive moments of rich and intense quality provide each individual with his or her direct encounter with life.

Not even Buddhism has excelled Hartshorne's struggle to awaken men and women to depths and ranges of awareness for the enjoyment of which our potentialities have barely moved beyond the most primitive range. Hartshorne speaks like a Buddhist in arguing that what we experience in the present moment is the fundamental reality, in comparison with which all else is an abstraction.

This convergence of philosophies separated by thousands of miles and years, and by radically different cultural systems, stands unmatched in the history of the species. The strange upsurge of process thought in Western civilization, strange in the light of the West's cognitive bias and almost hypnotic fixation with theoretical structure from the time of its emergence among the amazing Greeks, could probably not have happened at all without the concurrence of three remarkable transformations in the intellectual and cultural atmosphere of the United States, where modern process philosophy in its systematic formulation - best represented by the thinking of Charles Peirce, William James, Josiah Royce, John Dewey, and Alfred North Whitehead - first appeared.

The first of these historic transformations was the quantum revolution that shook physics during the first quarter of the present century and led to the rejection of many of the dominant ideas of Western thought, such as the rigidly determined world subscribed to by virtually all philosophers in the West, and the concept of a permanent, self-identical, not-further-analyzable substance. The second great transformation came when no traditional cultural identity was able to survive the rub of radically different racial, ethnic, linguistic, and cultural systems brought to the "new world" by the immigrants whose descendants form the overwhelming bulk of the population.

A nation had emerged out of a spontaneously self-chosen population, initially from Europe but eventually from every part of the planet. During the two centuries following Jamestown and Plymouth Rock, intercultural communication became a law of life. The vast problems of settling a continent forced a polyglot population to turn its back upon all European models of civilization and to place the emphasis upon the original experience which individuals here were sharing with one another in everyday life. As Dewey later eulogized this radical departure from ancestral ways, "of all affairs communication is the most wonderful. That the fruit of communication should be participation, sharing, is a wonder by the side of which transubstantiation pales."

The third and final factor is that many of the central ideas of the "Classic American Philosophers" had been anticipated in philosophers whose contributions might still be neglected and even forgotten except for the role they came to play in American process thought: Samuel Alexander's and C. Lloyd Morgan's "emergent evolution," Henri Bergson's classic view of the opposition between perception and conception, Étienne Boutroux's compatibility between causality and chance, Charles Darwin's famous repudiation of fixed species, Gustav Fechner's self-surpassable deity (dismissing the idea subscribed to throughout the European tradition that deity cannot change), C. Judson Herrick's aphorism that "making novelties seems to be nature's chief industry," Jules Lequier's equally provocative notion that "Thou hast created me creator of myself," and even more novel discoveries by David Hume, Sigmund Freud, Karl Marx, and Friedrich Nietzsche. Though none of these germinal thinkers was yet thinking of his work as "process philosophy," the term now everywhere in vogue, all were feeling out a world where creativity is an ultimate notion.

Like the other two process philosophies, which made their appearance in northern India and in Heraclitus's Greece, process thinking in its American mode constitutes a deep revolutionary challenge to the dominant ideas in which most inhabitants of this continent are reared. Like the other two philosophies, its central point is the tension between what is concrete, spontaneous, immediate, original, evanescent, and free in human experience, as Peirce puts it, and the almost irresistible pressure of every established order to force human experience into the linguistic and institutional system already in place.

The upsurges that shake the settled structures of individual and social existence bear witness to a deeper-than-conventional presencing of life. "The history of thought," Whitehead writes, "is a tragic mixture of vibrant disclosure and of deadening closure. The sense of penetration is lost in the certainty of completed knowledge. This dogmatism is the antichrist of learning." Philosophers in the West have been, for the most part, unaware of the perils of abstraction. Heraclitus in Greece has been a voice in the wilderness.

Every effort to describe and conceptualize novel forms of awareness must be false to them, and in the last resort, humanly destructive. In the concrete experience of William James the point became a matter of life and death. "Yesterday," he writes, "was a crisis in my life.... Hitherto, when I have felt like taking a free initiative, like daring to act originally, without carefully waiting for contemplation of the external world to determine all for me, suicide seemed the most manly form to put my daring into; now, I will go a step further with my will, not only act with it, but believe as well; believe in my individual reality and creative power." Whitehead and Peirce made this point throughout their careers. "The willful adherence to a belief," Peirce writes, "and the arbitrary forcing it upon others must be given up." As Whitehead was to put the point later on, "Life refuses to be embalmed alive."

Especially in its American mode, process philosophy is an effort to bring to the forefront of attention the outrage inflicted upon individualized experience when the contrived world of intellectual and institutional form is imposed upon the most precious of all natural resources - the incandescence and power of what is vivid in the momentary now. The formative events in the shaping of the American culture - the nation's territory tripling in less than two hundred years, its population multiplying fifty times, its resources growing with its sudden new sources of gold, railroads, and land - brought Americans face-to-face with the process in which a new society is born. "They know, because they have seen them made," Donald Cary Williams writes, "that societies are artificial combinations engineered by private citizens for their own ends."

And so a philosophical revolution has been needed, to complete what was commenced in the political one, presupposing as a matter of course the goals already so nobly advanced - freedom from inequitable taxation, from control by an established church, from constraints on social improvement - and calling into question the more fundamental form of bondage that it is the business of philosophy to expose - the rule of unchosen abstractions over the original individualized experience of the momentary now.

The ways of cultural imperialism are here exposed in their inexhaustible techniques of military, economic, political, linguistic, and, particularly, conceptual aggression. The age of a vast population deaf and dumb to the concreteness of their own experience can now recede into its European past. The idea has been germinating in American process thinking for a very long time that in the concreteness of things no man or woman is incapable of adding to the quality of life, whatever his or her racial or ethnic origin or background.

The new declaration of independence in this philosophical revolution was written by a transplanted Englishman who had been invited, after a distinguished career at Cambridge and London in mathematics, logic, and physics, to teach philosophy at Harvard, something he said at the time "he had always wanted to do," at the age of sixty-three. Addressing his Harvard colleagues about that institution's future, Whitehead carries the unfinished American Revolution beyond the limits of the past.

"For three centuries," he argues, "European learning has employed itself in a limited task. Scholars, in science and in literature, have been brilliantly successful. But they have finished that task - the possession of clear ideas, woven into compound structures, with the attributes of truth, or of beauty, or of moral elevation.""European learning," Whitehead continues, "was founded on the dictionary; and splendid dictionaries were produced. With the culmination of the dictionaries the epoch has ended." And further: "All the dictionaries of all the languages have failed to provide for the expression of the full human experience.... Experience does not occur in the clothing of verbal phrases."

In this statement the Europeanization of the earth is called into question. A new awareness has dawned that conscious symbolic processes are not the primary vehicles of learning. A cognitionbiased, definition-minded, concept-oriented, over-intellectualized European tradition stretching backward to the amazing Greeks is here effectively challenged. The world no longer exists to be known. The intellect is no longer the highest level of the soul. The attention has been shifted decisively away from a world of timeless truths, away from abstract systems of law, politics, and ecclesiastical form, over to a more fundamental way of experiencing the world.

William James, Josiah Royce, Charles Peirce, John Dewey, Alfred North Whitehead, and their penetrating and judicious auditor Charles Hartshorne constitute this kind of fundamental break with the past, calling into question the dominant tendencies in Western philosophy - the search for ideas that no amount of empirical experience can ever falsify, the enthrallment with abstract reason over concreteness, the pursuit of some Archimedean point from which to move the world, the general denigration of the burgeoning present, and the entrapment in language which Wittgenstein found to be an almost irresistible matter of "bewitchment."

In American process philosophy, creativity and freedom have found a home. Here, the happiness and value in the world are found in individuals: they alone enjoy and suffer the qualities of the fleeting instant; they alone give institutions whatever purposes they pursue. We, therefore, face the task, Whitehead writes, of providing for a universe that is without bounds, for a learning that is worldwide, and for an emotional life with springs lying below conventionalities. Civilizations are produced, according to Whitehead, "not so much by community of bare ideas as by community of feelings by which ideas are 'emotionalized' and become beliefs and motives."

Such feelings, however, "are not in the first instance ours," Hartshorne argues, "but belong especially to creatures making up our bodies. The 'ocean of feelings,' each with some self-determination and some participation in previous feelings, is reality itself." These original qualities of the fleeting moment, furthermore, encounter their death-trap in the rule of convention: "A learned orthodoxy," Whitehead warns, "suppresses adventure," exhausting the creative springs of originality that are essential to civilization.

The creativity and freedom found in American process philosophy cannot, however, be limited to each individual's experience; experience must be shared by all. Peirce frames the point in terms of logic and science: "Logicality," he writes, "requires that our interests shall not be limited, must not stop at our own fate, but must extend to all races of beings with which we can come into immediate or mediate intellectual relations." And Dewey's "reconstruction in philosophy" directs attention away from what James called the "block universes" of European thought over to the shared individualized experience that in the very nature of the case is always beyond the reach of the sociological communities to which individuals belong.

Process philosophy in the American mode, therefore, turns Plato, Kant, and Hegel upside down, the main line of reality lying in no conception of anything in or beyond the world, reality being created from one moment to the next and inherited in its vast interrelatedness in memory and perception. The greatest single contribution to American process philosophy is Whitehead's revolutionary concept of prehension, one of the three concepts that constitute the core of "Whiteheadianism," the other two being creativity ("the universal of universals") and the actual entities of momentary occasions ("the really real things which in their collective unity compose the evolving universe, ever plunging into the creative advance"). Whitehead defines prehension in his famous statement that "the many become one and are increased by one."

Clarifying how the one experience in the fleeting moment synthesizes many past events, Whitehead's concept of prehension is an unprecedented theory of the way the world proceeds, only vague approximations being found in Bergson, Peirce, and Buddhism. To make the concept possible, many careless habits of the Western tradition had to be overcome: its thingification of the world, its simple-minded submission to ordinary language and common-sense assumptions, its suspicion of new concepts, its confusion regarding the symmetrical nature of past and future, its prejudice with respect to an "inextended" mind and the dualisms naturally resulting therefrom, and its queer propensity to look beyond the tops of the highest mountains to something more fundamental than time and space and history could ever contain.

Reality is thus a new single event related to and partly constituted by many events of the past. Whitehead's world is self-creative, a balancing act between causality and change; creative change is an ultimate notion (as Peirce writes at great length). Whitehead's concept of prehension points to a form of causal efficacy at work in the deeps of human personality weaving new textures of shared experience into the deepening and widening community of life. It is here where men and women find their reality and their truth. In these prehensions we coexist much more than exist, influence others and are influenced by them, carry forward in time the funded experience of the species, and participate in the power that is acquired by caring, suffering, and remembering compassionately what is happening and has happened in the life of the world.

Long before we know what our novel forms of togetherness portend, we are caught in their opalescent grasp. There are many things in this mysterious world for which we bear responsibility, but the forming of our conscious minds is not one of them. Changes of mind are native growths within a living organism, nurtured in the relational origination of things rather than summoned into existence. "To prehend," as Hartshorne says, "is to sympathize with or participate in the feeling of others."

In its most fully developed American form, process philosophy speaks to us of a world that is always forming itself through the creative communication of individual persons and things. Reality is most unambiguously given, not at the verbal or institutional levels of life, but in those novel forms of togetherness that find their way into what is coming to be. Our own more or less intense unverbalized experiences are the clearest and most indubitable instances of what is actually real, a view that differs from the ineffable experience found in European doctrines of mysticism because here it is an empirical process present in everyday life, an empirical process responsible for ordering the form of everything that is coming to be.

Deeper than the matters that separate individuals from one another, the common bond of our togetherness is found at this experiential level, feeling the feelings of one another and communicating out of an original experience in its nonverbal social growth. This is the same fundamental fact Guenther finds in Tibetan Buddhism - "its communicative unifying thrust."

"The total concrete reality in a personal existence," Hartshorne says, "is new each moment," the latest in the career of an individual's life; it contains all there is to the unity of the self in whose personal character it occurs. Because this concrete reality emerges as a subliminal upsurge coming out of the individual's relations with fellow-creatures and the organic wholeness of the world, it is the basis for our sense of being "members one of another," including the speechless world's fellow-creatures. ("The Buddhists had this in mind for many centuries," Hartshorne writes, "and in all branches of Buddhism; I think they have a precious lesson to teach Christians at this point.")

Process philosophy in the American mode is not as largely a historical miracle as it may seem. It is the positive contribution of a handful of Western civilization's most powerful minds, working over insights of a European legacy usually ignored and drawing out for the first time the implications of physical research conducted in places like CERN (Conseil Européen pour la Recherche Nucléaire) and the Fermi Institute at Batavia, Illinois. Even more crucially, a new historical matrix created for the first time on American shores had the possibility from the very outset of curing a human community of an affliction carried by civilized form and structure.

More important by far than installations of high-tech research and discoveries in outer space, the chief discovery of the American community is the concreteness in the process of life. People here were simply unable to understand each other and solve their problems together as long as they allowed their minds to be shaped by their radically different ancestral linguistic and cultural backgrounds. Slowly but irresistibly, they came to accept the necessity of relating directly to one another's original experience in the new world. Their awareness of one another's "prehensions" became the occasion for influencing and being influenced by one another. They gradually stopped clinging to a world that had been projected for them by their ancestral traditions.

What Buddhism calls "relational origination," therefore, found in the American community its first cultural embodiment in the West. And this cultural fact, rather than any grasp of the Buddha's teaching, is the source of Whitehead's embodiment of so many distinctive Buddhist perspectives. In numerous explicit references to Buddhism he displays the most erroneous views. Insights were forcing themselves to the surface that Whitehead was deliberately attempting to clarify, helping this community to think freely about the novel possibilities here and the futility of trying to transplant European cultures to American shores.

Questions were being clarified here that had never been answered: What is it that men and women experience concretely, in relation to which everything else is abstract? What is experience as originally given, without the overlay of sensory form or the intrusion of conscious thought? These are but two of the devastating new questions shaking existing institutions of law, government, philosophy, and religion.

Process philosophy in the three modes presented in this chapter represents the return of the native to the concreteness of the living moment, to the flow of quality within an organism acting as a whole, brain contemporary with the body, the complex amplifier that transforms vague feeling tones into the more vivid ranges of experience where men and women in the instantaneous present are memorably and vitally alive. Process thinking returns the individual from the high abstractions of conscious thought - following Aristotle's lead, Western philosophy simply could not see that the final, fully concrete units of reality are momentary, unit instances of becoming, rather than of being.

Thinking in the process mode, we are returned from the wholesale institutionalization of our lives, from the stereotyped ways we perceive the world through cultural clichés, and from the even more artificial data of the senses. Process philosophy is an effort to give individual men and women a foothold in a universe of which they are an organic part, a universe that enfolds their freedom with the implicate order of the whole.

In its process form, philosophy has achieved a new relationship to human experience. Alphonse de Waelhens puts this point clearly in his recent survey of contemporary thought: "No longer an explanation from afar of the world and of consciousness, philosophy henceforth becomes one with this experience; not satisfied to shed light on man and his life, it aspires to become this life, now at the stage of complete self-awareness." In America, process philosophy approaches this stage, the creation of a community of immigrants who are still exploring the vast continent of their experience on the crossroads of an interdependent world.

6

The Buddhist Implications

THE TRANSFORMATION

The idea of scale is useful because historians agree that religions such as Buddhism, with their "karmic eschatologies," emerged during India's "second urbanization" (the first of course associated with the Indus valley civilizations). During this period small communities were linked to each other by trade networks and the imperialist designs of emergent empires. Similar, although not identical, social changes were occurring in the small Greek city-states, although the scale of change was not as great as in India. Avoiding terms like high and low, primitive and civilized, great and little, literate and preliterate, class and classless, and other such dichotomies, I will construct transformational models to deliberately reduce the rich complexity of the empirical world and to narrow down and then highlight the critical differences among the various rebirth theories presented in this book.

Birth transfers the individual from some otherworld to the visible human world. Rites of passage at birth assist this transition, helping one to overcome the perils of the soul (wherever such an idea exists) and of conception and fostering the nurture and protection of the fetus and the mother. The neonate is born into a family and a kin group for whom he or she is an ancestor returned. During the course of the individual's life, rites of passage assist transitions into critically important roles-for example at puberty and marriage. Each of these transitions, as ethnographers have consistently pointed out, can be viewed as a symbolic death and rebirth or, in Robert Hertz's words, as"exclusion" followed by an "inclusion."

When real death occurs, funeral rites serve to transfer the individual once again into the invisible world of the ancestors. We can now posit an important feature of this otherworld, namely, its essential temporality, because a person must eventually leave this otherworld for the human one, and this must go on and on. In fact the only enduring thing is the rebirth cycle itself, which in principle at least can go on forever. There is little ethnographic data to indicate whether the temporal character of the otherworld and the perpetual recurrence of rebirth cycles are given existential meaning and significance in the eschatologies presented earlier, as they are in the Indic idea of samsara or in the Greek ideas of the processes of rebirth, variously conceptualized as metacosmesis, metensomatosis, or metempsychosis.

The otherworld may not exist, however, in a few of the eschatologies examined in this work, among some Greek Pythagoreans and the Druze; and in some of the Amerindian ones it might on occasion be bypassed. Consequently, one can ask: how is this otherworld structured? In all of the small-scale societies presented earlier, the otherworld is structured on the model of the only world everyone is familiar with, namely, one's own society.

Thus the architecture of the otherworld replicates the key features of the earthly social structure, or, more often, human beings utilize structural principles that govern the social world for constructing a new society of ancestors. Yet precisely because otherworlds are constructed by the human imagination, one can express through them one's wishes for a utopia or a paradise, a place where suffering and privation are eliminated. "It is or can be the realm of the ideal," says Hertz. The Trobriand eschatology defined by Tomwaya Lakwabulo is a good empirical approximation of this paradisiacal ideal; a few of the Northwest Coast societies come close to it in their idea of a land with abundant food.

Although the idea of a world of ancestors (paradisiacal or otherwise) is omnipresent, this is not so with the idea of a hell or a similar place of punishment. Occasionally there is a place where violators of taboos and those guilty of heinous acts such as incest and sorcery are confined, but there is no hell to which the bad are condemned. Most often, as with the Igbo, such persons are punished by being denied a human reincarnation. Entry into the otherworld rarely depends on the ethical nature of one's this-worldly behavior. With the exceptions already noted, entry into that otherworld is a privilege available to all, and this entry is achieved by the correct performance of the funeral rites.

To imply that small-scale societies have no ethics and on the contrary, their social morality might be complex, even stringent, but except in a very few cases this morality does not affect the fate of the soul after death. Malinowski put it rather bluntly in respect to Trobriand reincarnation: "There are no moral ideals of recompense or punishment embodied in their reincarnation theory" (FPP, 44). It is certainly the case that were I found guilty of offenses such as adultery or theft, I would be punished by a variety of punitive or restitutive sanctions meted out by some duly constituted legal authority in my group; but it is rare that would expect to be punished again, in the otherworld, for these offenses against public morality.

This does not imply that some lack a religious evaluation of moral action. The Northwest Coast Amerindians and the Igbo, as well as other West African groups, for example, have agencies such as ancestors or deities who will punish (and reward) in the here and now those who have violated (and conformed to) certain moral rules.

Here the ancestors punish transgressors in a manner that parallels decision making in secular courts. As with secular courts there is an immediacy of punishment, but this does not affect the person's entry into the world of the ancestors after death. Further, insofar as these ancestors afflict malefactors with illness and other misfortunes, they act, as Simon Ottenberg says, very much like the individual's conscience, punishing a person for the violation of the patriarchal values of the group.

In religions such as Buddhism and Christianity one can have all of this; yet there is in addition the critical feature of delayed punishments or rewards that are meted out only after death. In the rebirth eschatologies the absence of such consequences means that the otherworld into which one enters after death is valued positively, and so is the ensuing rebirth on earth. This positive attitude is expressed in our topographical models in terms of plus signs.

By contrast, in religions like Buddhism and Christianity violation of a moral precept of virtually any sort implies *ipso facto* a violation of a religious precept and to use the term ethicization to conceptualize the processes whereby a morally right or wrong action becomes a religiously right or wrong action that in turn affects a person's destiny after death. Ethicization deals with a thoroughgoing religious evaluation of morality that entails delayed punishments and rewards quite unlike the immediate or this-worldly compensations meted out by deities or ancestors.

The Amerindian religions reflect profound ethical concerns in such beliefs as the interdependence of all species' existence, the value of the physical environment, and so forth. Yet these religions do not hold that their social morality is anything but social. By contrast, in the so-called historical religions or, as Jaspers puts it, those religions that developed with the "Axial Age" during the sixth century b.c.e. and after, this secular social morality is redefined as an intrinsic religious morality that has profound implications for society, culture, and the conscience.

Christians and Buddhists generally think that the morality expressed in the Ten Commandants or the Five Precepts is of a truly unique nature. Quite the contrary: the moral rules enshrined in them are very conventional for the most part and found virtually everywhere in small-scale societies because such rules are required for the minimal operation of an orderly society. Their unconventionality lies not in their substance but in their ethicization. It is ethicization that produced an important break or turn in the history of religion.

Because ethicization in my definition entails the conversion of a moral code into a religious code that in turn affects a person's after-death destiny, one must now ask whether such a process is reflected in the ethnographic material. The answer is that although some religious evaluation of moral action exists, it is not systematically carried through into life after death. On the other hand, in Buddhism and the great monotheisms virtually all morality is by definition religious and implicated in otherworldly recompense.

Perhaps the clearest example of ethicization in any rebirth eschatology comes from the Tlingit recorded by Frederica de Laguna. We noted that the afterworld of these Tlingit consists of three "layers": k'iwa'a, the heavenly abode of those who have died in war; the abode of those who die normally, located in a space near earth itself; and a "dog heaven" (actually a kind of "hell") located beneath the earth for those who have done wrongs. (According to some Tlingit groups "Raven's home" takes the place of the dog heaven.)

It is in relation to the dog heaven that compensatory ethics seem to surface. One informant told de Laguna that the dog heaven is the abode of those who commit suicide, whereas another claimed, "The people who get killed in war or in accident go to the real khiiwwaa'âa, way up above and the spirits are seen in the Northern Lights playing shinny…. Then between them and the earth, right on the clouds, the clouds going all around with them- this is where the dog spirits go, and they live among the dogs, suicides, and witch doctors [(witches?); the witch doctors] who are killed go to kheetl-khii-waa'âa," where they will live among the dogs.

Others said that those who wasted food by killing what they did not need, especially small animals and little birds, went to dog heaven. Some also believed that those who went to dog heaven could not be reborn on earth. Another remarked, "It's almost like the Bible, what they used to teach the young child when he was just learning to talk. They would say that bad people who kill a man, or who steal, will go to Dog Heaven … Just the bad people. That's why people are afraid to do anything wrong…. I'm surprised when I start to read the Bible. It's just what my grandma taught me".

In most of these cases only special instances of wrongs are listed, except for the last informant, who tended to include in the dog heaven all violators of social morality. As far as the good heaven is concerned, most informants thought it was a place for warriors who died in battle. Yet this good heaven of the warriors has also been influenced by Christianity, according to de Laguna.

Since K'iwai'a is sometimes confused with the Christian Heaven, we might note that one of my informants did dream of her dead daughter in Heaven. This occurred on Easter Sunday, about a year after the girl's death. In her dream, Heaven appeared as a beautiful garden where the daughter reported that each good person has his or her own flower garden, the success of which depends upon the moral conduct of living relatives.... Every day they open a big book in which writing appears of itself to record all the bad things done by the living.

The Christian influence on Tlingit beliefs lends some support to my hypothesis that systematic ethicization is associated with "universalizing religions." Although the otherworlds of the societies discussed tend to be occasionally ethicized, it is rare that ethicization extends to rebirth in the human world. The Qiqiqtamiut Inuit of Belcher Island tend to exclude in a kind of negative reaction the immoral from rebirth in the human world, very much like the Tlingit and the Igbo. "Those who have led exemplary lives are thought to be assured that their name spirits will be conferred on new societal members. Those who have led opprobrious lives or who have died by violence are thought not to be recycled- for the reason that any bearer of the name will live a life of misfortune."

In this case what constitutes an "exemplary" or "opprobrious" life is not spelled out, nor is there any specification of the moral rules involved. By contrast, Rasmussen's inland Inuit of eastern Canada seem to have a concept of punishment and reward that echoes the Indic notion of karma, at least as far as rebirth in the human world is concerned: "They are very little concerned about the idea of death; they believe that all men are born again, the soul passing on continually from one form of life to another. Good men return to earth as men, but evil doers are reborn as beasts, and in this way the earth is replenished, for no life once given can ever be destroyed."

If these Inuit pushed their ideas of ethical recompense further, they would have invented their own version of a karma theory. But there is not enough ethnographic evidence to show that they did. Instead there is evidence that surrounding groups did not think animals were a lower form of existence; therefore, it could well have been that Rasmussen's Inuit were influenced by the ethics of the missionaries in their midst. Whether or not these Inuit were influenced by the missions, the example does illustrate the rare instance in which a rebirth eschatology develops into something like a karmic one.

Sometimes it is an individual rather than the group who gives a strong ethical slant to rebirth. Thus John, one of Mills's Gitksan informants, appears to reinvent some Greek and Indic notions of purification through the rebirth process. "Have you ever asked why there is reincarnation? It is a purification process. You bring back with you the good and the bad. It is like forging gold. In each life the other metals get burned off until there is pure gold". But John's theory of purification remains an idiosyncratic one: there is no conception of otherworldly rewards and punishments in his scheme.

THE KARMIC ESCHATOLOGY

When ethicization is systematically introduced into any rebirth eschatology that rebirth eschatology must logically transform itself into a karmic eschatology and some detail the logically expectable changes or transformations that emerge with the introduction of ethicization into the ideal type or topographical model of the rebirth eschatology.

1. With ethicization morally good or bad actions are systematically converted into religiously good or bad actions. Inasmuch as any social morality must punish those who commit wrong and reward those who conform, so must a religious morality. Implicit in these notions of reward and punishment are such ideas as religious merit (the Buddhist punya karma) and "sin" (or the Buddhist papa karma). That is, the consequences of the rights and wrongs for which being rewarded or punished can be conceptualized for present purposes as "merit" and "sin."
2. A purely social morality is concerned with the earthly existence of human beings, but that must change drastically

with ethicization might well be punished here and now for the wrongs or might suffer the pangs of conscience; but beyond this, religious rewards and punishments must extend to the whole eschatological sphere through the operation of what *the call the principle of the conditionality or contingency of reward.* Let me explain what I mean by this. In the rebirth topography the transfer to the otherworld depends on the proper performance of the funeral rites. But when there is ethicization, entry to the otherworld must be *conditional*, depending on the ethical nature of one' s this -worldly actions. When ethicization occurs, one cannot say that a person who has committed wrong can unconditionally enter the otherworld.

3. What then is the logical effect of the principle of the conditionality of reward on the structure of that otherworld? The otherworld must also be transformed into a world of retribution and reward. There can no longer be a single place for those who have done good and those who have done bad. The otherworld must minimally split into two, a world of retribution ("hell") and a world of reward ("heaven"). Heavens and hells have to be invented in any ethicized eschatology, and we see them in religions such as Buddhism, Christianity, and Islam. This crucial topographical transformation is step 1 in the ethicization process; the "occasional ethicization" mentioned earlier stops for the most part at this point. Step 1 of ethicization can be represented in plus and minus signs. It is therefore possible to have a system of rewards and punishments in the otherworld and then to leave it at that, which I will show later is how Platonic rebirth formulated this issue. In this case a person could be fully compensated in the otherworld for the good and bad he or she had done while alive; then the person could be reborn into this world with a clean slate, as it were.

4. In any rebirth eschatology the soul's stay in the otherworld is by definition temporary, or on some occasions the otherworld might be bypassed entirely as the soul seeks a human reincarnation. Note, however, that owing to ethicization the earthly society into which the soul arrives is

a place where ideas of sin, merit, and the contingency of reward have already been developed. Therefore when ethicization is systematically pursued, there is a critical step 2, which requires that the next rebirth also be ethically conditioned. This conditioning inevitably takes into account one's actions in the preceding life. In other words the same principle of the contingency of reward that operated in respect to the otherworld must, in the context of systematic ethicization, also operate in respect to a person's rebirth in this world. This means that the human world into which one is born must also split into a good rebirth and a bad one, which can, once again, be topographically represented in plus and minus signs. Thus the human world into which the individual is reborn also becomes-in a kind of "protokarma" theory-a world of retribution and reward as a result of the second movement of ethicization. In principle and in practice step 2 of ethicization could exist independently of step 1. I will refer later to eschatologies in which the soul at death simply bypasses the otherworld and is immediately reborn in this world and is punished and rewarded for ethically relevant actions committed in the previous life.

5. To continue with our argument regarding step 2 of ethicization: If the person is assigned a good or bad rebirth that depends on the quality of his or her moral actions in a previous existence, then any prediction of the person's reincarnated status is rendered doubtful. One can no longer guarantee that a person will be reborn into his or her own lineage or family or kin group; there is a dis-location consequent to the person's rebirth that, rather than being based on kinship affiliations, is determined by and commensurate with his or her load of sin or merit.

Further, the continuation of group identity so significant in small-scale societies is ruptured; so is it with gender identity. Rebirth into the same group, gender, or location is possible but not expectable in general. Associated with this break in expectations is another transformational feature: the individual now reborn cannot be the same person he or she was in previous existence. The new persona is based on the load of sin and merit acquired in the individual's previous incarnation. This is easily illustrated from Buddhist societies where people claim that they could be born anywhere in their known world, depending on their good or bad karma.

The story is about a female ascetic who, having achieved nirvana in around the second century b.c.e. in Sri Lanka, recollects some of her past existences.

> In former times I fell from human estate and was reborn as a hen. In this state of existence my head was cut off by a hawk. I was reborn at Rajagaha [Ganges valley], retired from the world, and became a wandering nun, and was reborn in the stage of the First Trance. Passing from that state of existence, I was reborn in the household of a treasurer. In but a short time I passed from that state of existence and was reborn as a young sow. Passing from that state of existence, I was reborn at Suvannabhumi [Burma, in a royal household]; passing from that state of existence, I was reborn at Benares; passing from that state of existence, I was reborn at Kavira Port [South India, in the household of a mariner]; passing from that state of existence, I was reborn at Anuradhapura [Sri Lanka, in the household of a nobleman]; passing from that state of existence, I was reborn in Bhokkanta village [in south Sri Lanka].

1. In some rebirth eschatologies several ancestral spirits can be incarnated in the body of the neonate, particularly if the neonate belongs to an influential group. Alternatively, there could be double or multiple "souls," as with the Amerindian groups discussed earlier. With ethicization and the development of individual moral responsibility these features must necessarily drop out of the eschatology. The reincarnated person is a single individual who is responsible for his or her own ethically meaningful actions, but these actions in turn have the effect of changing the very character and life trajectory of that reincarnated individual. Thus the compensatory ethics associated with ethicization state that I am morally responsible for what I did in my past existence, yet that very responsibility means that I am also a different person. Buddhism carries this expectable logic to its extreme: here individuality is created without the need for naming and other devices.

2. Once reborn into a world where an ethicized morality already exists, individuals must continue in their life trajectory, doing good or bad, acquiring sin and merit. Then at death they are pushed once again into the otherworld and the cycle keeps going. Thus, ethicization of rebirth eschatology, pushed to its logical extreme, connects one lifetime with another in a continuing series of ethical links. When this happens, a concomitant epistemological shift takes place: it appears to those who live in these societies that rebirth is not a thing in itself but a product of the ethical nature of one's actions. Rebirth cannot be divorced from ethics; it looks as if it is generated from ethics.

Translated into Buddhist terms this means that the karma theory has fully developed, and it is karma that fuels the rebirth cycle known as samsara. In other words, if ethicization is carried out to embrace the whole eschatological sphere constituting the otherworld (or -worlds), as well as the human world into which one is reborn, and if this is followed through into finite or infinite rebirth cycles, then one will have created a theory like that of karma. Furthermore, this theory of impersonal and lawlike ethical compensations and rewards (or karma) cannot give primary consideration to immediate punishment. That is, I cannot be punished for the wrong I do now in this very same existence without converting the karmic eschatology back into rebirth eschatology. The logical effect of any impersonal ethical law that punishes or rewards me straightaway for what I have done empties heavens and hells and good and bad rebirths of any ethical significance.

For that reason immediate karmic punishment is rare in Indic religions except for especially heinous sins, and even these must be expiated again in the life after death.

The success of this operation depends on whether the rebirth topography constructed is, to use Weber's phrase, "objectively possible," that is, whether the conditions stipulated in the model violate or contradict empirical features of existent rebirth eschatologies. For the model to be "nomologically adequate" (another of Weber's terms), it must possess logical consistency and persuasiveness and must not contain features that are against the grain of empirical possibility. Now let me address this issue of objective possibility and nomological adequacy in some depth.

1. The rebirth topography fits most of the Amerindian cases in my sample but with one important qualification. Almost all existent eschatologies from the Northwest Coast and Inuit recognize the existence of parallel rebirth cycles for humans and animals; in some it is possible for a human to be born as an animal and vice versa. I have omitted animal rebirth from the topographical model at this point because Trobriander and Igbo rebirth also can be fitted into this scheme without too much violation of the empirical record. Other reasons for the omission will be discussed later in this chapter.
2. In most cases a dead person's "soul" goes round and round in endless cycles of existence and reexistence. It is an automatic process, one might say, and only in exceptional cases is there any deity or other force to prevent it. The soul does not die; it might change form at the very most, but otherwise it goes on being reincarnated. This ineluctability or automatism, if one could formulate the soul's progress in this manner, is recognized in the rebirth topography. When this topography is ethicized, the system of rewards and punishments also takes on this automatic or axiomatic character.
3. Is there any force or agency that can put a brake or roadblock on this ineluctability of the soul's continual, if not continuous, reincarnation? I have already noted ethicized instances in which the souls of the wicked are not permitted to reincarnate (as with the Igbo). It is not clear, however, whether this happens axiomatically, where the bad by virtue of their actions are denied reincarnation, or whether there is an intercessory deity that prevents the bad from reincarnating. In parts of West Africa, and at least among the Qiqiqtamiut Inuit, there is a Creator God or a powerful intercessory deity who might have a role in preventing the bad from being reborn or in other ways block the inevitability of the rebirth process. One ought to deal with this possibility by imagining a model in which the

automatism of the rebirth process is compounded by the active agency of a superordinate deity. Perhaps the early Christian heresies, influenced by Platonism, had to reconcile the notion of rebirth with the reality of an omnipotent God. So did the Druze and other Isma'ili-influenced sects.

THE EARLIEST INDIC MODEL

The beginnings of ethicization in Indian history by reflecting once again on the Brihadarayaka and Chandogya Upanishads texts that affected an important epistemic break in the dominant Vedic tradition. There were two figures that introduce rebirth into the Upanishads, the Brahmin sage Yajnavalkya and the Ksatriya Pravahana Jaivali. Let me come back to the more developed version of the "fire-water doctrine" by the Ksatriya sage.

In this version the king discusses three paths available to souls at death. First, there is the path to Brahmann for those who have true knowledge; they are fully saved, and they know no return or rebirth. This path is, however, called the devayana, the path of the gods; the soul goes to the world of the gods and stays there for an indeterminate period and then goes into Brahmann. Second, there is the path of the Fathers, or ancestors, the classic Vedic pitryana. This is for those who have offered sacrifices in the old Vedic sense; they are reborn in the human world and keep going round and round in a cycle.

Not all are continually reborn though, or in the same manner, according to the second Jaivali text, which affirms the fire-water doctrine but adds that those who live good and bad lives realize a good and bad rebirth, either as one of the twice-born vara categories or in a "foul womb." I noted that ethics have entered into the picture, even if they are the ethics of vara.

They do not negate the ethics of karma based on the vara scheme but simply affirm the most deadly of the "sins" from the point of view of the priestly class: the one who steals gold, drinks liquor, kills a Brahmin, fornicates with his teacher's wife, and all who associate with the above. Finally, there is the enigmatic category of insects that will never achieve a human rebirth. This category resists easy interpretation; it might refer to the Sûdra or, more likely, to those outside the pale of the vara scheme, the so-called Untouchables.

There is not much difference between these two Upanishadic thinkers: both believe in knowledge leading to Brahmann; both believe in a lesser path, where one can be reborn according to one's karma, even if karma refers to vara ethics; both accept the fire-water doctrine of rebirth for unliberated souls; both articulate karma and rebirth with the major soteriological ideal of the Upanishadic tradition, the merging of atman with Brahmann. Yajnavalkya presents "joyless" conditions at death for those who have violated vara ethics; Pravahana Jaivali does not mention this.

Yajnavalkya is a Brahmin sage who takes his pupil aside as he enunciates the idea of karma and rebirth that he does not want to talk about "in public." "In public" surely does not mean in front of the general populace because no Upanishadic text talks to the public in that sense. The "public" in this context must refer to other Upanishadic seekers of salvation-teachers and their pupils. In this text Yajnavalkya imparts this knowledge to Arthabhaga privately. Implicit is the idea that knowledge of karma and rebirth is something new in the broader Vedic tradition- as if this is the first time these ideas have appeared.

By contrast King Pravahana Jaivali assumes a different discursive posture. He clearly states that these doctrines are not new but that they were unknown to Brahmins; they are the prerogative of the Ksatriyas, and that is why "government has belonged exclusively to royalty [ksatriya]." The dialogues dramatize an important theme: that the rebirth theory is something new or ignored in the Brahmannic tradition but that it was well known to the Ksatriyas.

If this is so, there is a historical question that must be answered even as informed guesswork. From where did the Ksatriyas gain this knowledge? The only reasonable conclusion one can make is that these doctrines have come from some source outside the Vedic tradition and have been creatively incorporated into the Upanishadic tradition, although not into its mainstream.

The scholarly opinion in general is that these early Upanishads were composed in the upper and middle reaches of the Ganges, where Brahmins were relative newcomers. I suggest that the Ksatriya sage as a dramatis persona was voicing popular beliefs about rebirth that were known to many persons in this region and recasting them in a frame that might seem acceptable to Vedic thought. Brahmins either were indifferent to these ideas, which violated early Vedic eschatology, or did not know them.

The early heartland of Brahmannic power was further west, in what was known as the Aryavartha, the region of the Aryas (noble ones). Hence the enigmatic statement of the king: that because the Brahmins were ignorant of these ideas, "government has belonged exclusively to royalty." This statement, I think, implies that knowledge of the rebirth ideas of large masses of people was necessary for dominion over them. Knowledge is power.

It should be remembered that the great religious innovators of the Ganges valley, such as the Buddha and Mahavira, were also Ksatriya sages. Jaina traditions in particular emphasized that Mahavira belonged to a line of sages, and his teachings were partly based on those of a previous sage, or Jina, named ParMvanatha, who, according to some scholars, lived around 850 b.c.e.

If so, the Jainism of Mahavira's time was the culmination of a longer process of religious exploration. Pursuing this line of guesswork, one might argue that there was a tradition of Ksatriya sages in the region of the Ganges valley and that Pravahana Jaivali of the Upanishads was an early representative of that tradition.

In Pravahana Jaivali's scheme the way of the gods leading to union with Brahmann is fully within the innovative soteriology of the early Upanishads, breaking away from the primacy of the sacrifice of the Brahmana s and the soul's journey into the realm of the Fathers (ancestors). In the Upanishadic transcendental state of the union of atman with Brahmann there can be no further rebirth. The way of the Fathers, which was the goal of early Vedic thought, is now downgraded. It is no longer a paradisiacal realm where the souls of the dead comport with their ancestors but a temporary way station in the rebirth cycle.

The left side of the figure illustrates the trajectory for all those who have performed sacrifices, have given gifts to Brahmins, and have led good lives. They go to the realm of the Fathers, although they are not equal in ritual and moral status. Following the logic of rebirth theory the stay in the world of the Fathers is temporary; the caterpillar-like soul must move on.

The relative good and bad done by people are recognized in the next human rebirth as they achieve reincarnation as one of the twiceborn castes (Brahmin, Ksatriya, or Vaiya) via the complicated processes described in the texts (the fire-water doctrine). But what about those whose karma was bad, that is, those who did not follow the proper ritual and moral injunctions? The right side of the figure illustrates their fate: they bypass the desired world of the Fathers and achieve a low human or animal reincarnation. Fundamental Brahmannic values have been creatively transformed and ethicized.

THE BUDDHIST INTERCONNECTIONS

Between the early Upanishads and the later religions of the Ganges valley there might well have been a period of at least a hundred years. If the former contain only the briefest references to rebirth and karma, the latter are saturated with them. It is impossible for us to figure out what happened in the intervening period. The Buddhist texts, perhaps, can give us clues as to how ethicization as a historical process might have occurred.

To begin let me continue to follow my perverse strategy and shuttle back and forth from the empirical world to the model, using Buddhism as my example, in order to investigate four interrelated problems: the kind of rebirth eschatology that existed prior to Buddhism; the problematics of vegetarianism; the problematics pertaining to sentient existence; and finally the role of animals and plants in rebirth eschatologies in contrast to Buddhism (and other religions of that period).

The last three elements are interlinked through the differential role of animals in rebirth and karmic religions. Following the practice of some Indological scholars I will introduce the term samanic to describe the "new religions" of the Ganges valley in the sixth or fifth century b.c.e. and the already familiar term Brahmannic to designate the orthodox Vedic tradition up to the period of the Upanishads.

INVENTING A PRE-BUDDHIST TRADITION

It is virtually impossible to bring direct evidential support for the argument that this transformational process did in fact occur in history. When direct evidence is not available, as is often the case with the historical sciences, it is necessary to bring forth indirect evidence to substantiate the hypotheses formulated.

The notion of an affinity between Indic religions and the rebirth eschatologies to ask the following question: Which among the various rebirth eschatologies comes closest to the Buddhist? An important feature of Buddhist and samanic eschatologies in general is that humans can be reborn as animals as a consequence of their karma. Jainism, following more closely on the two Upanishadic cases, goes even further than Buddhism in postulating that plants might also possess sentience, even though one cannot be reborn as a plant. It is certainly possible that the Buddhists and Jainas invented these ideas, as some Indologists claim; on the other hand the ideas might have been inherited from preceding eschatologies.

The only empirical cases similar to the Buddhist among small-scale societies outside the Indic area are those of the Northwest Coast Indians and the Inuit, because the Igbo and other West African groups and the Trobriand islanders have no notion of animal rebirths, parallel or cross. Amerindians and Inuit also occasionally recognize that plants too are forms of sentient existence, even though they are outside the rebirth scheme. Hence my conclusion: if it is indeed the case that Upanishadic theorists, Buddhists, Jainas, and other nonBrahmannic religions of the time did not invent the idea of animal reincarnation and the sentience of plants but inherited it from a preexisting tradition, then it is likely that that inherited tradition was similar to the eschatologies of the Northwest Coast Indians and Inuit.

One cannot therefore entirely discount the idea that the circumpolar distribution of these rebirth eschatologies might well have extended from Siberia down into central Asia and then to the Indian subcontinent, although diffusion of ideas and the impact of "influences" are not directly relevant to my project.

The conclusion that the Indic religions show the closest structural similarity to the Amerindian-Inuit necessitates that we add the feature of animal rebirth to our topographical model and include this feature. When this model is ethicized, it produces not just any theory of karma but specifically the Indic one.

THE LOGIC OF VEGETARIANISM

Having narrowed the focus of our inquiry to the rebirth eschatologies of the circumpolar regions and the karmic ones of the samanic religions which deal with issues that arise from the idea shared by both-that humans and animals (and occasionally plants) give expression to a universal "species sentience." In the examples of rebirth eschatologies from the Inuit and the Northwest Coast and the omnipresence of animalto-human transformations and vice versa. To eat animals, however, was both necessary and desirable, and eating was prefaced by a double act, first of killing the animal and then of ensuring its reincarnation.

Animal consumption, then, is a reverential act, yet at least on an unconscious level there is guilt in recognizing the possibility that one may be eating an ancestor or someone closely related. In those rare cases of cross-species reincarnation it is not possible to escape the guilt pertaining to endoanthropophagy. Such a dilemma can be better dealt with in the Ganges valley of the sixth and fifth centuries b.c.e., where forests had been cleared and rice cultivation had been established. There was no need to eat one's ancestor; hence the samanic religions (and perhaps the rebirth eschatologies that preceded them) either had a vegetarian diet or expressly forbade the killing of animals.

The attitude toward animals depended on the paths of ethicization taken by the different samanic religions. It should be remembered that only selected animals incarnate as humans in the rebirth eschatologies. Perhaps the samanic religions universalized this idea to include all animals. One thing is clear though: in Buddhist ethicization, with its strong emphasis on motivation, it is the intentional killing of the animal rather than eating it that is at issue, whereas Jainism forbids not only killing but also eating animals, as well as selected sentient plants and vegetables.

By contrast the Brahmannic religions right up to the period of the Upanishads permitted the killing and eating of animals. We also know that goats, sheep, and cattle were eaten in the religion of the Vedas, and huge numbers of cattle and horses were sacrificed in Brahmannic rituals for kings. Henk Bodewitz shows that the early Dharmasûtra texts, particularly Gautama (not to be confused with the Buddha, also called Gautama), probably compiled soon after the period of the Buddha, posit the doctrine of ahimsa, or noninjury to living things, although the word itself appears only once. He thinks that these texts have been influenced by the ideologies of the samanic religions.

Further, even Gautama permits Brahmins as well as renouncers to eat the "the flesh of animals killed by carnivorous beasts." Apastamba, another early Dharmasûtra authority, lists specific animal foods that Brahmins might eat; Vasistha is even more liberal, permitting "food given by a hunter" and such delicacies as porcupine, hedgehog, hare, tortoise, iguana, and some unspecified domestic animals except camels. These facts force us to draw an important conclusion: insofar as the karmic eschatology posits universal species sentience and respect for animal life, one can conclude that the early Brahmannic religion, with its killing of animals for the sacrifice, could not possibly have had any inner affinity with that model. This adds substance to our assertion that rebirth ideas came into Indic religions from a source outside the main Brahmannic tradition.

Some might reasonably argue that as far as the Indic traditions are concerned, vegetarianism is a direct effect of the ahimsa doctrine rather than the ahimsa doctrine itself being based on the doctrine of species sentience and the dread of endoanthropophagy expectable from my model. But the relationship between vegetarianism and ahimsa is not straightforward. The Jainas have the strongest convictions regarding vegetarianism, which directly ties in with their theories of nonviolence, but some plants were taboo as food because they contained a life-essence.

The Buddha permitted the eating of animals that were accidentally killed or that died of natural causes, much like the other Gautama of the Dharmasûtras. And the Brahmannic texts that came later incorporated vegetarianism rather than ahimsa per se into their encompassing conceptions of purity and impurity. Thus, although the equation expectable from my model suggesting "endoanthropophagy: vegetarianism: ahimsa," might be problematic, equally problematic is the direct tie-in between vegetarianism and the ahimsa doctrine of noninjury or nonviolence.

Now let me turn to a more complicated illustration of the relationship between rebirth and endoanthropophagy by examining once again the developed version of the fire-water doctrine of the Chandogya Upanisad. We noted earlier that the souls that take the lesser path pass into the smoke, and after various other transformations they reach the world of the Fathers and then the moon, where they become the food of the gods. Then they follow a downward trajectory that takes them into a human rebirth: passing into the wind and to the sky and into rain and from the rain to earth, where they become food, that is, plants and cereals. Man repeats what the gods did previously; he consumes these foods, and they are converted into semen, which he injects into a woman's womb to beget children.

Consider the implications of this fascinating theory. In Presocratic Greek theory, a soul could be reborn in plant form; but insofar as the plant is an incarnated human soul, one cannot eat that particular species and similar ideas underlie Jaina theories of the sentience of plants. But the Upanishads have a complicated solution to this problem of endoanthropophagy: the soul gets embodied and transformed many times over until it becomes a plant or a cereal, not any kind of plant or cereal but those that humans eat. Consumption is a creative act that reproduces the previous archetypal act of the gods: eating human souls that have been transformed as divine food.

These human souls are reborn and continue to do good or bad. Those who do good are reborn to replenish the human species of the first three orders, or varas. However, those who were bad ("of foul behavior") could be reborn in a "foul womb" as animals such as pigs or dogs, or as an outcaste, or, according to some unclear statements, as insects or creepy-crawlies.

To develop the hidden implications of this theory in terms of our models first, it seems that eating vegetarian foods is a form of endoanthropophagy but also a reverential act like that of the Amerindians, entailing a transvaluation but not a transubstantiation of ordinary food substances. Hence, as with Amerindian eating of animals, I would hesitate to call it a sacrament analogous to the Eucharist. The Upanishadic theory transvalues the doctrine of species sentience in a specific direction by postulating that plants and cereals, at least those we eat, are permeated with a mystical sentience.

Wild plants that do not possess this form of sentience could presumably be eaten anyhow. Second, following this originary condition is the next incarnation, when those who did wrong are reincarnated directly after death in foul wombs as pigs, dogs, insects, and such. They are in effect the souls of recently dead humans; they are also those that Brahmins (and the three vara classes) would not eat, or ought not to eat. Eating them would be tantamount to endoanthropophagy. But what about well-known domestic animals such as goats, sheep, cattle, and horses? The texts do not mention them.

But silence is a symbolic language that demands interpretation. Although all sorts of sacrificial animals are mentioned in Vedic texts, the most regularly sacrificed were goats, sheep, cattle, and horses. It would not do for human souls to be reincarnated in the "foul wombs" of these creatures without raising for the higher classes the deadly possibility of endoanthropophagy unmediated by the complicated changes that vegetables and cereals undergo. Hence the texts make no reference to human beings reborn as domestic/sacrificial animals.

Finally, take the case of wild animals. One must presume that the Ksatriyas hunted some of them and ate others; so did the Vaiya classes; and some wild animals were permitted as food for Brahmins. These creatures are also not mentioned as carriers of souls in the texts discussed earlier. The presumption is that they are good to eat. But one text hints that such eating may not be entirely acceptable. This is the third Upanishad that deals with rebirth-the Kausitaki-which clearly indicates that rebirth as animals was a much wider phenomenon than reported in the Arayaka and Chandogya Upanishads.

This text says that the rain brings down to earth the souls of those who do not know the true knowledge, and, following the dictates of karma, they are incarnated "as a worm, an insect, a fish, a bird, a lion, a boar, a rhinoceros, a tiger, a man, or some other creature." Thus the unliberated ones can be reborn as any kind of being, including wild animals, but the text leaves open whether these other creatures include the domestic animals ignored in the other two Upanishads.

If this text reveals the hidden or silent message in the other two Upanishads, then it means that eating certain specified and unspecified animals, including wild animals, is in effect eating a former human being, a direct and vile anthropophagous act quite unlike the creative act of eating cereals and vegetables. The later Brahmannic taboo on meat eating and the high valuation of a vegetarian diet develop from this model, not from one based directly on the doctrine of noninjury, or ahimsa.

ETHICIZATION AND SPECIES SENTIENCE

The rebirth eschatologies of small-scale societies postulate a universal species sentience that can lead to the recognition of a spiritual equivalence between humans and animals. With ethicization, however, animals get "demoted." A person who does bad or commits "sin" (papa karma) might be punished by being reborn as an animal or some other lowly creature. Thus, in the samanic religions, there is a peculiar aporia whose poignancy appears only when we compare those religions to the simpler rebirth eschatologies: although humans and animals belong to a common order of sentient existence, the latter are relegated to an inferior existence in ethicized samanic religions, and they lose the elevated status they had before.

This "fall" is nicely expressed in folk versions of the Vessantara Jataka, the birth story that deals with the penultimate birth of the Buddha, where, as Prince Vessantara, he epitomized the perfect generosity of the seeker for Buddhahood who gave away as slaves to a greedy Brahmin what he most loved and valued-his two children and later his wife. In this story the wife goes in search of the missing children and asks the animals their whereabouts (in beautifully poignant poetry in the texts of the popular tradition). The animals, sympathetic to her plight, tell her what they know; but in doing so they inadvertently hinder the salvation quest of the Buddha, so they lose their capacity for speech!

The Vessantara Jataka itself is one of the most popular tales from the compendium of 550 "birth stories" known as the Jataka tales, which deal with the past lives of the Buddha. These tales in turn come from a miscellaneous collection of texts called the Khuddaka Nik a ya (Minor collection), thus named to distinguish it from the major collections of the discourses of the Buddha. Scholars agree that the Jatakas were originally folktales circulating within a larger Indo-European orbit. Precisely because the Jatakas come from the folk repertoire, they do, I think, contain ideas from traditions that predated the samanic religions.

One of the striking features of the Jatakas, prior to the penultimate Vessantara Jataka, is that in many of them the Buddha himself appears as an animal, for example, as an elephant, a lion, a monkey, a lizard, a parrot, a pigeon, a hawk, a swallow, a cock bird, a peacock, a dog, a hare, a fish, a deer, a water buffalo, a bull, a horse, a goose (hasa), an antelope, a mallard, a frog, a garuda, an iguana, a snake, a sea sprite, a partridge, a vulture, a woodpecker, a quail, a rat-almost always to express the nobility of the creature. There is little in these texts to indicate that animals were a degraded species or that the Buddha was an animal owing to his bad karma.

Animals have the capacity for speech, live in the same kinds of societies as humans, and are represented by a range of good and bad characters. These conceptions are similar to those of the Amerindian eschatologies in my sample and suggest that the samanic religions ethicized an eschatology that had either parallel-or cross-rebirth cycles for animals or that this idea is reflected in the texts of the folk traditions embodied in the Jatakas.

BUDDHISM AND THE SENTIENCE OF PLANTS

It is well known that Buddhism, unlike Jainism, does not teach the sentience of plants. Plants do not have centers of consciousness as animals do; therefore, taking the life of a plant is totally different from taking the life of an animal. However, in an important essay Lambert Schmithausen has shown that early Buddhists might well have believed in the sentience of plants. Whether Schmithausen is correct is not as germane as his demonstration that such an idea was part of the popular culture and that Buddhism and Jainism dealt with it in different ways.

Schmithausen starts with a passage from the Patimokkha, the Buddhist "confessional" for monks, which says: "If [a monk or a nun] is ruthless with regard to plants, this is an offence to be atoned" (PSP, 5). In a detailed exposition of this passage Schmithausen admits that it is not clear whether the text refers to plant sentience. The discourses (suttas) themselves contain several statements to the effect that monks should abstain from injuring seeds or plants, although these have sometimes been taken to mean a prohibition on agriculture.

The Patimokkha rule, however, is clear that injury to plants is equivalent to injury to animals. The commentary of the Patimokkha gives two reasons for this rule: the first is that by cutting the tree the monk injured the child of the deity inhabiting the tree; the second, more germane to our argument, is that "this action was disapproved by the people as an act of injuring because they regard trees as living beings (jivasannino … rukkhasmi F)" (PSP, 14). The monks themselves did not accept this view, but they observed the rule out of respect to the public, a feature of ascetic decorum adopted by Buddhists.

Similar prohibitions are found elsewhere. In the Khandhaka section of the Vinaya Pitaka (Book of the discipline) the Buddha blames monks for cutting young palmyra and bamboo leaves to make sandals. "Here, too, the reason adduced is that people consider trees to be living beings, more precisely: living beings with one sense-faculty (ekindriya jiva), and hence object to the monks cutting off shoots … as an act of injuring a living being. Here, too, the implication seems to be that the Buddhist monks themselves do not believe in the sentience of the plants concerned".

These kinds of plants are not normally the habitat of deities, and it is not likely that "living beings with one sense-faculty" refers to deities. Not all plants possess sentience; however, the prohibition on bamboo and palmyra suggests that plants producing shoots and, in other instances, grains capable of germination were viewed as especially sentient, although only possessing "one sense-faculty". Therefore, although it may be wrong to destroy certain plants, it is not possible to be reborn as a plant. Similar ideas are found in Jainism: perhaps following some enigmatic Upanishadic precedents, monks and nuns are not allowed to consume bulbs, bulbous roots, or other plants, such as sugarcane, that are capable of sprouting. In later Jaina thought they are even said to possess souls.

To sum up: there are at least three forms of plant sentience recorded in the Indic literature. First, there are those plants, already mentioned, that possess a single center of consciousness; because they are living beings, they must not be destroyed. It is not clear how these plants achieved sentience in the first place. Second, there is the Upanishadic form in which the spirit of an ancestor gets into certain plants that are creatively consumed by humans. Third, there are the well-known Indic cases in which a spirit can reside in especially large trees (such as a banyan) as the deity of the tree. Injuring these trees is a sin as far as orthodox Buddhist doctrine and popular beliefs are concerned.

THE SAMANIC RELIGIONS

To bring in detailed evidence of a slightly more direct sort to show that the historical process subsumed under the term ethicization did in fact occur in the samanic religions of the sixth (or fifth) century b.c.e. The contemporary "tribal" religions in India exhibit little or no ethicization and not to argue that the presamanic religions of India were tribal. If small-scale societies in India are not concerned with ethicization now, it is unlikely that they would have been concerned with it then. I will also show that the Brahmannic traditions that preceded Buddhism were relatively unethicized.

The evidence to suggest the existence of relatively unethicized yet complex rebirth doctrines prevalent among the contemporaries of the Buddha and the positive evidence for ethicization in the historical development of Buddhism at the time of its founding and conclude with a more sweeping view of ethicization in Buddhism and the Axial Age monotheisms.

The word tribe is in disfavor now. A convenient alternative is a div a si, "the ancient residents," the Indian government's official definition of tribe, even though this is a literal translation of the English aboriginal, a concept that never existed in South Asia. Negative connotations unfortunately do not wither away through a change of terms, but the term adivasi does contain a historical truth in that it refers to people in small-scale societies in India who have often resisted incorporation into larger socioeconomic and cultural structures.

Christoph von Furer Haimendorf, the foremost ethnologist of Indian adivasi society, says that those groups least influenced by Hindu thought have "amoral" religions. Regarding the Chenchus, Haimendorf says: "Supernatural sanctions, though not easily evaluated, came to play a comparatively small part in promoting conformity to the accepted moral standards.... There is little to suggest that moral lapses are subject to supernatural sanction" (MM, 23). The Reddis: "deities demand from man the observations of certain taboos ... but the relation between man and man are to them a matter of indifference; there is no divine retribution of crime or reward for virtuous behavior" (MM, 43). "The Kamars' attitude to adultery is much the same as that of the Reddis" (MM, 45).

The Daflas: "While an appeal to supernatural powers is used to strengthen a peace-pact, there is otherwise no suggestion that gods and spirits are concerned with the moral conduct of human beings" (MM, 69). "The Apa Tanis are sensitive to social approval or disapproval, and the fear of being 'shamed' is a powerful incentive to conformity. There is, on the other hand, no sense of 'sin' and no corresponding desire to acquire 'merit' in a system of supernatural rewards.... [Daflar and Apa Tanis] do not ascribe to their gods a general interest in the moral conduct of man" (MM, 79).

Although some adivasis, such as the Gonds, do have notions of "sin," Haimendorf speculates that these are newly introduced notions. Haimendorf's material is extremely interesting because he wrote without any reference to the logic of ethicization. In fact, my idea of ethicization is much narrower than his views of adivasi morals and merit. Haimendorf speaks of supernatural sanctions in general, including punishment by deities for wrong or immoral behavior, whereas the narrower sphere where moral ideas are converted into religious ideas that ipso facto are related to a system of otherworldly rewards and punishments.

Yet it is clear from his account that ethicization, or rather its lack, is not simply a structural feature of my topographical models but is also a feature of at least some adivasi religions of India and to demonstrate that ethicization is also alien to the Indic religious traditions prior to the samanic religions of the Ganges valley, as the studies by Arthur Berriedale Keith, Paul Deussen, and others indicate. The scholarly work of "colonialist" writers is under critical scrutiny nowadays, and one might wonder whether Keith's attribution of a lack of ethicization in Brahmannic religion is influenced by his orientalist presuppositions.

It is indeed true that Keith, E. W. Hopkins, and Deussen think that there is something morally dubious in the Indic tradition of constructing amoral religions. But this is not a feature of orientalism per se because even emancipated contemporary scholars have similar views and assume that the lack of ethicization is symptomatic of a moral lack. Most of us have been raised in traditions that make a virtue of ethicization. The question of what morality is will lead us into a methodological bind from which it will be impossible to extricate ourselves.

Consider the Rig Veda, the oldest stratum of Brahmannic religion. The soul at death, driven by a chariot or on wings, takes the route of the Fathers and reaches a place of eternal rest. The Rig Vedic notion of heaven is a paradisiacal one: "there is light, the sun for the highest waters, every form of happiness, the Svadha, which is at once the food of the spirits and the power which they win by it, their self-determination".

As is well known, the major deity of the Rig Veda is Indra, who, along with other divinities, enjoys material luxury, intoxicants (sura), milk, ghee, honey, and soma (the drink of immortality), as well as the delights of love. There is also music and singing and a celestial fig tree where Yama drinks with the gods. This eschatology is a paradisiacal, not a retributive, one. Keith notes that even Yama and Varuna, who sometimes might appear as ethical deities, do not "punish the dead or judge them for their sins" but grant a kind of unconditional pardon. Consequently, "the idea of a judgement of any kind is as foreign to the Rg Veda as to early Iran."

He then adds that the notion of hell "was present in germ" in the Rig Veda (RP, 2:409). It is a place under the earth into which Indra and Soma are to hurl evildoers, these being the enemy, robbers, or demons. The Atharva Veda (c. 800 b.c.e.), which succeeded the Rig Veda, has the word narakaloka (bad place), which was later identified with ethicized hells known as niraya or apaya.

This was a blind, black place where female goblins, sorceresses, and murderers were confined; here persons who injure Brahmins sit in streams of blood eating their hair. This bad world is similar to Igbo conceptions; those committed there have been guilty of specific offenses rather than the general categorical ones of ethicized religions. The Atharva Veda depicts at best a minimally or occasionally ethicized eschatology. Here also the otherworld is for all and is contingent on the performance of the correct rituals rather than on the moral nature of one's this-worldly actions.

Keith's brief summary of their ethical stance: "The most convincing evidence of all regarding the almost ritual character of goodness in the view of the BrahmanJas is that their concept of torment is inextricably bound up with the correct practice ... of the ritual". It is true that at death a person is weighed in a balance to test the good and the bad, but this judgment is based primarily on violations of taboos and ritual interdictions.

This comes out clearly in the vision of Bhgu in the Tatapatha and Jaiminiya Brahmannas, where the persons confined to hell are those who cut wood without offering the agnihotra and those who kill and eat animals and even herbs without performing the correct rituals. In the Kausitaki Brahman the animals will take revenge on a person in the next world unless he or she performs the correct ritual. In the Brahman as also there is occasional ethicization, but for the most part these texts are concerned with the violation of taboos and ritual interdictions.

The Upanishads, although belonging to the Vedic tradition, prove that a sophisticated speculative religion need not concern itself with otherworldly ethics, except for the few instances discussed earlier. This fact has dismayed scholars who are conditioned to think that a speculative soteriology must also entail an ethical soteriology. Thus Paul Deussen, in his exhaustive discussion, points out the absence of a moral concern in the Upanishads except for specific scattered injunctions. His own explanation is rather naive: "Lack of generalization, as well as the rarity of such warnings in Upanishad literature, proves that offenses of this character were not common."

He also argues that ethics have no objective or external work to do in the Upanishads, misjudging their ethical nature, because European religious traditions emphasize external, nonsubjective ethics, that is, ethics that seem to exist outside the individual. But he forgets that both Buddhism and Jainism had an external (or a social) morality very different from the subjective, internal ethics of the Upanishads. The fact is that the Upanishadic seeker of salvation can in some instances go beyond everyday morality. In the Kausitaki Upanisad the man who attains Brahmann after passing by the river of immortality casts away his good and bad deeds; he is above all morality, even above such heinous deeds as the slaying of an embryo and the murder of a father or a mother, a position unthinkable in religions like Buddhism and Jainism.

This kind of thinking goes back to such texts as the Jaiminiya Brahmana referred to earlier and anticipates the late Upanishadic texts of renunciation, such as the Bhiksuka Upanisad and the Bhatanyasa Upanisad. In these later texts the renouncer is no longer part of the social world and is indifferent to its mores; hence he makes "no distinction between right and wrong." Or, as the injunction in the Bhatanyasa Upanisad states: "Abandon right and wrong; abandon truth and untruth. Having abandoned both truth and untruth, abandon that by which you abandon."

The renouncer, we know from the work of Patrick Olivelle, gives up the everyday life in a series of powerful symbolic actions, and in doing so he gives up everyday morality, the very morality that religions like Buddhism ethicized. The only place in Buddhism where a parallel situation seems to obtain is in the story of Vessantara, who gives away his wife and children to the greedy Brahmin Jûtaka, ignoring the norms of everyday morality.

In this text, however, the reader or listener knows that the gods are going to rescue the Bodhisattva's wife and children, much as the Christian knows that Isaac is not going to die. But there is no such escape clause in the texts on renunciation. Consequently one can accept Keith's characterization of the Upanishadic tradition in general without accepting his value judgment that "there is no attempt to make the theoretical philosophy a ground of morality of any sort".

THE DOCTRINES OF THE AJIVIKAS

My experimental transformation of the rebirth eschatology into the karmic one only stipulates that good and bad actions have religious effects known in Indic thought as karma; it cannot specify whether these actions have to be intentional or otherwise. Interestingly enough, Buddhist reform has given karma intentionality (cetana) such that if I do something unintentionally I do not reap a karmic consequence (karma phala, "the fruit of karma"). Jainism took yet another route; it stipulated that karma produced irreversible effects, whether intentionally motivated or not.

One would expect speculative thinkers to have produced not only ideas that transformed preexisting rebirth eschatologies into rationalized karmic ones (Buddhists and Jainas) but also rationalized doctrines that were nonkarmic or nonethicized. There is some evidence from Buddhist and Jaina texts for the existence of rebirth eschatologies of the latter sort. Indologists have rightly seen these as contemporary religions opposed to Buddhism and Jainism and as carrying on an argument with them.

In one of the most important texts of Buddhism, the "Samannaphala Sutta" (The fruits of the life of a recluse), the parricide King Ajatasattu seeks healing for his troubled conscience by visiting the Buddha. The Buddha questions him about the other teachers he has consulted, and Ajatasattu delivers a synopsis of their teachings. Ajatasattu refers to six teachers belonging to the samanic schools; most of them seem to take the doctrine of rebirth for granted but not the doctrine of karma as the Buddhists or Jainas understood it.

There is no doubt that their doctrines have been oversimplified and distorted by the Buddhists, but for our purposes the outlines of their theories will suffice. Thus, according to Ajatasattu, the first teacher he visited, known as Pûrana Kassapa, taught that the practice of good or bad deeds has no karmic consequences whatever. The Buddhist disapproval is forcibly expressed in that part of the text that is supposed to represent Pûrana Kassapa's views:

To him who acts … or causes another to act, to him who mutilates or causes another to mutilate, to him who punishes or causes others to punish … to him who kills a living creature, who takes what is not given … who commits dacoity, or robbery, or adultery, who speaks lies; to him thus acting there is no guilt [that is, no bad karma]. If a discus with a sharp edge like a razor should make all the living creatures on the earth one heap, one mass, of flesh, there would be no guilt thence resulting; no increase of guilt would ensue. Were he to go along the north bank of the Ganges giving alms, and ordering gifts to be given, offering sacrifices or causing them to be offered, there would be no merit there resulting, no increase of merit.

No wonder Pûrana Kassapa gets a bad press in a religion that extols ethical causality! Ajatasattu tells the Buddha that this theory is one of nonaction, or akiriya F vy a k a si, the belief that there are no karmic consequences. Pûrana Kassapa, however, is also hitting at religions like Buddhism, not only by denying the karmic effects of the Five Precepts, as is evident in the earlier quotation, but also by speaking against some of its higher ethics insofar as they produce karmic effects. "In generosity, in self-mastery, in control of the senses, in speaking truth there is neither merit nor increase of merit."

Pûrana Kassapa is simply one among many teachers arguing against a view of ethical causality based on karma. Buddhists are wrong in assuming that Kassapa was an immoralist; he is simply saying there is no such thing as an ethical notion of karma. It is quite likely that he subscribed to an older view that the good or bad a person does has nothing to do with his or her fate in the afterlife. He surely knew that it could matter in this life because anyone who has committed the horrendous crimes he lists will certainly be punished by the secular authority.

Kassapa's teaching makes sense only if we consider the context in which it is made. He does not deny rebirth, unlike some other teachers of the period. Instead he is saying that although rebirth is a reality, there is no otherworldly retribution for immoral acts of a most deplorable kind. It seems to me that his teachings are a defense of unethicized rebirth eschatology, one that must have existed as a "background religion" of the time. He was probably arguing against thinkers who insisted, as did the Buddha and Mahavira, that the violation of a social morality constitutes a "sin."

He is also in effect telling Ajatasattu that his actions will have no bad karmic consequences. Finally, one must not forget that the Buddhists also had some interest in representing a rival teacher as a total immoralist rather than as someone subscribing to a secular code of ethics instead of a karmic one.

A. L. Basham, in his influential book History and Doctrines of the Jivikas, says that the most important thinker subscribing to the theory of rebirth but denying ethical causality is Makkhali Gosala (Makkhali of the cowshed), whose teachings survived up to about the sixth or the eighth century c.e. in parts of southern India. Basham shows that Pûrana Kassapa was also a Jivika, although not necessarily a follower of Makkhali Gosala. Because both Pûrana Kassapa and Makkhali Gosala believed in rebirth, it is not likely that a third "heretic," Ajita Kesakambili (Ajita of the hair blanket), was also a Jivika, as Basham thinks, because Ajita, an uncompromising materialist and "annihilationist," clearly did not subscribe to such a theory.

In my view the Jivikas rationalized pre-existing rebirth eschatology without bringing in karmic causality. Makkhali Gosala fully recognized the impersonal nature of the rebirth cycle and then gave it philosophical elaboration and conceptual formulation. He seems to have asked, what keeps the universe going in this manner? He suggested that an impersonal cosmic principle, or niyati, determines continuity.

This doctrine denies an ethical theory of karma but does not deny orderliness to the universe-what the Greeks called cosmos. But Makkhali Gosala added another element in his own rationalization of the rebirth eschatology, stating that the rebirth cycle cannot go on forever but will simply run out after many eons, at the end of which the soul will have attained bliss or salvation. I will argue later that this journey of the soul is not a fortuitous element in his teachings but is related to the double vision of salvation that Makkhali Gosala, along with other thinkers of the time, formulated: one mode of salvation for the world-involved laity and another for the virtuoso.

His teachings as depicted by Ajatasatru in the "Samannaphala Sutta" of the Majjhima Nikaya:

> There is neither cause nor basis for the sins of living beings; they become sinful without cause or basis. Neither is there cause or basis for the purity of living beings; they become pure without cause or basis. There is no deed performed either by oneself or by others (which can affect one's future births), no human action, no strength, no courage, no human endurance or human prowess (which can affect one's destiny in this life). All beings, all that have breath, all that are born, all that have life, are without power, strength, or virtue, but are developed by destiny, chance, and nature, and experience joy and sorrow in the six classes (of existence).

The text then lists, in a very schematic manner, the multitudinous rebirths the soul undergoes during its long journey. There are 1,400,000 chief uterine births, 6,000 and 600; 500 karmas, 5 karmas, 3 karmas, a karma, and half a karma; 62 paths; 62 lesser kalpas; 6 classes (of human existence); 8 stages of man; 4,900 means of livelihood (?); 4,900 ascetics; 4,900 dwellings of nagas; 2,000 faculties; 3,000 purgatories; 36 places covered with dust (?); 7 sentient births; 7 insentient births; 7 births from knots (?); 7 gods; 7 men; 7 pisaca (births?); 7 lakes; 7 knots (?), and 700;

7 dreams, and 700; and 8,400,000 great kalpas through which fool and wise alike will take their course, and make an end of sorrow.

There is no question of bringing unripe karma to fruition, or of exhausting karma already ripened, by virtuous conduct, by vows, by penance, or by chastity. That cannot be done. Samsara is measured as with a bushel, with its joy and sorrow and its appointed end. It can neither be lessened nor increased, nor is there any excess or deficiency of it. Just as a ball of thread will, when thrown, unwind to its full length, so fool and wise alike will take their course, and make an end of sorrow.

This is the earliest and most detailed statement of Jivika thought by a contemporary, and although it is meant to be pejorative, even satiric, it does contain the elements of Gosala's thought, in Basham's opinion. The force that propels the rebirth cycle or samsara is niyati (Destiny or Fate), which is similar to karma in its impersonal and lawlike quality. Associated with niyati is sagati (chance) and bhava (nature). Later jivika thinkers identified Svabhva, or bhava, with niyati itself. Here are two Jaina commentators on the importance of bhava. Jnanavimala: "Some believe that the universe was produced by Svabhva, and that everything comes about by Svabhva only.

Gunaratna: "What makes the sharpness of thorns and the varied nature of beasts and birds? All this comes about by Svabhva. There is nothing which acts at will. What is the use of effort?" This means that "nature," very broadly defined, incorporates everything in the sentient world, including all forms of human action. From a Buddhist point of view these kinds of thinkers are ahetukavadins (believers in causelessness) and akriyavadins (disbelievers in the efficacy of works). What is striking about the Jivika theory is that it does recognize "karma." Makkhali uses this word and describes the various kinds of karmas in almost casuistic fashion.

Basham thinks that the Jivikas recognized karma on the nominal level but rejected it at a deeper essential level, a distinction well known in Indian thought. I do not think this is correct; Jivikas used the term but not in its Buddhist and Jaina sense. They were having an argument with their opponents in order to show that their "karma" was different from that of the others. It is highly unlikely that Makkhali would have given the term Jaina and Buddhist meanings because that would radically have undermined the theory of niyati and (sva) bhava. He used the term karma to deconstruct it or to deny that karma was ethical and purposive.

Any purposive theory of action, be it karma or God, is anathema to the Jivikas (HD, 233). Instead, each person goes through a variety of rebirths in fantastic time cycles, and these rebirths include those of humans, animals, supernatural beings, even plants. It seems that the Jivika doctrine, more than any other known religion of the time, possessed a systematic notion of species sentience. Thus all beings must pass through all known forms of sentient existence. Ultimately this cycle stops "like a ball of thread that has unwound itself." Concomitantly, all persons will eventually achieve salvation, defined as the purity of the soul, irrespective of the quality of their thisworldly actions.

A man might think he is a free agent, but this is an illusion because even the belief in free will is determined by Destiny, Fate, or niyati and constitutes part of a natural process (bhava or svabhava). The stages of human life are controlled by Destiny, and so is life after death because "a new body is not obtained by anything else such as karma .... Under the compulsion of Destiny they experience various repulsive conditions, such as being humped-backed, one-eyed ... a dwarf ... death, disease, and sorrow".

By formulating his own version of "karma" Makkhali Gosala can carry on debates with his opponents who believe in another kind of karma. Nevertheless, irrespective of what he means by karma, Makkhali Gosala is not denying that those who violate moral norms will be punished or rewarded in their present existence. It is difficult to imagine a sophisticated thinker being so ignorant of the realities of the world we live in. What is denied is a system of rewards and punishments that affect rebirth; instead, the rebirth cycle goes on according to natural principles, or bhava, until it too, likes time, must stop.

There is another crucial issue pertaining to Jivika religion that scholars and commentators have not satisfactorily explained.

Is the system totally and irrevocably deterministic? If everything must work itself out, according to principles of niyati, what is the significance of the extreme asceticism assiduously practiced by the Jivikas? The logically expectable answer that asceticism, like everything else, is determined by Destiny is not satisfactory. According to Buddhist sources the Jivikas divided humanity into six classes, and each class was given a particular psychic color. For example, black is the color of those who live by slaughter and cruelty, such as hunters, fishermen, thieves, and jailers; and white is the class that contains Jivika ascetics of both sexes.

The purest color is "supremely white," but this class contains only three persons: Makkhali Gosala and two other Jivika leaders, Nanda Vaccha and Kisa Sakicca. Basham rightly thinks that this class also contains the arahants and Tirthankaras of Jivika soteriology. Nevertheless, if it is the case that all persons go through the same scheme of reincarnation and eventual salvation, why are there two special classes of highly advanced spiritual virtuosos? Why the preferential treatment? The answer, it seems to me, is that the Jivikas probably believed that the only thing that could hasten the salvation of the individual is asceticism.

Asceticism cleanses the soul and permits the achievement of salvation even in this life. The idea of the jivan mukta, the person who has achieved salvation in this very life, is common to the soteriologies of other samanic groups like the Jainas and Buddhists. This reinterpretation of Jivikaism permits us to postulate two key features of its soteriology: a belief in niyati, or Destiny, that irrevocably and with unrelenting slowness brings about an eventual purification of the soul and with it an automatic end of the samsaric cycle; and a belief that this slow salvific process can be dramatically shortened by the purifying processes of extreme asceticism. My reformulation renders intelligible the similarities that scholars have noted between Jivikaism and Jainism.

The difference is that Jainism has an ethical theory of karma, as in Buddhism. Yet in a unique departure from Buddhism, Jainism postulates that karmic actions produce a material component that taints the soul and weighs it down in both a physical and spiritual sense. Cleansing of the soul is through extreme asceticism. Here then is Jainism's resemblance to Jivikaism: even though Jivikaism did not subscribe to the ethical theory of karma as in Jainism, it probably believed with Jainism that "karmas" have a material component and hence can be classified casuistically.

More important, it believed in the power of ascetic practices to purify the soul and thus achieve "nirvana" even in this life, as Jainas do, but through a form of nonmoral effort. Thus the Jivika ascetic, like those of other samanic religions, abolishes the rebirth cycle after the achievement of nirvana. Ordinary people will also eventually achieve nirvana but only through the long-term operation of niyati, or Destiny. Because Jivikaism did not subscribe to the karma theory, it in effect permitted everyone to achieve eventual salvation. This is probably why it became popular in India and at one time was a contender with Buddhism and Jainism.

Although Jivikaism is closer to the rebirth eschatologies of small-scale societies in its rejection of karmic ethics and its conception of an impersonal cosmic process, it has inner affinity to the samanic religions in postulating a notion of salvation or nirvana outside of samsara, that is, by stopping the cycle of rebirth. The idea that even a nonethicized and antikarmic religion like Jivikaism had a soteriology that brought it in line with the rationalizing spirit of other samanic religions of the time tempts me to reexamine the significance of "purification" and its relation to asceticism in Jivika thought, particularly because similar conceptions prevailed not only in India but also in Greece.

Buddhist Jataka texts refer to Jivika soteriology as sasara suddhi, which can be translated as "samsaric purification," because the soul will eventually become purified and achieve salvation. "There is no short cut (lit. door) to bliss, Bijaka. Wait on Destiny. Whether (a man has) joy or sorrow, it is obtained through Destiny. All beings are purified through transmigration [rebirth], (so) do not be eager for that which is to come." This quotation, in my view, refers to the ordinary road to salvation and is typical of the advice given to laypersons even by such thinkers as the Buddha to remind them that their time of salvation will eventually come and to encourage them to be patient. In my interpretation purification by asceticism in Jivikaism takes the place of the ethical notion of karma, whereas in Jainism, the religion closest to it, there is a coexistence of karma and purificatory asceticism.

One Jivika purifying practice is especially significant for my examination of Jivika ascesis. According to the Jaina text Aupap a tika Sutra, the noblest Jivika ascetic, the uttiya samaa, entered a large earthen pot in order to do "penance." Aupap a tika is the Sanskrit form of the PaliBuddhist opap a tika, that is, birth outside of normal bodily processes. In the context of this Jaina text would interpret the action of the uttiyasamaa not as a literal nonbodily rebirth, as the term aupap a tika implies, but a symbolic one. If the large earthenware pot symbolizes the womb, then the Jivika virtuoso practicing asceticism in such a vessel is reborn into a higher salvific state through a form of purificatory asceticism, subverting Destiny and abolishing the normal process of slow salvation available to all.

CONTENTIOUS DISCOURSES IN BUDDHIST THOUGHT

Recent scholarship has shown that the institution of world renunciation conjoined with asceticism had low priority in Brahmannic thought until the Upanishads. The Brahmin priests themselves were rarely given to renunciation; their later sympathy for renunciatory practices resulted from the influence of the Upanishads and the religions that labeled samanic. There is some evidence that yogic practices were known in the Indus valley civilizations from seals that depict ascetics in poses similar to those practiced by the later Jainas. It is certainly possible that with the abandonment of this civilization, renouncers (who by virtue of their vocation were relatively free of the sociopolitical order) might have moved along river routes into the Ganges valley, perhaps joining other population migrations.

The Vedic tradition essentially extolled the household life-marriage, earning, and the begetting of children-whereas the renouncer has rejected those very values to become a homeless one or an anagarika, to use a Buddhist term. The well-known division of Hindu society into four stages of life, or aramas-student, householder, hermit, and renouncer- was formalized by the time of the Dharmasûtras (c. fourth century b.c.e.). But Brahmannic thought produced contentious debates regarding the "legitimacy of the renouncer's aM rama" and the value of the householder's life traditionally praised in the Vedic literature. These debates continued "even during the medieval period."

One text says: "As all rivers, both great and small, find a resting-place in the ocean, even so men of all orders find protection with householders"; and Baudhayana, who thinks that the demon Kapila invented the fourfold division of the life cycle, adds: "there is one arama only, because the others do not beget offspring." The renouncer came to be fully incorporated into the Hindu worldview only after the institution of world renunciation had been established in the samanic traditions and had begun to be accepted by large segments of the population.

The general term for ascetic renouncers was paribb ajaka (Pali) or parivrajaka (Sanskrit), which means "those given to wandering," a term appropriated by the samanic traditions. Other terms, like samana (sramana) and yati, emphasize "effort," namely, an ascetic mode of existence, whereas bhikkhu (or bhiksu) refers to a mode of living through "begging." The term sanyasin (someone who has "thrown away" all possessions) was used more or less exclusively in the Brahmannic tradition. To quote Olivelle: "A parivra jaka was a person who had left home and family had no fixed abode and lived on alms. His life had a basic religious dimension, since its final aim was the discovery of his individuality and his personal liberation."

Sukumar Dutt, who did the pioneering work on these wandering ascetics, says that the begging bowl was the symbol of their vocation; Brahmancariya (a difficult term with many meanings that here could be glossed as "salvation quest") was their spiritual aim and dharma their religious doctrine. The Buddhists sometimes make a distinction between samaas, to which they belong, and the general category of ascetic wanderers, the parivrajakas, whom they despise, although at other times these distinctions are blurred.

The Buddhist texts provide descriptions of the public life of these recluses. The Majjhima Nikaya (Middle length sayings) has an entire section titled "The Division of the Wanderers," which gives us valuable information on the various schools of wanderers. For example, in one text the wanderer named Sandaka is reputed to be staying "in the fig tree cave with a great company of wanderers, with at least 500 wanderers." A wanderer named Uggahaman had a following of three hundred.

The Buddhists despised these particular wanderers and felt no need to exaggerate their importance, although the rounded numbers are not to be taken literally. The texts clearly show that several schools of wanderers-like the Buddhist, Jaina, and other samanas-had large numbers of followers, and many other wanderers lived alone. All of them were a familiar feature of the social landscape of the Ganges valley and were generally highly regarded and patronized by the great, including kings and the newly emerging merchant classes.

There were special areas of the cities reserved for them. The "Mahasakuludayisutta" states that celebrated wanderers such as Anugara, Varadhara, and Sakuludayin stayed in the wanderers' park at the peacock feeding place near Rajagaha. They also congregated in other places for debates: thus the Buddha debated Vacchagotta the wanderer in a special park, ekapu Jarika (single white mango tree park), near Vesali. In the city of Savatthi was Queen Mallika's park, within which was a specially demarcated place "set around with a row of tinduka trees" and known as "One Hall."

The greeting with which Upaka, the naked ascetic, addressed the Buddha soon after his Awakening (Enlightenment) suggests a convention quite unlike the Brahmin one of inquiring about one's caste and lineage upon meeting a stranger: "On account of whom have you, your reverence, gone forth, or who is your teacher, or whose dhamma do you profess?"

The kinds of places listed above were not only resting places but also arenas where rival groups debated each other or expounded their own doctrines, or dhamma. The wanderer Sakuludayin gives a vivid account of the diverse schools of the time locked in debates with each other during the rain retreat.

Sometime ago, revered sir, when divers members of other sects, recluses and Brahmanns, were gathered together and were sitting down in the debating hall, this chance conversation arose: "Indeed it is profitable for the people of Aga-Magadha ... that these leaders in religious life, heads of companies, heads of groups, teachers of groups, well known, famous founders of sects, held in high repute by the many-folk, have come to Rajagaha for the rains-residence. This Pûrana Kassapa is a head of a company.... This Makkhali Gosala too ... This Ajita of the hair-blanket too ... This Pakudha Kaccayana too ... This Sanjaya Belatthi's son too ... This Nataputta the Jain too ... This recluse Gotama too is the head of a company, head of a group, the teacher of a group, he is well known, the famous founder of a sect, held in high repute by the many-folk; he too has come to Rajagaha for the rains-residence.

In another very interesting account Kunjaliya the wanderer tells the Buddha that after Kunjaliya has his morning meal, "I roam from park to park, from garden to garden ... [and] there I behold certain recluses and Brahmins debating on the profit of freedom from controversy and the profit of wrangling." It seems therefore that this period was bustling with intellectual activity, the spirit of which extended even to some householders.

The latter also listen to sermons and engage in conversations with religious leaders such as the Buddha and Mahavira, and apparently there were debating assemblies set aside for the laity also. The Buddha himself idealized "full and frequent assemblies" of the sort he was used to in his own home "republic" of Kapilavastu. The public debates practiced by religious virtuosos were called vada-vivada (arguments and counterarguments) and were often very acrimonious. One gets a feel for the rhetorical strategies employed by contestants from the disparaging remarks made by Buddhists on the casuistry of "eel-wrigglers" and "hairsplitters" and other dialecticians.

It is out of this intense intellectual activity that the great speculative religions of the sixth and fifth centuries b.c.e. emerged, particularly the Upanishads, Buddhism, Jainism, and many lesser-known intellectual and religious movements described in Buddhist and Jaina texts. The period was conducive to philosophical and soteriological probing and the systematization of thought (what Max Weber called the "rationalization" of the religious life). Nevertheless, speculative and systematic thinking need not produce ethicization.

The Upanishads produced a great speculative soteriology that was not concerned with ethicization. What then is the critical feature of religions like Buddhism and Jainism that was conducive to systematically converting a social morality into a religious one? The answer is that these religions were not simply those of the "homeless" interested in their personal salvation, as with the Upanishadic virtuosos; they were also concerned about the welfare of the ordinary person tied to a home. Buddhists extolled the renunciatory ideal that leads to salvation, but, in the spirit of Vedic thought, they also believed that the household life was necessary and desirable for those not driven by soteriological aspirations.

Thus Buddhists and Jainas established connections with the lay community in a systematic manner and developed stable congregations of lay supporters. Quite the contrary. These connections were probably created or imagined by others also. Just as an experiment has to be imagined before it can be created in a laboratory, so it is with ethicization. Thinkers must imagine a lay congregation before they actually create one, but even imagining such a community is impossible or meaningless if knowledge is secret or esoteric or if the salvific goal is for exclusive elite. Buddhist texts give us insights regarding the processes whereby religious innovators established connections with the lay population.

Many groups of wanderers had the general support of the laypeople in their midst but were, like the Upanishadic ascetics, not interested in lay conversion. I suggest that it is in relation to a lay community that ethicization of the moral life occurs. This should not surprise us because ethicization is the conversion of the morality that governs the life of ordinary people into a religious one. Religions like Buddhism and Jainism simply continued this concern with ordinary or everyday ethics, but they projected these ethics onto a religious or eschatological plane. Let me spell these ideas out in respect to the contrasting ethical orientations in Buddhism and the main body of the Upanishads.

Whether etymologically justified or not, Indian writers usually define Upanisad as "rahasyam" (secret). The term rahasyam captures the idea of an esoteric doctrine that the guru imparts to his pupil questing for salvation, similar to what the Greeks called paradosis, a transmission of esoteric knowledge, often on a one-to-one basis. Upanishadic paradosis often took place in an araya (forest); hence the term a rayaka was also used.

Certain physical gestures also indicate this esotericism, as, for example, when Yajnavalkya of the Brhadarayaka Upanisad takes his questioner aside to discuss the nature of his doctrine. The seeker of salvation goes to a guru and learns the "secret" knowledge-rahasyam-which is also true of many of the wanderer schools of that time. But the term rahasyam must not be taken literally; knowledge is communicated, although in a special way. Rahasyam is the way of "paradosis," of which Deussen gives many examples:

Chandogya 3.11.5: "Therefore only to his eldest son shall the father as Brahmann communicate it (this doctrine), but to no one else, whoever it may be."

Tvetavatara 6.22: "Give it (this supreme secret) to none who is not tranquil, who is not a son, or at least a pupil."

Bhadarayaka 6.3.12: "This (the mixed drink, mantha, and its ritual) shall be communicated to no one except the son or the pupil.

Nisiarvatapaniya 1.3: "But if a woman or a Sûdra learns the SavitKi formula, the Lakshmi formula, the PraJava, one and all go downward after death. Therefore, let these never be communicated to such. If anyone communicates these to them, they and their teacher go downwards to death."

Ramapûrvatapaniya 84: "Give it not (the diagram) to common men."

What one finds in the Upanishads (and similar doctrines among both Indian and Pythagorean Greeks) is a preoccupation with the individual's personal salvation; the values of the society are irrelevant to the issue and in extreme cases of renunciatory asceticism, they can be openly rejected. By contrast, in the samanic religions, such as Buddhism and Jainism, there was an additional interest in the soteriological-cum-ethical welfare of common men, women, and Sûdras, that is, of the larger lay community.

The theoretical significance of these divergent ethical orientations was neatly stated by Durkheim in his classic essay "The Determination of Moral Facts": individuals, he argued, cannot be moral objects unto themselves because the ground of morality is established in a social network.

One must qualify Durkheim somewhat and reaffirm that by morality we mean the kind of values necessary for the orderly conduct of social life- such things as respect for elders and injunctions on theft, adultery, lying, and violence, among others. It is possible for someone to reject a social morality for a "higher" ethic, hence my reluctance to enter into axiological judgments. If social morality of the sort I have described is established only in our relationships with others, then one cannot expect it to have salience for any individualistic salvation quest. In such quests social morality is at best irrelevant, even a hindrance, insofar as social morality links a person to his or her group, whereas salvation entails removal from it.

Weber was therefore clearly wrong when he said that Buddhism emphasized the personal certitudo salutis rather than the welfare of the neighbour. Although the doctrine of homelessness and ascetic withdrawal from the world was central to it, Buddhism was additionally concerned with conversion and the constitution of a lay community. This linkage was so powerful that the Buddhist salvation seeker could not be indifferent to morality; failure to adhere to conventional moral standards as stipulated in the Five Precepts will hinder the achievement of nirvana.

The ascetic withdrawal from the world with its goal of personal salvation must be reconciled with the establishment of communication between layperson and monk. Buddhism insisted that the monk should live "lonely as the single horn of the rhinoceros"; but he should also be concerned about the "welfare of the many." Although there have been problems reconciling the goal of ascetic renunciation with the demands of the laity, there is not the slightest doubt that Buddhism was never Max Weber's exclusive "monks' religion." In a major Buddhist text Gautama, the Buddha of our era, was faced precisely with this dilemma. Here he recognized that the doctrine is difficult and meant for the few, and he was reluctant to preach it to the world. By not preaching it he would have opted for the goal of personal salvation.

This model does exist in Buddhism in the person of the pacceka -Buddha, a Buddha who has achieved true knowledge but is not interested in proclaiming his message. Such Buddhas have existed before and will appear again; they have realized nirvana, but they make no dent on the world. Gautama wondered, according to this text, whether he should adopt this path but then made his decision clear when Brahman himself interceded and urged him to proclaim the doctrine for the "welfare and the happiness of the many." It is no accident that the Buddha's decision to save the world was a later thought.

Although the Buddha discovered the main doctrinal tenets of Buddhism during his first tremendous meditative experience, or Awakening (Enlightenment), the Five Precepts pertaining to lay ethics were not one of them. They were invented when the early Buddhists, like the Jainas, decided to convert the laity. The Buddhist discourses (suttas) are replete with statements that the doctrine is for both monk and layperson. Let us take a crucial text, the "Maha Parinibbana Sutta," which deals with the death of the Buddha.

Here Mara, the personification of the world's ills, tells the Buddha that he should die straightaway, but the Buddha replies: "I shall not come to my final passing away, Malignant One, until my bhikkhus and bhikkhunis [monks and nuns], laymen and laywomen, have come to be true disciples-wise, well-disciplined, apt and learned, preservers of the Dhamma, living according to the Dhamma, abiding by the appropriate conduct, and having learned the Master's word, are able to expound it ... and preach this liberating Dhamma."

The Buddha then says that this statement was uttered by him to Mara soon after the Buddha's Awakening at the foot of the goatherds' banyan tree, creating an impression that this has been a consistent position from the very beginning of the Buddha's career: "I shall not come to my final passing away,

Malignant One, until this holy life taught by me shall become successful, prosperous, farrenowned, popular and widespread, until it is well proclaimed among gods and men."

It therefore seems incontrovertible that early Buddhism and Jainism involved preaching to the world and establishing communication with the lay community, not only as a means of finding recruits for the order but also to create congregations. Communication with the laity was facilitated by the development of monasticism. When the Buddha entered a city, the monks there gathered to meet him, an indication that monastic communities, great or small, were inextricably associated with the development of early Buddhism.

With the establishment of the "rain retreat" (vassa) monks had to stay three months in one place, generally in small shelters erected by lay devotees or with friends and relations "but always close to a village or town." These lay congregations assemble to hear the Buddha preach. Hence, a crucial feature of early Buddhism was the public sermon, which has remained to this day a vehicle for the communication of doctrinal tradition to laypeople. These public sermons were open to all, unlike the closed esoteric world of the Upanishadic guru and his pupil.

7

Ethical Transformation and the Axial Age

This body is gnawed by eighty thousand worms. The worm that relies on the hair is called "hair-iron." The worm that relies on the skull is called "swollen ear." The worm that relies on the brain is called "maddener." In this class there are four kinds. The first is called ukurimba. The second is called shibara. The third is called daraka. The fourth is called dakashira .... The worms that rely on the heart are of two kinds. The first is called sibita. The second is called ubadabita. The worms that rely on the root of the heart are of two kinds. The first is called manka. The second is called sira .... There are three kinds of worms that rely on the two lower orifices. The first is called kurukulayuyu. The second is called sarayu. The third is called kandu pada. Thus one should recall minding the nature of the body through "worms" [while meditating]. -Upatissa Thera, The Path of Freedom (Vimuttimagga)

If Weber was wrong in characterizing Buddhism exclusively as an apolitical status religion, "a religious 'technology' of wandering and intellectually schooled mendicant monks," he was equally wrong in his estimate of the Buddha as a "prophet." "We shall understand by 'prophet' to mean a purely individual bearer of charisma, who by virtue of his mission proclaims a religious doctrine or divine commandment." Weber includes as prophets those who renew an older religion and those who proclaim a new one, for they merge into each other. Yet he is interested in a more fundamental typological distinction between two kinds of prophets, "one represented most clearly by the Buddha, and the other with special clarity by Zoroaster and Muhammed" (SR, 46).

The former is an "exemplary prophet" who by "his personal example demonstrates to others the way to personal salvation," whereas the latter is an "ethical prophet" who becomes "an instrument for the proclamation of a god and his will, be this concrete command or an abstract norm. Preaching as one who has received a commission from god, he demands obedience as an ethical duty".

Developing this idea further Weber wrote that "the prophet, in our special sense, is never to be found where the proclamation of a religious truth of salvation through personal revelation was lacking. In our view, this qualification must be regarded as the decisive hallmark of prophecy". In a beautiful passage Weber described the prophet presenting to his followers "a unified view of the world, derived from a consciously integrated and meaningful attitude towards life. To the prophet, both the life of man and the world, both social and cosmic events, have a certain systematic and coherent meaning. To this meaning the conduct of mankind must be oriented ... if it is to bring salvation" (SR, 59). The prophet attempts to "systematize all the manifestations of life, regardless of the form it may take in the individual case" (SR, 59); or, as Arthur Mitzman felicitously put it, he becomes a "tool of the divine will."

Although Weber brilliantly described the nature of ethical prophecy, his understanding of Buddhist "exemplary prophecy" is not very helpful. As Weber realized, all prophecy, whether the ethical or the nonethical oracular prophecies found in many societies, entails "possession" by a deity and/or some notion of "divine revelation," whereas for Buddhists such ideas contradict their ideal of a self-reliant individual dependent on no external support for salvation. It is impossible for the Buddha to become a tool of the divine will because no such will exists in the religion.

Further, prophecy entails proclaiming the future or prognosticating the past; although the Buddha practiced both features of prophecy, these were not as central to the religion as in the case of ethical prophecy. Although the Buddha was "exemplary" in showing the path to salvation for others, the Buddhist tradition upholds the idea that he was a special person, a maha purusa, or great being, impossible to emulate but one whose conduct helps ordinary persons to reflect on their own imperfections.

Most important, by polarizing ethical prophecy and exemplary prophecy, Weber underplayed the intrinsically ethical nature of the latter. If I were to distinguish the Buddhist ethical reform from that of the biblical tradition I would characterize it as "ethical asceticism." Asceticism is not necessarily ethical or even necessarily salvific; often it is to acquire spiritual powers through bodily mortification. Indeed the Buddha's criticism of extreme asceticism was often on ethical grounds.

I now want to briefly refer to the ethical reform taking place in an adjacent civilization, namely Iran, by the great reformer Zoroaster. The Zoroastrian reform was the southern furthest reach of what Weber calls ethical prophecy. We know there were broad similarities in the larger IndoIranian cultural area prior to the sixth century b.c.e. In both the Indic and the Iranian traditions there was a systematic rethinking ("rationalization") of the preexisting traditions, the Indian through the samanic reform of ethical asceticism and the Iranian through "ethical prophecy".

A beautiful example of this ethical orientation is found in a hymn describing Zoroaster's vision of God, which transported him back in time to the creation of the world: "Then, Mazdah, did I realize that thou wast holy when I saw thee at the beginning, at the birth of existence, when thou didst ordain a (just) requital for deeds and words, an evil lot for evil (done) and a good one for a good deed." At the risk of some oversimplification let me now deal with the contrasting orientations of ethical prophecy and ethical asceticism, focusing on ethics, not soteriology.

1. The crux of ethical prophecy is that the prophet is the vehicle of a transcendental and unitary deity whose soteriological and ethical message he communicates to the world. The ethical ascetic, by contrast, discovers the truth

of the world and of salvation from his own inward contemplation but the ethics he formulates have no transcendental quality. They are not eternal truths but guidelines for right conduct.

2. The nature of the prophet's message flows from the character of the deity: because it comes from God, it is a proclamation of the divine will. The prophetic ethics that ensue constitute "commandments." By contrast, the ascetic's ethical message does not come from God; it is a precept to be followed because of its inherent rightness. For example, Corinthians 7:6 makes a similar distinction in respect to marital ethics: "I speak of this by permission, and not commandment." The distinction between commandment and precept was crucial to the respective religious traditions in which ethical prophecy and ethical asceticism were institutionalized.
3. Because the prophetic message is from God, the command brooks no compromise. Thus ethical prophecy contains within it an uncompromising attitude to the world. Zoroaster sees his opponents as evil incarnate; in the extreme case no mercy or quarter is shown to nonbelievers, as in forms of Islam or Zoroastrianism and in many sectarian traditions of evangelical Protestantism. The preexisting religion is viewed with intolerance, regarded as the worship of sticks and stones. Thus, Zoroaster denounces the soma drinkers, very much in the spirit of the angry Jehovah and his prophets: "Wilt thou strike down this filthy drunkenness with which the priests evilly delude the people?"In ethical asceticism, by contrast, the ethical message, insofar as it is based on practical considerations, is vulnerable to compromise and revision. The rules of the monk order underwent constant revision until the formalization of the canon around the second century c.e.; such revision is extremely difficult to do with God's commands. In ethical asceticism the attitude to lay religion is tolerant, skeptical, and seen as folly rather than as evil. Contrary to the opinion of some scholars Buddhism does not contain a theory of radical evil like that found in the monotheisms. The basic contrast is that for the monotheisms the preexisting (or alien) religions are evil, whereas for the Buddhist they are folly.

4. The uncompromising attitude of the ethical prophet almost inevitably leads him into conflict with the secular order. The prophet ethicizes a preexistent religion, and this often brings him into conflict with the established priesthood and the secular authority that is legitimated by that priesthood and religion. This was true of Jesus and of Mohammed and Zoroaster, at least in the initial period of their reforms. By contrast, ethical asceticism, lacking an uncompromising posture, does not threaten the secular order. Religions like Buddhism and Jainism have compromised with the secular authority. Buddhism, for example, was strongly critical of caste (vara), but it nowhere attempted to reform the social order based on it. However, it did not provide any kind of validation for the caste order either.
5. The respective attitudes that I have sketched above affect the tone of the religious message. The prophet's message is intense, emotionally charged, and conveys a sense of urgency. It is expressed in condensed poetic language and metaphor, whereas the Buddhist suttas are expressed in ironic, reflective, and dialogical discourses containing seemingly endless repetitions and long discursive similes.

The repetitions are mnemonic devices, yet, as Walter Kaufmann says, if a person "does not want to take the time to listen slowly, the Buddha might say, it will take him a long time to achieve salvation." If in the suttas the technical and conceptual language is framed within a dialogical setting, not so with the commentarial tradition, the Abhidhamma, the third part of the canon, which has elaborate classificatory schemes and technical terminologies that have influenced the texts on meditation, such as the famous Visuddhimagga (Path of purification) by Buddhaghosa and the lesser known text quoted at the beginning of this section.

THE TRANSFORMATION OF THOUGHT

It is tempting to see ethicization as a (causal) variable; consequently, the methodological significance of my imaginary experiment would be to show how one kind of model or structure changes into another owing to the operation of the variable "ethicization." Model a (the rebirth eschatology) is transformed into model b (the karmic eschatology) as a consequence of the operation of x (ethicization), the causal variable. All this can be expressed elegantly and parsimoniously in verbal or figural form, yet it seems to me this way of representing social facts is misleading precisely on account of its oversimplification or "parsimony." The social reality of ethicization is far too complex to be isolated as a "cause."

It has to be re-presented in such a way that the complexity is maintained; this can be done through descriptions of historical or social process. At best one could represent ethicization initially as a causal variable, but then one must unscramble and "complexify" it because, as I see it, the goal of the human sciences is not only to simplify the world but also to understand its complexities and existential predicaments. The Buddhists rightly say that conditionality is everywhere; one cannot compress that pervasive conditionality into a single causal variable or into isolatable "factors."

In line with these methodological precepts let me then use these models to further illustrate the complexity of the historical process during this period of intense intellectual activity and the usefulness of Karl Jaspers's idea of the Axial Age transformation of the religious life without attempting any rigid periodization. In Jaspers's and in Shmuel Eisenstadt's recent reformulation this transformation entailed a preoccupation with soteriology and an ethics that transcended the world of everyday reality and the preexisting forms of religious life localized in the small community.

The Axial religions of India, as elsewhere, tended to be "universal" in the sense that their soteriology was meant for all. Following the creative thought of mathematician turned Indologist D. D. Kosambi, one could relate that expansion of thought to the changes taking place in India's "second urbanization." This period saw profound changes in political and economic life in India that I will now briefly describe.

First, two new emerging empires, Kosala and Magadha, violently swallowed the many small independent Ksatriya "republics," like the Buddha's own place of birth, that had collective decision-making assemblies known as sanghas or ganas. To deal with this threat some small republics banded together in a loose political alliance known as the Vajjian confederacy, but this too was short-lived. Other republics lasted much longer. The "full and frequent assemblies" of these sanghas and ganas were so idealized by the Buddha that he not only named the Buddhist order after them but also borrowed their organizational principles and transferred them to the monastic assembly, as did his rival Mahavira, the spiritual leader of the Jainas.

Second, there was the emergence of new cities and the development of trade and commerce and concomitantly a new class of wealthy traders, bankers, and entrepreneurs generally known as setthis. Many of these setthis supported the new salvation religions. Kosambi argues that the development of trade and the movement of caravans transcended local groups and traditional political boundaries. Two caravan routes were especially significant: the uttar a patha, the northern route into the Indus region of Brahmannic culture, and the daksi Japnatha, which went south into the modern Deccan, both routes providing access for Buddhist monks and other teachers to spread their faiths.

These trade routes needed policing, which the new empires provided; thus was forged, says Kosambi, an alliance between the merchant classes and the kings. He adds that the time was right for the emergence of universalizing and transcendent religions that paralleled the obsolescence of older political communities and the creation of wider ones. I think it reasonable to assume that the breakdown of traditional social forms and the rise of new empires gave concrete embodiment to the older notion of a "universal ruler," or cakravartin. These changes in turn paralleled the outward-looking and universalizing orientations of the new religions, the one probably influencing the other.

But an "orientation" cannot account for the content of a doctrine; therefore a direct tie-in between economic and political change and the thought of the new religions of the Ganges valley is difficult to substantiate. Some scholars have suggested that the sense of pessimism and the emphasis on suffering that these religions formulated can be related to the social disruptions and dislocations of traditional life-forms of the sort that Durkheim conceptualized as anomie. But one can as easily argue that such conditions could lead to a preoccupation with hedonism instead of postulating a world of impermanence and hopelessness. Indeed, it can be demonstrated that the Buddha's own life, as reflected in myth, represented recognition that hedonism is no solution to the ills of the world.

What seems to have occurred at this time is the emergence of thinkers questioning preexisting values and proposing a variety of salvific and nonsalvific solutions to the problems of existence. The Buddhist texts describe nonreligious thinkers such as various kinds of materialists, sophists, and nihilists. Many practitioners of extreme asceticism aimed, through the mastery of the world, at the mastery of the body of the world; others aspired to realize some kind of transcendent reality beneath the flux of everyday existence; yet others combined any number of these forms of religious and nonreligious speculations.

The social changes of the time provoked thinkers to deal with a variety of existential issues, almost all geared to general and universalized knowledge that transcended, although they did not necessarily replace, the values and ideals of the local community. For example, the Buddha borrowed the model of the sangha from the republican organization of the time; but his sangha was no longer tied to a specific political unit; it was the universal church, "the sangha of the four quarters." So it was with the religious doctrine, or dhamma: it was not localized in any specific community or groups either but contained a salvific message for all. The figure of the founder is also not exempt from this process.

Once the Buddha decides to become a renouncer, he ceases to be a member of the local community; furthermore, as the Buddha he is the seventh, twenty-fourth, or twenty-eighth (depending on which texts you choose) of a long line of redeemers, previous Buddhas. Thus the three main axes of the religion-the Buddha, the Dhamma, and the Sangha-are all universalizing conceptions.

Here then lies a major difference between the Axial Age religions in general and the eschatologies of the small-scale or adivasi societies. None of the latter is involved in the universalizing process. It is certainly the case that after European colonization their physical worlds and geographic horizons drastically expanded, but the missionary religions took over the universalizing function, leaving little space for native intellectuals to forge larger worldviews out of their own localized religious traditions. This historical process is by no means closed, and native intellectuals might yet create new universalizing religious forms.

Is there any concept that one can employ to designate the multiple strands of the Indic reform that I have highlighted thus far? These ideas, namely, ethicization, the universalizing (and transcendental) thrusts in soteriology, and "axiologization" , are part of the systematization of thought and life-forms that one might, following Weber, label as "rationalization."

Weber used the term rationalization in a bewildering variety of ways and think it fair to say that one important sense of rationalization is "systematization of thought." However, this meaning of rationalization is useful only for identifying the general or totalizing sweep of thought unless one can specify some of its components, as I have done. Weber did have a restricted and more useful definition of rationalization as the kind of intellectual action that "the systematic thinker performs on the image of the world: an increasing theoretical mastery of reality by means of increasingly precise and abstract concepts." I will resurrect the term conceptualism from medieval European scholasticism as the intermediate position between realism and nominalism and give it a different meaning to designate the invention and use of abstract terms and formulations. Thus conceptualism is not synonymous with rationalization but is one component of it.

The mastery of the world through the systematic imposition of abstract concepts makes fuzzy the conventional distinction between philosophy, science, and religious thought that Western epistemology has enshrined and permits us to focus on ratiocinative operations that are common to all three of the aforesaid domains, namely, the impetus to understand the nature of the world or the world of nature through the mediation of abstract concepts. It is difficult to believe, however, that conceptualism cannot occur in a multiplicity of cultures, small-scale or large; its occurrence and importance have to be demonstrated in context.

Although conceptualism is intrinsically associated with the systematization of thought or rationalization, one can have the systematization of thought without conceptualism. The unifying worldview of the ethical prophet can be seen as a systematization of thought. Yet, although the prophet had abstract ideals, he hardly used abstract concepts to understand the world; indeed, he shunned such concepts or found them irrelevant to his passionate and intense soteriological vision. Conceptualism is rarely found in the Bible; it is only in the Platonic heritage of later Christian and Islamic thinkers that one encounters careful and deliberate conceptualism.

To conclude: what is unique to Axial Age religions is a form of "rationalization" that includes the development of transcendental and universalizing soteriologies, and ethicization is a basic feature of that universal and transcendental vision. These soteriologies do require systematic probing into the nature of existence, but they need not necessarily involve "conceptualism"; the latter entails the supervention of abstract concepts for grasping the nature of the world, and it is religions such as Buddhism (and the tradition of Greek soteriological thought that I will delineate later) that exemplify it. In the Buddhist doctrinal tradition the conceptual imperative is so strong that one could reasonably speak of a "Buddhist Enlightenment" that parallels the Greek and the European.

The argument can be restated thus: the unique feature of Axial Age development in Indic religions is that their thought took a direction that ethical prophecy did not. Like later European philosophies or Pythagoreanism the samanic religions of India developed a set of abstract terms to grasp the transcendentalizing vision of their soteriologies. Hence one encounters such things as the Four Noble Truths; the doctrine of the impermanence of things; the five atomic principles, or skandhas, that constitute the body; the doctrine of "no soul"; the theory of causality known as paticca samuppada, or dependent origination; the idea of rebirth linking consciousness; complex theories of perception and consciousness; the classification and analysis of states of concentration or absorption (jhanas); and so on.

These ideas are rarely presented as purely abstract discourse until we come to the later philosophical and psychological analyses known as the Abhidhamma. Rather concepts are woven into the dialogues of the Buddha that deal essentially with the nature of existence and the transcendence of the everyday world. The Buddhist dialogues, like the Upanishadic ones, have dramatis personae whose roles must be unfolded before we can begin to appreciate their content. Yet, although Buddhist conceptualism is necessary for an intellectual understanding of the religion, it has to be abandoned at a certain point in the salvation quest, along with discursive thought in general.

One can get a feel for the kind of speculative thought characteristic of the period by getting back to the "eel-wrigglers" and "hair-splitters" mentioned earlier. The reference to these dialecticians comes from one of the most interesting texts in Buddhism, known as the "Brahmanjala Sutta" (The net of Brahman). In it the Buddha discusses eleven vada (false theories; lit., "arguments") about the soul. Among the dialecticians of these theories are the eel-wrigglers, who, when a question is put to them, "resort to equivocation":

> In the first place, brethren, some recluse or Brahman does not understand the good in its real nature, nor the evil [bad]. And he thinks: "I neither know the good, as it really is, nor the evil. That being so, were I to pronounce this to be good or that to be evil [bad], I might be influenced therein by my feelings or desires, by ill will or resentment. [The same with wrong]. ... [H]e will neither declare anything to be good, nor to be bad; but on a question being put to him on this or that, he resorts to eel-wriggling, to equivocation, and says: "I don't take it thus. I don't take it the other way. But I advance no different opinion. And I don't deny your position. And I don't say it is neither the one, nor the other."

Eel-wrigglers are familiar to those of us in academia; so are hairsplitters, a subclass of eel-wrigglers, who "go about, methinks, breaking to pieces by their wisdom the speculations of others". In fact, the next example of the language of these casuists seems like a parody of the Buddha's own:

> There is not another-world. There both is, and is not, another-world. There neither is, nor is not, another-world. There are Chance Beings (so called because they spring into existence, either here or in another-world, without the intervention of parents, and seem therefore to come without a cause). There are no such beings. There both are and are not, such beings. There neither are nor are not, such beings. There is fruit, result, of good and bad actions. There is not. There both is, and is not. There neither is, nor is not.

These kinds of dialectics are used by the Buddha himself when he deals with ideas that cannot be expressed in ordinary discursive language. Paradox and equivocation are part of the language the mystic uses to describe ineffable states, or the unity of self with god, or of all existence as refractions of the deity. It is "neither this nor that," in the language of Meister Eckhart, or the "not this–not this" of the Upanishadic formula. It is the language of T. S. Eliot's "Ash Wednesday." And it is the language of Parmenides in Plato's Parmenides:

> So if, in every way, something is one and other things are not one, then the One would neither be a piece of whatever is not one nor as a whole of pieces. Nor, in turn, could the things that are not one be pieces of the One, nor as wholes to the One, as a piece....
>
> Let this be said, then, and also that, so it looks, whether one is or is not, both it and the different things, both in relation to themselves and in relation to each other, all, in all ways, both are and are not and both appear and do not appear.

Although parodied by the Buddha because of the extremes to which they are carried, the dialectics of the eel-wrigglers and hair-splitters indicate a powerful rationalizing impulse in any society.

TEMPORALITY, IMPERMANENCE, NIRVANA

A middle path in order to show the interplay between the individual's freedom in creating new knowledge and the constraints imposed by the preexisting structures of knowledge curbing that very freedom. In this exercise two prior systems of knowledge, the unethicized and ethicized eschatologies of rebirth topographically.

Continuing to demonstrate the limitations that any kind of rebirth theory imposes on the soteriological innovations of thinkers such as the Buddha and the more drastic visions of those who followed them.

1. Built into rebirth eschatology is the idea that the soul goes through cycles of existence. It is obvious that one could impose a limit on the number of times one is reborn, as Makkhali Gosala, some Inuit, the African Benin, and the Greek Pythagoreans did. In both Trobriand and Buddhist eschatology the cycle is theoretically illimitable. Any innovative thinking must be contained within this unalterable parameter that takes for granted the continual or continuous cyclical journey of the soul.
2. With ethicization there is a qualitative change in the structure of continuity such that the rebirth cycle is propelled by ethics that now begin to generate good or bad otherworldly consequences. That too is given a name: karma. Karma fuels existence and reexistence that consequently begins to take new meaning and this is also given terminological recognition: samsara. The thinker does not invent these ideas; he has no choice but to invent them because, as we have already noted, when ethicization is introduced and systematically pursued through steps 1 and 2, the ideas of karma and samsara must necessarily follow. What the thinker does is to articulate ideas implicit in this scheme and give them terminological recognition (conceptualism). Once conceptualism occurs he can manipulate terms in new ways and invent related concepts, which in turn give him greater freedom to gain mastery over life, existence, or the world.
3. Take the first of the two interrelated terms forced on the thinker, namely karma, and consider its implication for his freedom to invent new ideas. One of the most interesting notions in Buddhism is anicca, or impermanence, and it is karma that provides the stimulus for that line of thinking. According to the karma theory every good and bad action I perform must have its fruit (phala) or consequence (vipaka).

Insofar as I cannot exist without continually performing good and bad actions, my "being" or spiritual state is also continually conditioned by karma. For example, my present existence is the product of my karmic actions in my previous birth and innumerable ones before that; this means that my present condition must continually change owing to the operation of these karmic fruits. So is it with my next birth, which is conditioned by the good and bad do combined with karmic residues from previous existences. Karma then is the great destabilizer, and it introduces the ideas of change and flux as part of sentient existence. "Impermanent are all conditioned things," say Buddhist texts, precepts, and practices everywhere. It is on the basis of karma that Buddhists have erected their radical theory of impermanence.

4. However, a theory of impermanence need not entail the denial of a stable entity that resists change, namely, the soul. There could exist a still point in the changing world, and Buddhists could easily have retained this idea from previous rebirth eschatology or from the prior Upanishadic tradition. Yet they did not; for them there is no permanent substrate in the person, and the "soul" itself is a product of constantly changing aggregates, or skandhas. This is a radical innovative break in the tradition of previous thought and is entailed neither by the instability that the karma theory produces nor by the idea of impermanence developed by thinkers on the basis of that karma theory. With this idea Buddhist thinkers have embarked on a daring and autonomous direction that in turn will produce new debates provoked by the angst that the idea of "no soul" must have on those religiously musical people who have invested emotionally in ("cathected") the soul's existence.
5. To deal with a crucial feature of"rebirth eschatology": it does not concern itself with "salvation." In other words innovative thinkers in the small-scale societies have discussed are not obsessed with the idea of an ultimate state of bliss, that paradoxical terminal state in which the world is transcended. Steps 1 and 2 of my imaginary experiment that produces the karma theory make no change in this situation; one can in

principle have a karma theory without the notion of "salvation," if by salvation one means "a state or condition in which suffering is eliminated." Weber rightly noted, "Not every rational religious ethic is necessarily an ethic of salvation. Thus, Confucianism is a religious ethic but it knows nothing at all of a need for salvation. On the other hand, Buddhism is exclusively a doctrine of salvation" (SR, 146). And one might add Jainism and forms of Hinduism. All these religions use a term like nirvana or moksa to designate salvation, but although the theologians of these three religions define nirvana differently, their definitions have one thing in common: nirvana has to be sought outside the cycle of rebirths, or samsara; it must result in the cessation of rebirth. Because salvation or nirvana is neither the concern of rebirth eschatology nor entailed by the karmic eschatology of our model, it has to be invented by the thinker. However, it is easy to show that once the thinker becomes interested in the idea of salvation, the rebirth eschatology imposes a restriction regarding its nature such that there is no other way to achieve salvation except outside the rebirth cycle; or, to put it differently, one cannot achieve nirvana except by abolishing rebirth, or samsara. Let me elaborate. In rebirth eschatology there can be no elimination of suffering, which is the sine qua non for any doctrine of salvation, Buddhist or Christian or Pythagorean or Whatever. There can logically be no permanent state of bliss. Why so? First, in rebirth eschatology the soul's sojourn in the otherworld must perforce be temporary. Second, one is eventually reborn in an earthly existence that by any definition must entail suffering. This sojourn is also temporary because after one is born on earth, one has to be reborn in another sphere of existence. If a rebirth eschatology had some notion of a blissful place (as in Trobriand), it is at best an alleviation of suffering, not its elimination, because rebirth in the human world clearly implies its presence. This means that within the rebirth cycle one cannot achieve salvation, defined as either a permanent state of bliss or an elimination of suffering or both. The karmic eschatology of my model makes no difference to the conditions listed above but only exacerbates them. Hence there is no way to define nirvana except in such terms as "the elimination of suffering" or "the cessation of rebirth" or "the abolishing of karma." To recapitulate: the seeker of salvation is a creature of the Axial Age; in the Indic context the truth seeker has no choice but to define salvation as something occurring outside the samsaric cycle. As Braudel put it: "mental frameworks too can form prisons of the longue durée."

6. Once a new concept has been introduced-in this case nirvana-it must loop back to the earlier concepts and infuse them with further meaning and significance. Such looping back and forth is intrinsic to the propensity called "conceptualism." Thus the introduction of nirvana adds new meaning and significance to the idea of karma. For example, karma ties one down to the cycle of rebirths, or samsara, whereas nirvana is the cessation or transcendence of samsara. The idea of impermanence also gets further existential power because there is now a new eschatological principle that is opposed to it, or transcends it, or is in a dialectical relationship to it. Finally, when nirvana is conjoined with karma, samsara itself gets a further load of undesirable connotations quite unlike those accorded it in smallscale societies in which rebirth is a good thing. This latter idea is partially retained in Buddhism, which recognizes that although samsara is undesirable, birth in a human world is necessary for salvation. Even the highest god must have had a human rebirth at some point in his or her moral career to achieve salvation.

THE APORIAS OF EXISTENCES

The karmic eschatology proposed that good and bad moral actions will have consequences for the after-death fate of an individual. The model postulates that if this logic is carried through, the samanic notion of karma will emerge. Once one has a definition of existence based on ethical causality of this sort, there seems on the face of it little freedom to maneuver for individual religious teachers-according to the logic of the karmic eschatology. Expressing it rather differently, one might say that a strict determinism of karmic rewards and punishments is an expectable inference from my model.

Yet what is expectable from an ideal scheme of things is never going to be replicated in empirical reality; even so, empirical reality cannot ignore karmic determinism because karma makes no sense without such a notion. Thus the ideal model, as Max Weber recognized, can serve as a means for assessing deviations from it; or, more reasonably, the ideal or utopian conditions postulated by the model might help us understand those complicating existential conditions that always occur in empirical reality.

Only a limited number of ideas could be introduced into the karma doctrine without necessarily affecting its strict determinism. In doctrinal Jainism one cannot escape karma's consequences, which operate irrevocably and mechanically. However, Buddhists gave the karma theory a different emphasis: only intentional and ethically motivated actions have karmic effects. Buddhists also added another dimension to karma by postulating that human pain and suffering can arise from nonkarmic causes.

For example, illness can be caused by karma, but it can also be caused through the sole action of the bodily humors. Thus, although karma is deterministic, it is not exclusively so as far as human existence is concerned. In practice one can reconcile the karmic with the humoral by saying that it is a person's karmic condition that permitted the humors to affect his or her health. These qualifications do not affect the claim that karma will eventually have its way, as the following statements from three different texts indicate:

1. Possessed of my own deeds [karma], I am the inheritor of deeds, kin to deeds, one who has deeds as a refuge. Whatever deed I shall do, whether good or evil, I shall become the heir of it. This is to be contemplated by woman, and by man; by householder, and by him who has been taken into the order.
2. Todeyya's son Subha asks the Buddha: "Master Gotama, what is the cause and condition why human beings are seen to be inferior and superior? For people are seen to be short-lived and long-lived, sickly and healthy, ugly and beautiful, uninfluential and influential, poor and wealthy, low-born and high-born, stupid and wise. What is the cause and

condition, Master Gotama, why human beings are seen to be inferior and superior?"...

1. The Buddha replies: "Student, beings are owners of their actions [karma], heirs of their actions; they originate from their actions, are bound to their actions, have their actions as their refuge. It is action [karma] that distinguishes beings as inferior and superior."
2. The King [Menander or Milinda] said: "Why is it, Nagasena that all men are not alike, but some are short-lived, some sick and some healthy, some ugly and some beautiful, some without influence and some of great power, some poor and some wealthy, some low-born and some high-born, some stupid and some otherwise?" The Elder [Nagasena, the monk] replied: "Why is it that all vegetables are not alike, but some sour, and some salt, and some pungent and some acid, and some astringent and some sweet?" "I fancy, sir, it is because they come from different kinds of seeds." "And just so, great King, are the differences you have mentioned among men to be explained." For it has been said by the Blessed One: "Beings, O Brahmann, have each their karma, are inheritors of karma belong to the tribe of karma, have each their own karma as their protecting overlord. It is karma that divides them into low and high and the like divisions."

The last example in this list, from The Questions of King Milinda, was composed in the Indo-Greek kingdom of Bactria several centuries later than the passage preceding it, but the basic position remained unchanged, even though some tinkering with the doctrine of karma had taken place. It seems that Nagasena uses the previous text (or a similar one) as his authority. In all of these texts it is clear that karma is a deterministic force; therefore, it is no wonder that nineteenth-century scholars, influenced by the science of that period, thought that karma appeared to Buddhists as a "natural law."

And even though nineteenthcentury scientific philosophy is outdated, Buddhist intellectuals, who rarely have moved out of that century, even nowadays refer to karma as a "natural law" in order to designate its determinate and impersonal quality. There is no way that one can affirm karma yet deny determinism in its operation. Nevertheless, it seems to me that with this determinism arise several existential puzzles, or aporias, that demand resolution; but the resolution of one existential puzzle leads to others, such that aporias are within aporias! Structuralists might formulate these aporias in terms of contradictions and their mediation. But I agree with Paul Ricoeur that to frame the issue in this way is to bypass the "aporias of existence" around which mythic and religious thought gravitates. Therefore let me frame for Buddhism some of the aporias that arise from the logic of karmic determinism.

KARMA AND PUNISHMENT

According to the karmic prescription something done ethically wrong will be punished in the future. What it is that have done ethically wrong, or whether done anything ethically wrong at all, is not clear from the punishment incur during my present existence.

That this has been an issue from the very start in Buddhism is clear from many Buddhist texts in which the Buddha tries to reverse the situation by specifying that such and such a bad rebirth was caused by a specifically bad karmic act; so is it with the good. On the popular level it has led to handbooks that specify a particular type of punishment for a particular karmic misdeed.

More significant is the related issue of whether in fact from punishment whether committed a bad karmic act at all. Let us now say that I am old, I have contracted a disease, and I am about to die. Does this mean that I have done something ethically wrong in the past? After all, everyone dies, and my disease may have nothing to do with my karma but simply be due to my inevitable old age and mortality. I think it is to resolve this aporia that early Buddhism postulated nonkarmic causes for misfortune that I have already mentioned, such as humoral and natural calamities and the effect of seasons and climates on people. Thus, although all karma must bear fruit (phala), not all "fruit" has been produced by karma. This is an escape clause formulated very early in Buddhism to meet this particular aporia produced by the karma theory.

THE PSYCHOLOGICAL INDETERMINACY OF KARMA

The problem with the karma theory is that although it is causally determinate (karma will pay), it leaves the individual in a particularly vulnerable position psychologically. According to karma the past determines my present condition, and my present karmic actions will determine my future-life fate. But here's the rub: my present life situation is, I am told, mostly, if not entirely, owing to what I have done in a past birth or births, but of this I know nothing. If I know nothing regarding my karmic past, then I will never know what my present existence holds for me. Consequently, sudden peaks and drops of fortune could occur as results of things I have done in a previous existence (of which I know nothing). Today I am a pauper, tomorrow a prince; today I am young and healthy, tomorrow stricken by a fatal disease.

In a religion like Christianity we are all born with a constant load of original sin; any sin or meritorious action I commit is something I am for the most part conscious of. The effect of sin is psychologically determinate, and I can do something about it through what the religion has made available to me: faith, sacraments, confessionals, and the like. Not so in karma theory; not only is the load of sin or merit that I am born with different from everyone else's, but I do not know what that load is.

Karma produces a psychological indeterminacy regarding the life contours of one's present existence that adds to the instability regarding one's moral and spiritual condition that I mentioned earlier. The only way to meet this situation is to know what that past was; but only the Buddha or the Jina or the arahants have the power to "retrocognize" the past. The former two are no longer present, and arahants, even if they are around, rarely proclaim their presence. Thus this problem cannot be resolved within the frame of Buddhist doctrine itself. Buddhists must perforce be satisfied with this indeterminacy, or they must go outside Buddhist doctrine to resolve it.

In my view this is where astrology comes in. Astrology charts the life trajectory of an individual, but although astrology is a deterministic theory (like karma), it is also psychologically determinate. The certainty of astrology compensates for the uncertainty of karma; the astrologer tells you that although you are a pauper today, you will be a prince tomorrow, or that fatal illness will strike you even though you now seem in perfect health. The need to resolve the aporia pertaining to karmic indeterminacy is so great that, in spite of the doctrinal condemnation of astrology as one of the "beastly arts," Buddhist monks have taken over the astrologer role without too much misgiving.

What the astrologer does is chart one's karma, and professional Buddhist astrologers will explicitly state this. One of Sri Lanka's most distinguished monks, the late Balangoda Ananda Maitreye, who claimed to be an aspirant for future Buddhahood, put it thus: "The child is born into an environment of planetary influences.... Therefore according to each one's karma they fall into different environments. The gravitational pull of planets, their changes and one's own karmic force are interconnected. With knowledge of astrology, one can understand the karmic force at birth.... Therefore, the planets influence a person in accordance with his karma."

This posture, however, leads to another problem: once one knows one's karmic condition through astrology, then it is only to be expected that one wants to do something about it. Consequently, something outside of doctrinal Buddhism must again come into the picture and subvert the karmic law, this being the popular rituals denigrated in the doctrinal tradition. There arises an aporia within an aporia owing to an attempt to subvert karma, which in principle cannot be subverted.

GODS AND THE SUBVERSION OF KARMA

The attempt to ward off karma produces some fundamental "contradictions" in Buddhism as it is practiced. The doctrinal tradition does not seem to have budged on this issue; the gods themselves are karmabound creatures in need of salvation. Yet, on the other hand, the existence of gods is clearly recognized everywhere in Buddhism; it is their power to subvert karma that is denied. The historical problem is easy to grasp; once the presence of the gods is recognized, as it is in early Buddhism, it is difficult to deny them the power they have always had in the consciousnesses of people who need their help in everyday existence.

Although the doctrinal texts affirm that one's present status is karma dependent, popular rituals everywhere give gods the capacity to bring weal or woe to individuals and the group. This simply means that the old life-forms that propitiated gods went on in spite of Buddhism- but only after the gods had been "Buddhicized."

The basic idea is that the major gods in a Theravada-Buddhist nation like Sri Lanka are Bodhisattvas, or Buddhas-to-be, and guardians of the secular and spiritual realms. People propitiate the gods and the gods help them; as a gesture of gratitude people transfer merit to the gods, whose own salvation will thereby be short-circuited. Although this theory has no justification in any of the texts of the doctrinal tradition, it appeared as soon as Buddhism became the religion of specific nations in South and Southeast Asia.

THEODICY AND THE PROBLEM OF SUFFERING

The previous aporia pertained to the problems of meaning that arise from competing notions of power. It deals with an issue in the ideological system of Buddhism itself. Translated into human terms it means that the gods ameliorate suffering, which everyone knows is overwhelmingly caused by karma. However much the doctrine says that "karma will pay," people are going to be much more ambivalent. Karma will pay, but.... In its contestation with Brahmannic thought, Buddhism had to directly confront this issue in its critique of a powerful god who could mitigate human suffering and pain. Consider this portrait of Brahman found in the Bhûridatta Jataka, from the Jataka Tales, that popular compendium of life stories of the Buddha:

- He who has eyes can see the sickening sight; why does not Brahman set his creatures right?
- If his wide power no limits can restrain, why is his hand so rarely spread to bless? Why are his creatures all condemned to pain? Why does he not to all give happiness?
- Why do fraud, lies, and ignorance prevail?
- Why triumphs falsehood, -truth and justice fail?

- I count your Brahman one the' unjust among, who made a world in which to shelter wrong.

It seems that even those Buddhist texts like the Bhûridatta Jataka that arose from the popular tradition and fed into it deliberately raised the problem of theodicy: the inability of Brahman, the all-powerful god, to account for the imperfections of the world. In their debate with the Vedic tradition Buddhists scorned Brahman and reaffirmed the universality of karma. By contrast, in later Hinduism it became orthodox for someone to subscribe to the doctrine of karma and simultaneously to the belief in a powerful god (Brahman, Visnu, Siva, or any of their manifestations), who has the power to subvert it.

The result is that in practice many Hindu movements, especially those influenced by bhakti devotionalism, are virtually (mono) theistic, so that karma becomes relatively unimportant and could be overcome by a single-minded devotion to god. But in Buddhism there is no such way out, and this entails a logical contradiction in the explanation of suffering: if the gods are powerful enough to ameliorate human suffering, then karma is not the deterministic doctrine it is claimed to be; if karma governs human suffering, then the gods cannot be powerful or capable of subverting it.

It seems to me that these types of contradictions cannot be ironed out by scholarly dialectical devices that often impel us to reconcile and systematize them in relation to the rationalizing imperatives of our own disciplines. These "contradictions" are a consequence of the aporias that arise from within an ideology and in many instances cannot be resolved. In Theravada Buddhist practice they are expressed and debated in multiple, open-ended discourses, some "authorizing" karma, some de-authorizing it-for example, in popular Buddhist stories, in monk sermons and lay responses, in everyday conversations, as well as on special occasions such as funerals, in discussions about natural and human catastrophes, endlessly.

These kinds of aporetic issues and the debates they provoke are not unique to Buddhism but are inherent in any systematizing soteriology.

DOCTRINAL RESPONSES TO POPULAR RELIGIOSITY

It now would seem apparent that aporias generate aporias; the "aporetic chain" is ultimately traceable to the problems that the doctrine of karmic causality unleashes on the world. It was fashionable in early Indological studies to see inherent contradictions in the belief system as a contamination of the "pure doctrine." But the pure doctrine has been "contaminated" from the very start in many ways.

One must not imagine that the aporetic questions arose "later" and were incorporated into later texts or exclusively into the popular religion. If these aporias are not always reflected in the earliest texts, one must not assume that these issues were absent in the controversies of the day. Rather, there was a strong resistance on the part of the orthodox tradition to deal with them (resistance being as much a weapon of the strong as it is of the weak). We know that some of these issues were dealt with in the earliest texts, but others were not.

Obviously, there cannot be a radical subversion of the karma doctrine that would undermine its totalizing embrace. Hence, little concession is made in the texts that would grant the deities power, and even late texts like the Bhûridatta Jataka affirm the doctrinal position. Nevertheless, the monks who composed texts dealt with this aporia of karma by rejecting the power of the gods and employing instead the recital of texts from their own tradition modeled on the Vedic practice of mantras, which gives power to the Word.

For Buddhism, however, the Word contains the truth of the doctrine, and it is the power of the truth that was operative in the development of its apotropaic verses, some of which come from the oldest stratum of the canon. These are known as parittas (protections), and they are recited by monks to bring blessings on people suffering from such things as illnesses, demonic incursions, and other misfortunes. If the intention was to provide a substitute for the propitiation of gods from the preexisting or popular traditions, it certainly failed because now people had one more way to overcome the inexorability of karma!

KARMA AND MERIT MAKING

The inevitability of karmic causality is rarely contested in the main body of the doctrine. However, texts such as the "Mahakammavibhaga Sutta." (The greater exposition of action) of the Middle Length Discourses could be used to justify the popular idea of counterkarma, the notion that good deeds could cancel the effect of the bad. In this text the Buddha muses on why those who do good might be reborn in good circumstances yet might also be reborn in hell:

> Either earlier he did an evil action to be felt as painful, or at the time of death he acquired and undertook [the] wrong view. Because of that, on the dissolution of the body, after death, he has reappeared in a state of deprivation ... even in hell. But since he has here [also] abstained from killing living beings ... and held [the] right view, he will experience the result of that either here or now, or in his next rebirth, or in some subsequent existence."

And for the same reasons (in reverse), those who do bad might be punished in hell, yet they might instead be rewarded in heaven. And the Buddha concludes: "Thus, Ananda, there is action that is incapable [of good result] and appears incapable; there is action that is incapable [of good result] and appears capable; there is action that is capable [of good result] and appears capable; and there is action that is capable [of good result] and appears incapable."

Additionally, a strong deed (balavakamma) can on occasion overcome a weak deed (dubbalakamma) and produce what is known in the doctrinal tradition as ahosi karma, that is, karma that has "lapsed" as a result of its inability to produce "results" (vipaka), generally owing to the operation of a strong counteractive karma. From here it is a short way for the popular tradition to reify the idea that a strong deed will cancel out the effect of the weak one and clear the path for merit making and for introducing an ethic of works that will coexist with an ethic of intention.

An important epistemic break occurs with those texts stipulating the three virtues conducive to the accumulation of good deeds or merit (punna), these being, in conventional order,

Dana (munificence), sila (morality), and bhavana (meditation). It would seem that these qualities are formulated in terms of the interests of laypersons because meditation, the great Buddhist value, comes last.

For the moment let us consider dana, or liberality, the most highly valued quality. Dana has the best effect when it is "sown" in the proper field. A well-known text says that just as seed sown in a "field that is undulating, rocky and pebbly, saltish, without depth of tilth, without (water) outlet ... is not very fruitful," so gifts [dana] given to monks and men of bad character are barren of result. Similarly, in a "field perfected, when the seed that's sown is perfect and the deva rains perfecting it," one will have perfect grain; so too "perfect alms in perfect precept given lead to perfection-for one's deed is perfect." And of course the best "field of merit" is the monk order!

The idea of the field of merit, with its symbolism of fertility, is obviously to keep the monastic order fed and looked after, but it seems that the doctrine has already tempered its ethic of intentions and opened the way for a Buddhist ethic of "works" whereby the acts of giving to hierarchically ordered fields of merit will have good effects. Thus, parallel with the theory of karma is merit accumulation through good works, a fundamental feature of popular religiosity in Buddhist societies everywhere.

The idea of merit making divorced from the ethic of intention was the major break that led to the mitigation of the harsh karma doctrine. Yet it is always possible to link merit making to intention and affirm that merit making has no real effect unless it is linked with intention. But the field is also clear for separating them and then for linking them up when expedient. Without the idea of merit making and its relative independence of the ethic of intention, there could not have developed the notion of "merit transfer," a key feature of the popular tradition.

Merit transfer is very popular in everyday life. It postulates that the merit one has made can be transferred to a dead relative in need or to a deity. Regarding the latter there is the case of Nanda's mother, who promised the deity Vessavaa (Vairavaa, the god of the northern quarter) to comply with his wish that when she fed monks the next day she should transfer to him the merit accruing from that act. Consequently, she offered alms to Sariputta, a senior disciple of the Buddha, and to other monks and then informed Sariputta:

"Reverend Sir, let all the merit (punna) in this giving be to the happiness of the Royal deva VessavaJa!"

And in that most important text dealing with the death of the Buddha, the "Maha Parinibbana Sutta," a similar sentiment is expressed in respect to food given to monks:

In whatever place the wise man makes his home, He should feed the virtuous leaders of the holy life. Whatever devas there are who report this offering, they will pay him respect and honour for this.

Neither text supports the popular idea of merit transfer to dead kin, but the popular idea can derive support from such texts. However, the idea is clearly present in late canonical texts formulated around the second century b.c.e., particularly the Petavattu that dealt with ancestors reborn as miserable spirits, or pretas (Pali, peta). In these texts the benefactor gives a gift to the monks "and declares the act of charity to be the peta's." It should be added that the pretas need human help. Persons who are dispatched to hell can expiate their bad karma and get reborn on earth, whereas the pretas and demons have no such luck.

Once in this miserable state they are in a bind: they have little or no opportunity to do good on their own, and they continue to do bad by causing hurt to humans; therefore, they cannot get out of their miserable state. The laity has little reason to transfer merit to the demons, but they have an obligation to help an ancestor reborn as a miserable preta. It is the case, however, that in Buddhist texts, early or late, merit transfer occurs only in respect to deities, good or bad, whereas ordinary Buddhists transfer merit to any dead kinsperson, enhancing that person's store of merit.

Does this mean that the Buddhists took over the idea of merit transfer from the texts and then extended it to include any dead kinsperson? I doubt this was the case; texts such as those I have quoted probably reflected monk responses to the demands of laypeople; and they tell us how the representatives of the doctrinal tradition were willing to meet those demands. Underlying these texts as we have them today are debates between monks and laypersons regarding the aporias that the karma theory has generated. Yet, as Richard Gombrich shows, the presence of a doctrinal position in turn has significance for lay religiosity also because sophisticated lay folk can refer to that position.

In conclusion, let me consider an idea that appears in both doctrinal and popular levels as the "death wish." Again the older texts unequivocally assert that deeds done or thoughts developed at the point of death may affect the next birth, based on the doctrinal postulate that the last thought conditions the next and that death is simply a thought moment. Texts like the "Mahakammavibhagga Sutta" would say that such "thoughts" have to be related to the karmic ethic of intentions.

But again is it not likely that the doctrine itself was developed under the influence of the popular thought that took the same idea (that between dying and rebirth is only a thought moment) and tried to condition that moment by apotropaic or magical means, such as the recital of paritta texts? The practices pertaining to merit are ubiquitous in Buddhist societies; but they are nothing new and must have made their advent in the early years of the founding of the religion.

KARMA AND EVERYDAY LIFE

The sage who is accustomed to living in distant places, the egoless and well-conducted one and the householder who supports a family-they are not equal. For the householder is unrestrained and destroys living beings; the sage is self-restrained and protects living beings. The blue necked peacock which flies through the air never approaches the speed of the wild goose. Similarly, the householder can never resemble the monk who is endowed with the qualities of a sage who meditates, aloof, in the jungle. -"Muni Sutta"

The ethicized moral injunctions that govern life are known in Buddhism as s i la s, generally translated as "precepts." Of these, five are specially designated as the panca s i la (five precepts). If there is anything that marks a Buddhist as such, it is the recital of the Five Precepts. Every Buddhist ceremony or sermon starts with their recital, and it is rare to come across a Buddhist who cannot recite them and gloss their meanings, even though the precepts are formulated in Pali. In Western translations they are sometimes expressed as categorical prohibitions of the "thou shalt not" variety found in Exodus 20:13–16.

But precepts, it should be clear from our previous discussions, are not commandments. In Christianity the violation of commandments, insofar as they are God's own imperatives, leads to alienation from God and, in principle at least, to a denial of salvation. This is not the case with the Buddhist precepts, which have little direct relevance to the soteriology.The Five Precepts have been translated by Saddhatissa as follows:

1. "I undertake the precept to abstain from the taking of life." This precept incorporates the Buddhist ethic of nonviolence, or ahimsa ("nonhurt"), which applies to all sentient existence.
2. "I undertake the precept not to take that which is not freely given." This precept covers much more than "theft" and includes all sorts of social responsibilities, as both Saddhatissa and Tachibana point out. Marxist monks use this precept to indict capitalism.
3. "I undertake the precept to abstain from sexual misconduct." This precept includes adultery, but it could mean much more than that, although nowhere in the doctrinal texts is this precept explicitly spelled out.
4. "I undertake the precept to abstain from false speech." This includes gossip, slander, and all forms of ill-mannered utterances.
5. "I undertake the precept to abstain from liquor that causes intoxication and sloth." It is interesting that the objection to alcohol is pragmatic; it causes mental sloth and should be avoided. No wonder this same precept could be used by both temperance workers and their opponents! This same pragmatic attitude to alcohol is found in the "Sigalovada Sutta," where the Buddha advises Sigala to adhere to

precepts one to four (abstention from the four vices of conduct) but refers to alcohol only in the pragmatic context of the "six channels for dissipating wealth."

It would seem that the Five Precepts do not have the specificity that characterizes the biblical commandments or, closer to home, the Jaina injunctions. The latter, no longer called silas (precepts) but vratas (vows) have an extraordinary specificity as befits a religion that enjoins asceticism for the laity. But the seemingly vague Buddhist precepts, like the seemingly precise Jaina ones or the Christian commandments, are nevertheless carefully thought out and constructed, and they possess two significant features.

First, there is the absence of a categorical imperative or specificity in formulation; second, it would be impossible to fulfill any of the precepts to the letter. These two features meant that the moral codes of the local community could be incorporated within the precepts and given Buddhist meaning. Therefore, the fact that people recite the Five Precepts surely implies an important affirmation of their belonging to a moral community of Buddhists; it is not necessarily an affirmation of ethical consensus, ideally or otherwise. For example, no one would disagree that adultery is a "sin," but it would be hard to find consensus among Buddhists in different societies on what constitutes "sexual misdemeanor."

Historically viewed, the Five Precepts showed a Buddhist tolerance for the values of the local community, which could, without too much conflict, are incorporated into the precepts. This in turn led to the spread of Buddhism among people with differing moral codes, such that one found Buddhism existing in easy harmony with, for example, polygyny and polyandry. In some key texts a courtesan like Ambapali is accepted without negative moral criticism or judgment. The tone of the texts that deal with lay morality is ironic, pragmatic, and lacking severity. Ethicization, in Buddhist societies, occurred without much social disruption or denigration of local values. This did not mean that Buddhist values had no impact. The injunction on ahimsa, or nonviolence, was particularly effective in the near elimination of animal sacrifices, helping in the long run to absorb hunting communities into pastoralism and agriculture.

Laypersons are those who are caught in the rebirth cycle, now defined as samsara; they are not expected to renounce the world, so the rewards of salvation are available to them only in the long samsaric run. Thus, as Weber put it, the Five Precepts are "an insufficiency ethic of the weak." One no longer can agree however with Weber's judgment that village Buddhism had no doctrinal sanction; the Five Precepts themselves are part of the doctrine, although invented with the laity in mind.

What the doctrine in effect denies to the laity is the practical possibility of nirvana through the Noble Eightfold Path. Thus the laity is given a moral code commensurate with their religious goals, and instead of the primary compensations of nirvana they are given the secondary compensations of a heaven and a happy rebirth. The Five Precepts constitute an ethical framework for right action and are designed for the orderly conduct of social life and the control of drives and passions. A layperson ought to lead a life that avoids bad karmic effects and produces good ones. The Buddha himself put it thus:

And, householders, there are these five advantages to one of good morality and of success in morality. What are they? In the first place, through careful attention to his affairs he gains much wealth. In the second place, he gets a good reputation for morality and good conduct. In the third place, whatever assembly he approaches, whether of Khattiyas, Brahmins, householders or ascetics, he does so with confidence and assurance. In the fourth place, he dies unconfused. In the fifth place, after death, at the breaking-up of the body, he arises in a good place, a heavenly world. These are the five advantages to one of good morality, and of success in morality.

It is clear that Buddhism does not prescribe asceticism or withdrawal from the world for the laity. Texts such as the "Sigalovada Sutta" and the "Cakkavatti Sihanada Sutta" contain explicit injunctions on how the good life may be led in the world; a virtuous, rather than a virtuoso, life was expected of the laity. A layperson is expected to form attachments; he or she need not renounce the world. A beautiful case of the soteriological gap between the layperson and the monk comes out in the conversation between Anathapijika, the great physician and friend of the Buddha, as he lay dying, and Sariputta, a senior disciple of the Buddha who consoled him with a sermon befitting the time of the "death wish."

When Anathapindika shed tears because he hadn't heard a sermon of that nature before, even though he had been closely associated with the monk order, Sariputta replied that laypeople cannot understand such things; only monks can. According to Walpola Rahula the commentary on this text states that "lay people have a strong craving and attachment to their lands and fields, gold and wealth, wives and children and servants and that they neither understand nor like to hear a talk that advocates the renunciation of these possessions." It is not surprising, Rahula adds, that one of the six duties of the monk is to show the way to heaven (saggassa maggam), but the way to heaven is not the way to emancipation (mokkhassa maggam).

The many heavens in Buddhism are drawn in graphic detail in such late texts as the Vim a navattu (Stories of heavenly mansions) and in the popular imagination. They are entirely sensuous, with women and music, dancing, and wish-fulfilling trees. Nevertheless, everyone in the lay community knows that these pleasures are characterized by impermanence. So are Buddhist hells, although a sinner can roast in them for eons before getting out. Although heaven titillates the senses and hells are nasty places that the virtuous should avoid, the truly serious lay preoccupation is with an imagined rebirth on earth.

Most people attach a prarthan a (formal rebirth wish) when they perform a merit-producing act and ask for material rewards-health, wealth, sensuous delights, power, prestige, high caste status-and, if the devotee is a woman, sometimes the wish to be born as a male. By contrast a bad rebirth is literally a hell on earth. People generally know that no one leads a life of unmitigated earthly bliss; everyone, rich and poor, suffers the vicissitudes of fortune. Part of this inevitability of suffering in any human rebirth results from the fact that the precepts are impossible to wholly fulfill; there is no way that one can not be a sinner some of the time. Hence human life as seen and experienced on earth excites the Buddhist imagination as a powerful moral scenario.

The beggar, the cripple, the destitute, the sick, and the ghostly spirits who haunt human habitations are all embodiments of suffering, symbolic representations of those who have sinned. So are animals, especially bulls (and, at one time, pack oxen), which, like the very poor, are destined to bear burdens; and those creatures, such as cobras, that creep into your house because of previous life attachments; they all affect the imagination in similar ways although not as powerfully as human sufferers. Thus the whole environment of humans and animals is an ethicized world-an ethicization that, we have already seen, is inevitable when the notions of "sin" and "merit" and the accompanying principle of the conditionality of reward is imposed on a rebirth eschatology.

ASCETIC RELIGIOSITY

Lay persons may be incapable of achieving salvation in this life, but they can achieve it in some future one. Thus the wish to eventually escape from the wheel of rebirth is part of the long-term soteriological motivations of most people. The renunciatory ideal itself is represented in the great ascetics of the Buddha's time, the "elders," or theras, after whom the religion Theravada is named. These monks have achieved nirvana and are therefore called arahants. The "arahant ideal" is a powerful conception in the imagination of the Buddhist laity, a measure by which ordinary people evaluate the virtue of monks.

Although unreachable for the many, renunciation is the ideal for all. Yet as an ideal it is represented in different ways and at different levels in those persons who have, temporarily or permanently, renounced the world.Let me begin with the situation on the village level in Sri Lanka; in virtually every village, nowadays, there are a few elderly laypersons known as up a sakas who have moved out of the daily routine of existence to adopt a special kind of asceticism. In the classical doctrine the term up a saka simply meant "lay follower."

But in the practical religion the upasaka is a lay devotee who, in middle or old age, has made a partial withdrawal from the world, generally after his or her children have grown up and married. The renunciatory thrust of the upasaka is expressed in the recital of the Eight or Ten Precepts (an artificial distinction because the Ten Precepts are only a reclassification of the Eight). The Ten Precepts are the more popular classification and include the Five Precepts plus five more:

6. Abstinence from eating at unseasonable times (that is, after 12 noon)
7. Abstinence from witnessing displays of dancing, singing, music
8. Abstinence from the use of garlands, unguents, scents
9. Abstinence from the use of a high or big bed
10. Abstinence from receiving gold and silver

The Ten are observed on the uposatha day, which occurs four times a month, corresponding to the four phases of the waxing and waning moon, the most important being the full-moon day. Popularly known as poya in Sri Lanka, the uposatha was a Buddhist adaptation of the Vedic upavasatha, in which the householder and his wife fasted one day every half lunar month while preparing for the sacrifice the next day. On poya the pious layperson is expected to devote the whole day to religious meditation and reading. Although this form of piety is theoretically open to all, irrespective of age and sex, its actual practice, until very recently, has been almost exclusively with the elderly.

The term Khastha up a saka is sometimes reserved for those who regularly observe the Ten Precepts. Grihastha is the householder stage in the Brahmannic fourfold scheme of life, but it refers here to those who have temporarily renounced the world while still being householders. A few of these people may decide to practice the precepts not only on poya days but consistently as a way of life and therefore are designated "the upasakas of the Ten Precepts."

Because the Ten Precepts are also the code for the Buddhist novice, or samanera, an "up a saka of the Ten Precepts" leads the life of a novice monk although technically a layperson. Sri Lanka does not have the institution that is omnipresent in Buddhist Southeast Asia, where young men get initiated as novices for a few months and actually live in monasteries. These temporary ordinations are again based on the ideology of renunciation and in turn, like that of the upasaka lifestyle, reinforce that ideology.

There are important differences between the Five and the Ten Precepts: with the latter the upaṣaka has moved into a form of life different from that of the ordinary layperson. First, precepts six to ten provide a specificity that the original five precepts lack. Second, the latter precepts require a partial suspension of lay living, a necessary requirement for the higher spiritual life. Thus the injunction on "gold and silver" requires one to withdraw from the economic life of the village.

Further, the third precept of the Five Precepts is categorically redefined; the "sexual misdemeanor" of the original is reformulated as total sexual abstinence. Third, insofar as the Ten Precepts prescribe shunning worldly pleasures, total abstention from sexuality, and withdrawal from the economic life of society, there is no way that these ethics could ever operate as general societal norms. Or, to put it differently, you cannot have a social order constituted on the basis of the Ten Precepts. They constitute not an ethicization of a preexistent social morality but an invention of a new renunciatory ethic modeled on it.

It must be emphasized that the rules themselves merely set the stage for the devout life; they help the upasaka to lead a life of piety and meditation away from the distractions of the world. It is generally the upasakas who can afford to ignore the gods and resolve that particular aporia because, having renounced the lay life, they rarely need the gods for help in worldly matters.

The demons, however, are not easy to refute because, at least in village life, their powers are being vindicated by the direct evidence of those who get possessed by them. In such instances upasakas can at least affirm that they are personally safe from harm owing to their belief in the dhamma or because only sinners can be harmed by demons. Some upasakas can even deny the efficacy of counter karma, although rarely that of merit transfers owing to the doctrinal support given to the latter. For others counterkarma can be important because it can support the whole institution of upasaka-hood, for according to counterkarma one can compensate for the indiscretions of one's youth by ascetic moral behavior in old age.

If the upasaka and the novice have only to practice the Ten Precepts, the fully ordained (upasampada) monk must adhere to the 220 rules laid down in the Patimokkha section of the Vinaya (the books of the discipline). All these rules are characterized by extreme specificity and are designed to move the monk away from the lay world and into the life of monastic asceticism. These special rules express the great soteriological gap that separates the monk from both the lay upasaka (and novice) and the layperson and set the stage for a further and more drastic move toward renunciation and salvation. Not by themselves sufficient, they help frame acts of renunciatory behavior that take the actor away from the world.

We now encounter one of the great paradoxes of Buddhist monasticism: the rules are designed to take the monk away from the secular society, but they cannot be effective for two reasons. First, the monk has certain parish roles to fulfill, such as preaching to the laity and officiating at death and commemoration ceremonies and paritta recitals (but never at puberty rites and marriage, at least until very recent times). Second, although the monk has escaped from lay society, he is caught up in the social structure of the monastic community, which in turn takes its bearing from the lay social order outside.

In the Buddhist world, as everywhere else, monks are involved in political conflicts and conflicts over power and position that operate within the order itself or between the order and the secular authorities. For example, monks are generally extremely inclined toward status and are addicted to titles and honorifics, which they love to display. Again: monks are expected to renounce caste, but in Sri Lanka, at least from the eighteenth century onward, the Siamese fraternity exclusively recruited its members from the high farmer (goyigama) caste, and especially wealthy temples tolerated chief monks from only the aristocratic segment of that caste.

The colonial period gave impetus for the aspiring lower castes in the maritime areas to assert their dignity, and soon they went to Burma and inaugurated two new fraternities, the Amarapura and the Ramanna. Although these fraternities were more open in their recruitment patterns, each temple or monastery tended to favor its own caste members. In all three fraternities small groups of very low castes, such as kinnaras (mat weavers) and roniyas (professional beggars), are not represented at all and in rare instances are not even permitted to enter the temples.

Monks from the traditional Siamese fraternity in the Kandyan areas often refuse to accept alms from them. Ironically, caste, status, and power distinctions within the order are important for the monks alone; for the laity in general anyone who wears a yellow robe is a "son of the Buddha" and worthy of respect. In fact, some high-caste groups may prefer to give alms to the Ramanna and Amarapura fraternities because they believe that they are more pious and less worldly than the monks of the dominant Siamese fraternity.

It therefore seems that the monk has escaped from one social structure only to get caught up in another. Moreover, that other society is also involved in the lay community, although in some historical periods more conspicuously involved than in others. If renunciation aims to remove the fetters that bind one to worldly affairs, the monk has not succeeded. It follows that although he represents a doctrine whose goal is salvation, he himself cannot achieve this salvation except in a later, even remote, rebirth.

He, like his lay parishioner, is caught up in a social system that inhibits the Noble Eightfold Path, which alone can guide him to his idealized goal. In the time of the Buddha the textual tradition asserts the goal of nirvana was realized by many arahants; not so with the routinization of monasticism. The arahant goal has become remote for monk, upasaka, and layperson alike. Yet nirvana remains the ideal still. How then can one reach the seemingly unreachable?

In later nondoctrinal religiosity it is said that one can achieve nirvana by being born in the dispensation of the next Buddha, Maitreye, and obtain release by listening to his sermons. It is not surprising that this doctrine of a future redeeming messiah should have developed. Many laypeople include this aspiration in their rebirth wishes, or pr a rthan a. But the interpretation of this doctrine is not uniform. For some laypeople listening to the sacred words of the messianic Maitreye alone might provide sudden illumination that leads them to the nirvanic path without renunciatory effort. But how is this possible?

The Greek Bactrian king Milinda (Menander) asked the monk Nagasena how and why thousands of lay devotees in the Buddha's own time achieved nirvana without really trying! Milinda's dilemma could be summed up: If people can achieve nirvana without effort by being householders or gods (gods being a species of laypersons), what is the use of ascetic renunciation?

Nagasena, the monk, replies that those laypersons who achieved nirvana did not do so without effort. In previous births they had performed the prerequisite ascetic renunciations, but the fruits of their efforts were realized only in the present rebirth. Hence ascetic renunciation at some point in one's samsaric career is absolutely necessary for salvation, but instead of being concentrated in one lifetime, it is scattered through many.

What then happens to the monk who wants to engage in the meditative effort that will hasten his salvation? The logical answer is simple enough: he must escape from his home in the monastery in a further flight into homelessness. This solution has in fact been institutionalized in the history of Theravada Buddhism in its two monastic orientations: the gramava sin (village dwellers), monks who live in temples and monasteries and perform parish roles, and the vanav a sin (forest dwellers), who pursue their own salvation with diligence away from it all.

The main task of the former is grantha dhura, the way of learning and parish activity, whereas that of the latter is vipassan a dhura, or meditative work. There is no question whatever that it is the vanavasins who represent in the public imagination the approximation of the arahant ideal.

The modern resurgence of the forest-dwelling (vanavasin) movement has been beautifully recorded by Michael Carrithers for Sri Lanka and by Stanley Tambiah for Thailand. In contemporary Buddhist nations these monks are found living in isolation in forest hermitages. But even for the most assiduous of them final escape from the world is not easy. Soon their fame as "good monks" and as true "fields of merit" spread. There is no way that they can escape the relentless piety of devotees who seek them out in their forest fastnesses, invade their solitude, and thus help destroy the very saintliness that they so much admire.

One such place in the late 1950s, named Salgala. Originally it was a place where a number of forest dwellers lived in caves and meditated. But soon their fame spread. Laypersons from all over the country wanted to come to Salgala to give alms (dana) to these virtuous monks. The pressures were so great that a local committee had to be formed to coordinate the alms-giving arrangements. Soon the caves and cloisters were floored with cement and a vihara (temple) was built in the forest.

This pattern is not at all unusual and can be seen in several ancient archaeological sites. Today this development can be bypassed altogether. Philanthropic donors build comfortable meditation chambers (kutis) in somewhat isolated places where monks, and nowadays pious lay people and salvation-seeking foreign tourists, can meditate for short or long periods. Some monks, still dissatisfied with these bourgeois arrangements, take refuge in other caves in less-known places. But their respite is temporary. Even the most isolated hermit must from time to time wander into outlying villages in search of alms. But then, as his reputation for holiness spreads, he finds it ever more difficult to escape the curiosity and zeal of the pious; and the historic cycle keeps repeating itself.

Bibliography

Aiyappan, A., and P. R. Srinivasan, *Story of Buddhism with Special Reference to South India.* Madras, India: Government of Madras, 1960.

Auboyer, Jeannine, *Buddha: A Pictorial History of His Life and Legacy.* New York: Crossroad, 1983.

Banerji, Aparna, *Traces of Buddhism in South India.* Calcutta: Scientific Book Agency, 1970

Bapat, P. V., ed., *2500 Years of Buddhism.* New Delhi: Government of India, Publications Division, 1956.

Basham, A. L., *History and Doctrines of the Ajivikas.* London: Luzac, 1951.

Basu, N. N., *Modern Buddhism and Its Followers in Orissa.* Calcutta, 1911.

Bechert, Heinz and Richard Gombrich, eds., *The World of Buddhism: Monks and Nuns in Society and Culture.* London: Thames and Hudson, 1984.

Cabezon, Jose Ignacia, ed., *Buddhism, Sexuality, and Gender.* Albany: SUNY Press, 1992.

Charles S. Prebish, ed., *Buddhism: A Modern Perspective.* University Park: Pennsylvania State University Press, 1975.

Conze, Edward, *Buddhism: Its Essence and Development.* New York: Harper Torchbooks, 1965.

Gellner, David, "Buddhism and Hinduism in the Nepal Valley," in Sutherland, Stewart, et.al., eds., *The World's Religions.* Boston: G. K. Hall, 1988.

Horner, I. B., *The Living Thoughts of Gotama the Buddha.* London: Cassell, 1948.

Jayatilleke, K. N., *Early Buddhist Theory of Knowledge.* London: George Allen & Unwin, 1963.

Joseph M. Kitagawa and Mark D. Cummings, ed., *Buddhism and Asian History.* New York: Macmillan, 1987.

Joshi, Lalmani, *Studies in the Buddhistic Culture of India,* 2nd rev. ed. Delhi: Motilal Banarsidass, 1977.

Karetsky, Patricia Eichenbaum, *The Life of the Buddha: Ancient Scriptural and Pictorial Traditions.* Lanham: University Press of America, 1992.

Keown, Damein et.al., eds. *Buddhism and Human Rights.* London: Curzon, 1998.

Kohn, Michael H., trans., *The Shambhala Dictionary of Buddhism and Zen.* Boston: Shambhala, 1991.

Lamotte, Etienne, *History of Indian Buddhism: From the Origins to the Saka Era.* Louvain-La-Neuve: Institut Orientaliste, 1988.

Lopez, Donald S., Jr, ed., *Buddhist Hermeneutics.* Honolulu: University of Hawaii Press, 1988.

Lopez, Donald S., Jr., ed., *Buddhism in Practice.* Princeton: Princeton University Press, 1995.

Malalasekera, G. P., ed., *Encyclopedia of Buddhism.* Colombo: Government of Sri Lanka, 1961.

Mishra, V. B., *Religious Beliefs and Practices of North India during the Early Mediaeval Period.* Leiden, Netherlands: Brill, 1973.

Morgan, Kenneth W., ed., *The Path of the Buddha.* New York: Ronald Press, 1974.

Nakamura, Hajime, *Gotama Buddha.* Los Angeles: Buddhist Books International, 1977.

Ñanamoli, Bhikkhu, *The Life of the Buddha.* Kandy, Sri Lanka: Buddhist Publication Society, 1972.

Narada Thera, *The Buddha and His Teachings.* Kandy, Sri Lanka: Buddhist Publication Society, 1988 (reprint).

Prebish, Charles S., ed. *Buddhist Ethics: A Cross-Cultural Approach.* Dubuque: Kendall/Hunt, 1992.

Thomas, E. J., *The Life of the Buddha as Legend and History.* London: Routledge & Kegan Paul, 1927.

Warder, A. K, *Outline of Indian Philosophy.* Delhi: Motilal Banarsidass, 1971.

Warder, A. K., *Indian Buddhism,* 2nd ed. rev. Delhi: Motilal Banarsidass, 1980.

Warren, Henry C., *Buddhism in Translations.* New York: Atheneum, 1963.

Index

T

U

W